LIVE

OR

DIE HARD

YOU ARE NOT A BARCODE

Introduction

Life Is Not About What You Can't Do

This book, in a sense, is a survival checklist that will become more valuable with each passing day. It will help you to rethink the patterns that have surrounded you since birth. It's time to rid all distractions and start focusing.

This book reveals the state of our society. It examines technology's impact on mankind. Are you killing yourself for a job where you can be replaced in a week? Where do you see yourself in the next five years? Have you ever sat down and asked yourself those questions?

Investigate the economic forces we're battling. Technology is playing the role of our master, we must learn how to take advantage of it instead of being enslaved by it. Discover the habits and learning patterns of the elite.

Learn how to use technology to your advantage instead of being enslaved by it. Discover the habits and learning patterns of the elite.

Society has made us into obedient automatons. We work for hours on end and only bits and pieces of ourselves are left for our loved ones. Continuous 'work harder' cycles are detrimental to our health and if we don't change soon, we won't have enough energy to make a difference. No one wants to reach retirement age and realize that they can't do what they love doing because of how fragile or broke they've become.

Don't you think life should be better as we get older? Don't you think you deserve the best out of life?

Why The Disruption Triangle Matters

Soon artificial intelligence will eliminate jobs and you'll be back at square one if you don't take charge of your life now. An average of 400 people compete for a single job in a day. The cost of living is skyrocketing and some of us are required to work multiple jobs to get by.

Read on to take full control of your financial life and make the best use of your time. You need to relieve yourself from the grip of that daunting job and life in general; There is a lot out there waiting to be explored by you!

Are you tired of living in a hallucination, being told what to believe, what to buy, and what to think? Don't allow patterns of behavior to control your life.

As we grow older we start to lose energy and we don't have the motivation to change. Don't wind up regretting your decisions. Instead, look back on your life and be proud of your achievements, be proud that you thought for yourself and chose yourself.

This book reveals how we are manipulated by the gods on Sandhill Road in Silicon Valley. How we are being manipulated like puppets by leaving digital traces behind us. Technology can be good or bad, it depends on usage and intention.

At times, the odds can seem impossible. You move to a new job but nothing changes except for the color of your cubicle. Don't get hooked on paychecks. Break the cycle and live a free life. Change your mindset and start thinking and acting as the rich do.

This book is for anyone tired of the limitations posed by routine nine-to-five jobs. It's for anyone seeking freedom, wanting to live life to its fullness, breaking through mental barriers society has imposed. It's for young adults wondering if there's truth in the saying 'one's economic security does not lie in the nine-to-five, but in power to produce, think, learn, create, and adapt'. It is for those who are ready to utilize their energy before it is too late. You are meant to live life, not to be programmed. Potential and creativity cannot thrive in a routine.

Financial Freedom Lifestyle

The financial freedom lifestyle can be a reality for anyone, regardless of the economic position which they are in. Financial freedom is the result of income generated without having to physically work, not to comply with a work schedule or be physically present. It seems complex but it's not.

Millions of people sacrifice their best years working jobs they don't enjoy. To keep faith in what they are doing, they trick themselves into believing that hard work guarantees a future reward. In reality, they end up deferring joy and then one day they wake up and realize that joy is never coming back. The path to financial freedom requires leaving your comfort zone and making that life-transforming decision to equal your efforts with your gains.

Becoming financially free does not mean you have to work long hours every day; A satisfying life is usually much cheaper and less strenuous than people think. What you need is mobility and flexibility - you need to be able to do what you want when you want. This is usually a smarter way of making money. Adopt this mentality and you can achieve your most meaningful goals.

This book will push you to face reality. We must plan for life, not death. You have one life to live and if you're exposed to chronic burnout and stress, your life expectancy will be shortened.

You were born free; Don't live your life trapped in a cubicle in some high rise. What distinguishes you from an inmate locked up in prison? In prison, the security guard has the access card; in your world, you have the access card.

The lessons ahead are the keys to freedom.

"To achieve goals you've never achieved before, you need to start doing things you've never done before."

-Stephen Covey

PS - I had an editor speed through the manuscript, while she did a great job you may still find some spelling and grammatical errors. If you find one, will you do me a favor and tell me what you find by sending me an email to andrew@andrewzee.com? Just note the page number, sentence and mistake and I'll fix it right away and thank you for your help.

If you love this, please post a review and share it with your close friends. If you DON'T like it, send me an email and tell me why. Please be kind. My children and their friends read about me online, we don't need any more negative thoughts on the internet. My direct email is andrew@andrewzee.com.

Copyright © 2020 Andrewzee

Andrewzee, Live Free or Die Hard: You are not a Barcode.

Table of Contents

Chapter 1 Rise of the Machines

"You die once but you get the chance to live every day. It is the accumulation of questions that you ask yourself which determine where you end up."

-Andrewzee

Live Free Or Die Hard

In small dark rooms across the country, the future is shaped by an elite group of people. Surrounded by pizza and soda cans with the dim glow of their laptop screens providing guidance, they slowly chart a course to a world that is becoming unrecognizable.

With the passion in which they strike the keys and bring together disparate lines of code, it is easy to conclude they hold all the answers. This is the greatest misconception of all. In truth, they have no real power and hold no real influence. They are simply building well-oiled machinery for the people pulling strings. The gods of Sandhill Road in Silicon Valley hold all the cards and they selectively play a game of poker with the world's future at stake.

Movies reminded us of how this game plays out - the ones who write the code and set the chain of actions that disrupt the world never actually win in the end. They are at the bottom of the ladder with the rest of the world, victims of manipulation and ultimately pawns in this callous game of chess.

The movie *Live Free or Die Hard* portrays this when Bruce Willis tries to stop a sinister plot led by a rogue government operative alongside a team of talented programmers who attempt to take over key government infrastructure like water, electricity, and gas to trigger a fire sale. The fate of this illicit agenda is left in the hands of a select few.

This is consistent with the narrative that continues to perpetuate itself today. In the grand scheme of things, there is only you. You must look out for yourself and live your best life every day.

The truth is, you will never live intentionally and free if you're tied to a cubicle. If your future self was to write to your present self, you would warn yourself and offer practical advice. You would remind yourself that all your education and experience was not for you to end up in a cubicle, slaving away for years until retirement. You would tell yourself to pursue your talents and passions. Your letter would help you realize that the joy of family, friends, and solid relationships outweigh long hours at work and constant stress. You would conclude by telling yourself to make a move, find the keys to living free, and start living!

You Against The Algorithm

Today's forecast calls for the elimination of 40% of jobs worldwide within the next twenty years. Even if you're a loyal employee that trusts your employer to stay out of the AI race, once the competition installs a few robots and eliminates 70% of jobs - what do you think your employer will do? If your company sits back and does nothing they will go out of business, leaving you to fend for yourself.

The push for company innovation comes from profit and utility. The future is a balance of providing maximum value to customers and profits to shareholders while minimizing the need for human labor and liability.

Any job that involves a continuous, repeatable process is endangered. Slowly but surely, AI will achieve complicated processes involving more discretion, emotions, and technical expertise.

Don't be surprised if your friendly neighborhood barista disappears. Just recently, Café X deployed a 10x10 metal container in San Francisco. When Café X opened its metal sliding door the robot performed slowly and it had a few drink mix-ups. By the second day, the robot was adjusted and updated and it began whipping out perfectly made drinks. With this level of automation in the coffee industry, where will temporary workers go when they are between jobs? The future forecast is filled with hundreds of startups using robotics to cut costs. It is clear that the future will be powered by creativity, strategy, and innovation, but these shifts will not be restricted to the future of transportation, it concerns the future of everything.

Consider the possibilities that automation could bring to McDonald's. How soon will McDonald's be able to automate the assembly of a hamburger? So far, McDonald's has installed machines to take your order. In the future, fast-food restaurants will probably employ mechanics instead of burger flippers.

When Uber launched in 2009, no one knew how much it would change the way we see the world and expect it to function. Uber tapped into a pressing need and created a tech-based, on-demand, ride service. The result disrupted the taxi industry.

Uber will continue to disrupt. The goal for the next two decades is to transform its fleet into one made up entirely of self-driving autonomous cars.

Elon Musk predicts that by the year 2037, autonomous driving vehicles will be the norm. Tesla does not want to miss out on this huge opportunity which is why they created their own autonomous truck that has the ability to move cargo across the country without a driver. Startups are transforming existing truck fleets into autonomous vehicles. These trucks will be able to follow each other very closely for the sole purpose of saving on fuel and minimizing wind drag. In the process, truck driving, the highest male-dominated industry will be disrupted.

Robots may also build the houses of tomorrow, replacing today's blue-collar workers. Australia's Fastbrick Robotics can lay 1,000 bricks per hour and construct the shell of a house in two days versus the six weeks it takes for regular laborers. A large cement 3D printer can continuously print a house without the need to rest. Recently, the Chinese company WinSun printed ten houses in under 24 hours.

Automation will continue to invade our lives. Instead of human housekeepers, you may have an AI-powered robot.

People will purchase robots to help with their daily tasks because, in the long run, they will be cheaper than their human counterparts. What will happen to those workers who might otherwise have been hired to help with those chores? If they fail to invest in themselves, they may not have other employment options. AI is impacting households and businesses everywhere. Are you and your children preparing for the approaching AI-powered future? Do you habitually turn off the internet at dusk to read a book or do you still have to pry your device from your child's hands? Are your habits any better than your children's when it comes to the tech addiction? These are important questions to answer as you attempt to prepare for and position yourself to profit from the impending automation take-over.

According to Forrester Research, 24.7 million jobs will be displaced by automated systems. Companies announce massive plans to mechanize their production process and automate desk jobs.

Entry-level positions aren't the only ones at risk. JP Morgan developed artificial intelligence to automate legal analysis work. As investments continue, previously unautomated industries, like law, will be replaced with AI. A law degree is one of the costliest degrees you can attain. Do your due diligence as degrees may be worth half as much in ten years.

Read what just a few prominent people have to say about the future of AI:

- **Stephen Hawking:** In his piece, *This is the Most Dangerous Time for Our Planet* [22] he warned, 'The automation of factories has already decimated jobs in traditional manufacturing, and the rise of artificial intelligence is likely to extend this job destruction deep into the middle classes, with only the most caring, creative or supervisory roles remaining... accelerating the already widening economic inequality around the world.'

- **Bill Gates:** In an interview with *Quartz*[23], he lent credence to the inevitability of job elimination and rising unemployment rates. He said, "You cross the threshold of job-replacement of certain activities all sort of at once. So, you know, warehouse work, driving, room clean-up, there are quite a few things that are meaningful job categories that, certainly in the next 20 years [will go away]."
- **Barack Obama:** At a Chicago farewell address at the end of his eight years in the White House, Obama reiterated the economic dislocations that should be prepared for as the world becomes competitively automated, and the need to mitigate the wide inequality it's caused. He said[25], "The next wave of economic dislocations won't come from overseas. It will come from the relentless pace of automation that makes a lot of good, middle-class jobs obsolete."

Artificially Intelligent Doctors

The medical profession has never been technology-shy, but AI is nothing like the traditional technologies that support the growth of the medical field. AI technology has the ability to gain information, process it, and give a well-defined output to the end-user, or in this case, the patient. AI in the medical field could cut out doctors, allowing people to correctly self-diagnose themselves and administer their own treatment.

The first step in healthcare management is compiling and analyzing information. There are over 10,000 diseases known to afflict humans, but at any given time, doctors can only remember a fraction of them. According to a 2012 John Hopkins study, over 40,000 people die in ICU as a result of misdiagnosis. This is not to blame doctors, they're simply human. As AI enters the medical field, this will no longer be the case. AI can be deployed to manage data, reviewing volumes of medical journals in seconds, saving time without the risk of forgetting important details like the human mind does.

In the near future, your smartphone could be your doctor. All you'll have to do is type the details of your illness into a program. The program will then search a database, diagnose you, and offer treatment. This is already happening in the UK with apps like Babylon that offer medical consultations through your device. Users report their symptoms to the app and it compares information against a database of illnesses, the user's personal medical history, and common medical knowledge. The app then gives recommendations based on its findings. These applications will reduce the time spent researching and analyzing patient data to make an accurate diagnosis. They are built to comb through data from the last 30 years and return results or diagnostic pointers to doctors in seconds.

Most hospitals would prefer to allocate funds to AI medical research, rather than expanding their workforce. For those studying to be doctors, this is no reason to despair. AI technology can't be developed in the medical field without the input of qualified medical personnel. Young doctors should seek to develop competence in developing AI software. Combined with their medical knowledge, they'll be able to create and control the tools that will define the future of medicine.

iPhone City

In Foxconn City, there is an assembly plant that resembles times past. There are over 700,000 contract workers working on iPhones, iPads, and laptops on non-U.S. soil. A Google image search of the facility reveals a huge factory lined with over three dozen rows, staffed by over 500 workers on both sides of tables that span the length of the factory. Employees are rewarded for installing components and tightening screws all day for months at a time. The facility has 230,000 employees, many of whom work six days a week, often spending up to twelve hours a day at the plant. Over a quarter of the workforce lives in company barracks and many earn less than $17 a day.

According to the Pulitzer Prize article *How the U.S. Lost Out on iPhone Work*, Foxconn can hire 3,000 people a day and convince them to move into the company barracks located on-site where iPhones are manufactured. It's no surprise that jobs are continually sent overseas.

If the elimination of U.S. jobs isn't bad enough, Foxconn also has plans to automate most of its Chinese workforce in three phases as mentioned in an article from Fortune.com. While this would make things interesting for the Chinese people, think of the ramifications for them and the rest of the world.

Computer Controlled Humans and Amazon

Pioneering software like MTurk gives us a peek at a future where machines take the place of HR personnel and wield the power to hire and fire.

What is MTurk? It stands for Amazon Mechanical Turk, a crowdsourcing online marketplace that allows you to coordinate and hire teams to perform tasks that computers can't. Such tasks include choosing a great picture from a collection, writing product descriptions, or identifying a piece of music. An employer can either post a job using an API (Application Programming Interface) or post it directly on the MTurk platform.

'Workers' on the MTurk platform are unlike conventional workers. They set their own hours and they are not obligated to accept tasks. They are contractors, not employees. They're responsible for withholding their own taxes, and they're not entitled to workers' compensation, minimum wage, or overtime. They are generally paid a dollar an hour. If a 'worker' rejects an assignment it could affect their reputation and their chances of getting a new assignment. International 'workers' are paid in Amazon gift cards. Americans receive payments directly in their bank accounts. Think of it as a virtual sweatshop, a throwback to when children were locked up in factories and forced to work for pennies. No one is really aware of this, because unlike actual sweatshops that can be raided by rights workers and investigated by journalists, these online sweatshops are invisible.

Most 'workers' were attracted by the idea of earning supplemental income, but they quickly found that it wasn't worth it. Robin, who signed up for the platform wrote, 'They make it sound like you can do just do a few tasks in your free time in between other things…But if you worked like that, I believe you would make about a dollar a day.' To earn a reasonable amount, you have to slave for long hours.

Rob, another 'worker' signed up for the platform close to two years ago. He thought he could make use of the time he normally spent watching television. So far, he has completed over 2,000 tasks with a 98% approval rate. How much has he earned so far? $157. He wrote, 'It's not worth it at all…Return an aluminum can and you'll make more money…You really have to be working all day long at top speed to earn minimum wage.'

This is just the beginning. Platforms like Amazon's MTurk are on the rise, a downside of the gig economy. This approach known as micro-tasking involves skills that are either too complicated for computers or require a high level of analysis that only humans are capable of but is too simple for skilled labor.

Amazon threatens jobs in more ways than one. They want to drive down the cost of 600k plus employees who are treated as bots themselves. Amazon warehouse employees face the constant threat of being fired. In these warehouses, cameras watch over the warehouse floor. A large screen displays the number of units each worker has packed in an hour; the target is nine seconds per item or 300 items per hour. If they pack less than two items per minute, they're fired. With such a grueling schedule, it should come as no surprise that ambulance calls are frequent to treat workers who collapse from exhaustion. Currently, humans are better at picking shelved items in

Amazon's warehouse but once AI catches up, what portion of its 130,000 warehouse workforce will feel that their jobs are safe?

Amazon has been running a contest to see who can create a robot that can handle picking items and packing them into a box. With the deployment of up to 100,000 robotic systems across its 25-plus fulfillment centers[17], they are going all-out to pioneer fully-autonomous warehouses. Efficient inventory management is a priority. They are a global giant in the virtual retail market and they work tirelessly to improve AI deployment. The drive for automation has led Amazon to acquire thousands of robots with amazing human-like agility and precision in its numerous fulfillment centers. Since their acquisition of Kiva Systems in 2012, Amazon continues to acquire industrial robotic startups with its latest being the 2019 acquisition of Canvas Technology.

They have already eliminated thousands of jobs due to the increased usage of robots, but they'd never admit it[20]. Moreover, those left behind are becoming increasingly redundant in their jobs as they get new roles[21].

Will the neighborhoods that surround the Amazon distribution centers eventually turn into uninhibited lands like Detroit motor city did when auto manufacturing left. Sure the lights will be on but the distribution center will be running on a skeleton crew. In the world of Silicon Valley you are as replaceable as a gear if the company even needs a gear. Humans will be as redundant as animals are to humans as mentioned in the book *Sapiens*.

Dangers Of Artificial Intelligence

While Technology is still a few years from making the average human intellect obsolete, rapid advancements in both hardware and software fields have been in line with Moore's law, which states that technology will grow at exponential rates every few years.

At OpenAI Five, AI plays 180 years' worth of games every day, learning via self-play. OpenAI Five is able to play complex video games that require teamwork and defeat human opponents of an above-average skill level at the game Dota 2. What is to stop corporations from releasing this AI in other sectors?

Artificial intelligence is used in large projects such as the human brain project, cognitive architectures, games, Google's Deep Mind, internet activism, and knowledge and reasoning with practical applications. AI was adapted in the 2016 presidential election with the use of Russian bots retweeting Donald Trump about 470,000 times versus Hillary Clinton at less than 50,000 times. If bots or AI are already influencing elections, there is much more to come.

In the narrow, well-tested area of application, such as driverless cars and medical diagnostics, the superiority of artificial intelligence over humans is established. Increased use of technology in these areas offers great potential like less traffic and accidents, as well as fewer mistakes in medical treatments and diagnoses, and the discovery of new therapies and medicines. In complex systems where several algorithms interact at high speed such as in the financial market or in foreseeable military uses, there is a heightened risk that new artificial intelligence technologies will be misused, or will experience unexpected system failures. There is also the threat of an arms race in which goals and values ought to be programmed into the AI algorithms with a guarantee that they remain stable and resist manipulation.

Many experts consider it plausible that this century will witness artificial intelligence surpass humans in all respects. The goals of such artificial intelligence could, in principle, take on any possible form and could influence the future of our planet in ways that could pose an existential risk to humanity. Our species dominates Earth because we have the highest level of intelligence. It is plausible that by the end of the century artificial intelligence will develop intelligence comparable to ours. Moreover, we cannot exclude the possibility of artificial intelligence developing phenomenal states (self-consciousness), subjective preferences, and the capacity for suffering, which would confront us with new kinds of ethical challenges.

In Peter Diamandis' TED talk *Abundance is our future*, he paints a compelling picture of a world with endless opportunities powered by technology. He talks up the prospects of AI, Robotics, 3D printing, nano metrics, and other fields.

He carefully broaches the topic of how these technologies affect us. He references a program named Watson that defeated humans in a game of Jeopardy. On the one hand, it's a great achievement. Humans were able to develop artificial intelligence to beat people at the game of Jeopardy. On the other hand, it is a cautionary tale of how far people have been left behind. Peter noted that the rate at which technology is advancing, we are becoming increasingly unmatched in a waiting game where we won't be able to make our move.

With computers and artificial intelligence improving faster than human brains can keep up, there is danger in staying static. The danger is the possibility that the technology we have strived to create and continually advance will take over our jobs, processes, and all the support systems we so desperately depend on.

Profits for the Tech Gods on Sand Hill Road

The jobs of their conceived future are determined by what will return the most profit. Automation and the use of artificial intelligence in key production is being held back by high cost and low demand. As demand rises, mass production will be actualized, driving down prices of robots and key software to automate processes worldwide. When production and price points settle, the only thing left will be effective deployment and phasing out jobs.

A lot of people hold on to the hope that they'll have a job that puts them in control of this new technology and that new jobs will cover the percentage of lost jobs. That is a model that makes no mathematical sense. The goal of automation is to cut labor costs and increase profits. To achieve this, human labor, even behind the workings of technology, will dwindle.

Shopping will be redefined and broken down into direct ordering from AI-powered shopping assistants. This might seem extreme and unimaginable but think back to a couple of years ago compared to now. Our present technology and growth rate looks like something straight out of a movie.

In the AI race, small businesses and the individuals have good reason to be terrified of operating in the shadows of technology behemoths like Google, Amazon and Facebook. As dollars continue to flow to these tech giants, business as usual will mean innovate or die. While Amazon stocks continue to spike the rest of the industry is slowly dying. This is aptly described by K.R Sanjiv CTO for Wipro in an op-ed for TechCrunch, where he wrote, 'As with all things strange and new, the prevailing wisdom is that the risk of being left behind is far greater and far grimmer than the benefits of playing it safe.'

No matter the motivation, this pace of human development is simply unsustainable and could end up creating a world that is simply unrecognizable. We may create a world where human beings are no longer at the top of the food chain, but struggling to survive and depending on stipends from the government.

Priced out of the choice areas, the bulk of the population will live in self-styled slums while the bustling cities will be overtaken by the new world superpowers; Google and Amazon. These two giants have created a market for expensive lifestyle pods that are firmly in their grip. These lifestyle pods are for the rest of the thinning human workforce to live in.

The governments of the world who refuse to submit to this new world order will slowly go underground to continue their resistance. The game will completely change and the machines will win.

If you for any reason think that the future charted in the preceding paragraphs is a nonsense notion, perhaps you should think again and consider just how much power Google and Amazon already have.

Sam Harris warns of thinking like this and avoiding the inevitable conversation in his TED talk, *Can We Build AI Without Losing Control Over It.* He warns, "We have a failure of intuition, our ability to detect any kind of danger from a scenario which is both terrifying yet likely to occur.

Swarms Engage In Unsustainable Behaviors

The moments before a locust swarm are the most breathtaking. The still silence remains, it is the light that goes out first. The swarm in the race to destruction has no brakes as it moves across the sky, blocking out the sun with common intent. What follows next is a terrifying force of nature, everything green disappears, and this loss of pigment is followed by almost tangible feelings of darkness, emptiness, and desolation.

When a colony of insects becomes too large, it's usually unable to sustain itself resulting in a disaster. The colony or hive thins out and dies until nearby resources are replenished, allowing a new colony or hive to rise in its place. This is what has helped insects live in an ecosystem for millions of years.

Scientists have long noted that studying the individual behavior of an insect or a human does not necessarily help in understanding how a swarm behaves. That's because a large portion of the swarm is guided by the behavior of those on the fringes. Human behavior is very similar.

Google and Facebook have built a framework for world domination. Their shared monopoly over advertising has granted them an incredible amount of power. They can subconsciously alter your tastes, track your spending habits, and determine what you buy when you go shopping.

Columnist Kashmir Hill of Fortune magazine mentioned in a 2012 article , "There's no need to get experiment participants to sign pesky consent forms as they've already agreed to the site's data use policy." Facebook unknowingly added positive and negative posts into a users feed which influenced their interaction with the site in the same way. And get this; over 600,000 users were part of the test. If it's free beware.

The role of tech corporations like Amazon and Google are likely to become bigger in the future since they understand technology better than the government and they're already in a place to begin influencing swarm behavior in humanity. Their ability to constantly give relevant content to people allows them a unique role in shaping the thoughts of entire generations. Who is really responsible for trending topics? How do you know if what you are reading is real?

Privacy is slowly eroded as the puppet masters of the internet find ways to manipulate your search results with the use of Pixel tracking. Ever notice a banner ad following you around the internet? A prime example of the power of information technology to influence unsuspecting people is seen in the Cambridge Analytica fiasco, where a single corporation was able to use data to influence the outcome of an entire election.

According to the Netflix documentary *The Great Hack,* approximately 32,000 voters were paid $2 - $5 to take an online personality and political test on Facebook. The app in the background not only collected their data but scraped all of their friends' data, estimating over 50 million Facebook users' data points. Traditional media advertising targets regions, channels, and time slots. With Cambridge Analytical data, advertisements can target demographics, location, age, interests, behavior, gender, and connections.

With this much data, unregistered voters can be influenced to vote in a particular way. The cost to reach 700 targeted views starts at $5. Donald Trump's 2016 digital campaign director claimed to have run 5.9 million visual ads on Facebook, compared to Hillary's Clinton's 66,000. The platforms created to connect us are being used against us.

Investigative journalist Carol Cadwalladr said in her Ted Talk, "Brexit was the petri dish for Trump." What millions of people around the world are missing is that they're in the middle of Silicon Valley swarms. Swarms are always working towards a common goal, gathering for as long as it takes to achieve a goal and they won't stop. Humanity is in danger of the same thing. In a quest to serve our needs, we have harvested forests, dug deep into the earth, and ruined our oceans without regard for how this will affect us. With climate change looming over our heads, we are still unable to stop our destructive behavior.

When it comes to humans, we have seen time and time again how groups of people are able to overcome situations if they have common goals. If the direction of goals can be manipulated, then control of the masses becomes a much easier task. Take Pokémon Go for example. A multitude of people put themselves at risk in order to play the game because they were so intrinsically aligned with a goal. This is a huge advantage for corporations that make mass-consumed software. They're able to create an ecosystem that influences the world in a swarm-like manner. The greed of these corporations will cause them to influence their user base for profit, regardless of the consequences.

The majority of the population will inadvertently begin to swarm and they'll be easily manipulated with minimal effort. This is where governments and corporations are likely to join hands to sustain populations. Corporations will earn huge profits from low-cost resources that don't ask for much, don't require much, and don't return much. It will become increasingly difficult to live on the planet if not bound to the benevolence of a business or corporation as a quasi-slave.

Despite this roadmap to extinction, everyday programmers continue to write thousands upon thousands of lines of code that will take us into total chaos. They are perhaps driven by the need to transform the world but without a doubt are also somewhat uncertain of the repercussions and far-reaching effects their work will have.

We are unwittingly caught in the middle of this swarming movement. Where there are no insects or aliens, but corporations run by humans and powered by technology and automation.

Universal Basic Income

"Robots will harvest, cook, and serve our food. They will work in our factories, drive our cars, and walk our dogs. Like it or not, the age of work is coming to an end"

-Gray Scott[1]

America has been through two major revolutions, the Agricultural and Industrial Revolutions, and each came with peculiar disruptions. Now we are in the Third Revolution and AI is undoubtedly the rave. It slowly but steadily revolutionizes the way things are done coupled with the knowledge driving those methodologies through its inclusion of ground-breaking information, integration, analysis, and usage for improved decisions[2]. Some categorize the AI wave as an industrial revolution itself[3], but not many agree. Either way, its effect will continue to be nothing short of revolutionary.

Be it transportation, health, legal, or education, AI is transforming the landscape. It's redefining what we know and what we think we know. Employees are in fear of losing their jobs[4] if they haven't already. Companies are cutting down on wage bills and the overall workplace striving for greater efficiency. It may take a few years for these AI-technologies to gain a foothold, but it is certain that will.

As technology advances, the things humans need to do are likely to dwindle to nothing, which means fewer jobs for lower-skilled people. The end result is that a large majority of people are likely to become surplus to requirements and will have to be taken care of by governments or large corporations.

A forward-looking mechanism to plug this perspective is Thomas Hobbes' *State of Nature,* where unemployment rates sky-rocket globally and the jobless become more nasty, brutish, and mean. Technocrats are proposing and experimenting with the idea of a Universal Basic Income to assist the displaced population.

The 2020 U.S. Presidential Candidate Andrew Yang sees UBI as a way out of the doom awaiting 1 out of 3 workers. He said[8], "Universal Basic Income (UBI) is a form of social security that guarantees a certain amount of money to every citizen within a given governed population, without having to pass a test or fulfill a work requirement."

Essentially it's a flat monthly wage paid to citizens whether or not they are working. Every citizen would be entitled to standard, non-variable social welfare payments that would cover basic needs like shelter, food, and health care. Quite similar to unemployment benefits, yet distinct for it is a flat-rate payment with no strings attached.

The idea of UBI is not a new one. Thomas Paine, one of America's founding fathers, referred to it as 'Natural Inheritance'. Thomas More (1478-1535) wrote about it in his book, *Utopia,* which was published in Louvain in the year 1516[9]. Political and financial will have been the only thing preventing the idea from becoming a reality.

In December 2016, the Finnish government took the bull by the horns and initiated a synonymous social remediation scheme by salarying 2,000 random unemployed citizens to cater to basic needs[10]. An analysis of the preliminary results dispelled fears about the scheme's negative impact on labor productivity. UBI advocate Scott Santens said in his analysis, "There was no discernible impact on employment, save for a small 2% boost in the self-employed."[11] This information provides evidence for the viability of the Universal Basic Income. Perhaps, that's why Canada, Kenya, Korea[12], India, and Russia, are blazing the UBI trails.

Regardless, the adoption rate of this scheme is still pretty low. The countries that have adopted it did so in the form of a pilot program with no subsequent decisive action. This lethargy could be attributed to governments' fight for capital-intensiveness. Nonetheless, we still need to prepare for the future and UBI is the best shot average workers have.

What entrepreneurs have to say about UBI:

- **Elon Musk:** The controversial CEO of the blazing autonomous-car company, Tesla, leads the pack of entrepreneurs who are in favor of and canvassing for the proliferation of Universal Basic Incomes. Well, that shouldn't come as a surprise since his company is one of those seeking to take jobs from the hands of drivers. At the 2017 World Government Summit in Dubai, he said: "Due to automation...we'll have to have a universal basic income."
- **Mark Zuckerberg:** The drop-out-turned-CEO of Facebook delivered a commencement address at Harvard in 2017. He heralded the importance of financial security on the home front, advising that "...we should explore ideas like universal basic income to give everyone a cushion to try new things."[14]. He affirmed this by stating that he probably wouldn't have tried out Facebook if he hadn't had a fail-proof, financial stability backup plan by virtue of his neurosurgeon father.
- **Andrew Ng:** Co-founder of the popular MOOC platform Coursera, and Chief Scientist at Baidu, lends his support to the UBI movement according to his statement in the wake of Donald Trump's victory at the polls. At the 2016 Deep Learning Summit in San Francisco, he mentioned:

"basic incomes deserve serious consideration[15] at this time, more than ever."

- **Steve Wozniak:** Co-founder of the global giant, Apple, agrees that there should be a sufficient set of income for everyone to meet their standard, basic needs. He further stressed that such income should vary since people in some societies are in more distress than others. In an interview at Stanford University, he said: "it [universal income] is more essential in this time than ever and...it should be very good."[16]

A cursory glance at this list would indicate a glowing endorsement of this income distribution system - where everyone gets paid for being alive in order to live a basic life. Justifiably, Silicon Valley executives should be the ones paying, since they are the driving force behind robotic automation that seeks to displace humans in the workplace.

Overpopulation

With the future of jobs evolving, the number of people competing for these roles also increases. This conversation is particularly important in the U.S, where we continue to experience a massive surge in population. The U.S. has grown from 269.4 million people in 1996 to 325.7 million people in 2016. This is a growth of 21% in 20 years. Overpopulation may be the genesis of unemployment issues.

There's a possibility that the problem isn't about the inadequacy of jobs, it's about too many entities and not enough opportunities. Pulitzer Prize author Edward O. Wilson said, "People born in 1950 were the first to see the human population double in their lifetime, from 2.5 billion to over 6 billion."

Today, most parts of the world are trying to figure out how best to manage human resources in the face of depleting natural resources like land and water. Thomas Robert Malthus wrote it in his *Malthusian Population Theory,* 'Exponential population vs. linear or perhaps, fixed resources. It's no gainsaying that most commercial hubs and geographies are past their bearing capacity and yet, people continue trooping-in in search of the golden fleece.'

We are left with one question: Are we on course to a future where our population will need to be strictly, geographically, separated between the working and the non-working class? Homeless people are already being distributed across the nation and we may begin to see this happen in a more coordinated effort.

Are we approaching a future where walls may be erected around an entire city like in the post-apocalyptic thriller *Escape From New York?* In the movie the entire island of Manhattan is turned into a maximum-security prison. Manhattan has a population twice that of San Francisco yet the city barely has 1/2 of the latter's land mass.

Clear the Logjam

Don't be surprised if we start seeing dedicated tent communities where the entire country dumps unemployed citizens. Tent cities are popping up due to unfortunate circumstances of individuals not being able to afford the high costs of rent.

Another method being used by some cities is to provide a free one-way ticket out of big cities to smaller ones in order to decongest homelessness. States including Florida, California, Nevada, Oregon, New York, and Washington are giving tickets to homeless people. The bright side is these homeless people are reunited with relatives in cities where the cost of everyday living is lower.

The poor people of Brazil aren't sitting too tight. They've taken matters into their own hands by building slums without government oversight known as Favelas. This, of course, is mainly for survival purposes. While America overbuilds in cramped cities to squeeze every last cent of profit from the planet, worsening the conditions for everyone around us. Does America really, innately care about its citizens and quality of life?

We are dealing with a global disease where the rich are getting richer and the poor are getting poorer. Furthermore the poor have to live farther and farther away from their place of work.

Where Will You Live

Ernest Cline, author of Ready Player One has gone from fan fiction guru to award winning author and now a prophet who is consistently painting with words the future of our lives as shaped by forward thinking technology and innovation.

For those who follow his work closely, this is not a new observation with many publications already crediting him for exploring the immense abilities of virtual reality as a technology and helping those who were already in the process of bringing it to life reimagined.

Cline's thoughts are seen through the living conditions of his protagonist; 'Wade Watts' who lived in the 'Stacks', a set of mobile homes stacked into the sky. These living conditions are a result of the pressure on the available housing space and the 'Stacks' are a creative attempt to create cheap opportunities for homes in prime locations that are close to cities.

It is about the future of living, where we would go to work, raise our families, build relationships, make memories and ultimately chase our dreams from a living space a ¼ the size enjoyed by our parents.

The problems that led to the creation of mobile homes in Ready Player One are anything but fiction. These problems are real and alive for the thousands of young professionals and new families who are struggling to find affordable housing, particularly in big cities where the costs of land or property continue to surge.

In San Francisco, California a two-bedroom house starts at 1.3 million. Within 10 years this number may blow up to 2.2 million. Oh yeah, don't forget you have to overbid to get your property with the money you do not have. A high tech worker is lucky to make $70,000 a year in the Bay Area, which is considered an average wage. So how does the next generation access safe and comfortable spaces to live and raise their families? You have to ask yourself early on in your career:

- Can I afford to live in my preferred city?
- Will I be able to buy or rent a house on my wages based on my current trajectory?
- What is my expected return on my educational investment (ROI) after attending college?
- Will I make more than I will owe for college?

People will not pay you to become rich. People will pay you to solve their problems and if you can scale solving people's problems, you have just taken the leap to an advanced mindset. If you truly love what you do it is not considered work.

According to *Business Insider*, the minimum income needed to rent a two-bedroom home in California is $30 an hour.

The solution that has taken the forefront is the use of micro-unit rentals. Ranging from 220 square feet to 500 square feet, micro-unit rentals are increasingly attractive to people who value location, living alone, and cheap rent.

This answer to the future of living still leaves us with many questions. How do we achieve a balance between professional and family life in these new living spaces? Will it affect the way our children will turn out? What impact would it have on building social skills and the development of human relations? Across

Europe and Asia, micro-units already represent a solution for bustling commercial hubs that have always grappled with the challenge of inadequate land, but nobody has figured out the answer to these questions.

For regulatory bodies and government, the questions are different. There is a worry that the rise of small, efficient spaces means an increased demand for public amenities.

Most micro-unit schemes are built without plans for parking spaces. There is a tendency for things to quickly spiral out of control, particularly in locations where parking is already limited. There have also been concerns about crime and the potential for these new housing micro-units to become breeding grounds for crimes and indiscipline. With a teeming youth population constrained in so little space, there is the likelihood that increased noise levels, crowding, and crime will make policing and safety part of this new conversation.

Perhaps we are overreaching and micro-unit rentals are not such a new thing in the grand scheme of things. Some would argue that we already live our lives in micro-units every day in our cubicles. In response to all the time we spend staring at our screens trying to get work done, we have made it our new home. Our pictures of friends and family are placed at vantage points on the desk, our drawers are skillfully stacked with essentials, and we have found a way to zone out and relax in these little spaces that are now home.

As population growth continues to surge forward, particularly in the United States, more people will turn to the cubicle lifestyle in search of their own space. Our office experience will merge with our home life as we begin to spend more time in these little spaces that we are already beginning to see as home.

Forward-thinking startups and even major companies have taken a leap by building workplaces in a way that closely resembles home. From sleeping pods to meditation spots to dining rooms, employers have already reimagined the future of work and living and they are trying to merge them.

It is not hard to imagine a future where home is work and work is home. With the lines blurred, it will be up to determine where work starts and ends. Setting career goals and personal goals, and deciding how we want to achieve them will even be more deliberate.

We must not only consider the rise of micro-unit rentals, but we must deliberately avoid being boxed into a future of living that envisions life in a little box. If we are to enjoy family life and provide a safe and comfortable space for our children to thrive, then the answer to micro-unit rentals is a no.

The future of living and the future of work are inextricably linked. According to a recent report from McKinsey, between 0% and 40% of hours worked globally could be automated by 2030. With big cities providing the biggest draw with lucrative opportunities, the key questions would no longer be how to move and where to stay, but whether you have the skills in this new world that makes you attractive to employers.

Going further, McKinsey projects the abilities to manage people, apply expertise, and social interaction will be skills in demand as automation will have a lower effect on jobs that require such skills. Essentially, our education has to put less emphasis on memorization.

Young adults can seize the future but they must learn to be creative. We need to embrace the joy of problem-solving and the blessing of teamwork to achieve future freedoms.

From the small corner of your micro-unit rental, you must remember to think in terms of a world that will continue to be disrupted. In constantly unlearning and relearning we can take advantage of a world with no boundaries.

Future Proof Yourself

When the Serengeti's water levels are low animals gather at the watering hole to take a sip. These animals face their predators head-on to avoid dehydration.

Well, the rain of jobs has slowed and decent employment is hard to come by. At the watering hole, you can see the dangers around you. You won't be eaten if you are standing at a job board but you may suffer from little to no responses from employers. Your fellow job applicant is not a lion, but they will travel more than 75 miles and take your job, as will the other 20,000 applicants that have moved into the area thirsty for work. Our struggle to survive is not in the Serengeti, it is happening over digital bits across the internet.

As we are priced out of our homes, we have to relocate further away from high-paying jobs. Depending on your industry, the need for your talent or service is challenged more every year. Due to overbuilding and population growth, we find ourselves on a never-ending path to scavenging for available resources.

A position that may have had 100 applicants in a week 15 years ago now has 400 or more applicants in a few days and as many as 150 applicants in a few hours. You must be thinking too many applicants right? Well, try the premium membership model on LinkedIN.com and you'll see the numbers for yourself. With a rapidly expanding working population, HR professionals are flooded with solicited and unsolicited applications.

If you're lucky you'll get to drink. In spite of all this competition, it is up to you to move forward. The question becomes, can you handle a 3 hour round trip daily commute? If you answer yes, this means you will sit in traffic for about 650 hours a year, that's about 16% of your life trapped in a car.

If you decide you don't want to commute, you might have to balance two or three part-time jobs to make enough money for rent, which leaves you pretty much without a social life. The urbanization effect on our planet will continue its downward spiral and we will continue to feel its effects for centuries.

One way to beat the curve is to become like the corporations that produce the goods and services we can't live without. We need to develop thinking that is productivity-oriented, not consumer-oriented. Tony Wagner, a Harvard Innovation Education Fellow, supports this idea in his book *Creating Innovators: The Making of Young People Who Will Change the World*: 'We've created an economy based on people spending money they do not have to buy things they may not need, threatening the planet in the process...We have to transition from a consumer-driven economy to an innovation-driven economy.'

Unfortunately, we can't count on the education system to equip us with the mindset and skills for innovation. The school system produces employees to service corporations. It emphasizes specialization, individual achievement, risk aversion, and passive learning, none of which are characteristic of successful entrepreneurs.

While I don't recommend you drop out of school, there are alternative education platforms that will be critical in shaping the mindset of future generations. We need to get used to innovating ourselves to stay ahead of technology. Online academies like Coursera, edX, and Udemy in collaboration with reputable institutions. They offer forward courses such as master coding fundamentals, protecting business innovations via patent, and digital competition in financial services. We also need to get in the habit of watching a few TED talks a week. This will exponentially unleash the creative intelligence of young people. The ideas pushed on the TED stage are unique and challenge audiences to search for personal innovation.

We need to take charge of our training so we are not forcefully molded to work for corporations. Unfortunately, impacting society is not on your school's agenda. Only by taking a high-level view of our own patterns with regards to everything that we are up against can we start to get traction and make an impact.

It is clear that the increase of robot workers has the potential to cause serious employment problems. It's important that our education and entrepreneurial system focus on teaching soft skills to prepare people for an evolving workplace where AI competition and management are to be expected. The real skills you need to succeed will involve more than traditional thinking. Creativity must be at its peak and we must be ready to provide urgent solutions to demanding problems. Here are some of the skills you need:

- The ability to interpret large amounts of data
- Organizing
- Marketing
- Contract negotiation
- Project management
- Adaptability
- Creative and critical thinking
- Technology literacy

Artificial intelligence is undoubtedly useful. As the world becomes more complex, we need to leverage human resources and high-quality computer systems. The idea that a machine might possess intelligence scares many. Most people believe that intelligence is something that makes us unique, which is what distinguishes humans. If intelligence can be mechanized, what is unique about humans? What sets it apart from the machine?

Artificial intelligence, more specifically, robotics, has both positive and negative impacts on employment. Most likely, it would be harder to get a job that a robot can also perform, as young people still lack basic work skills such as teamwork and problem solving, better suiting them for the role than a robot. However, the picture varies across different sectors, job types, and skill levels. Positions that can withstand the automation storm will involve thinking, quick judgments, none repetitive use of your hands, creativity, physical endurance, and experimentation. It's projected that some of the top careers for the year 2025 will be:

- Nursing
- Doctors
- Anesthesiology

- Dentistry
- Science
- Teaching
- Entrepreneurship
- Art / Creativity
- Athletics
- Law Enforcement
- Marketing ad creation
- Complex problem solving
- Computer programming
- Critical thinking
- Gardening
- Plumbing
- Drone Piloting
- Solar Installation
- Wind Turbine Technician

Getting Ahead

We live in a lopsided system that doesn't offer favors to people at the bottom. If anything, it is a reminder that you deserve more out of life. If there is anything to learn from this chapter, it's that you hardly matter in the grand scheme of the Silicon Valley gods.

You are more than a digital bit that can be turned on or off at your employer's will. You are worth more than a barcode that can be scanned and put to work for others.

At one point I noticed that I was hitting repeat on my life, like a mouse running on a wheel that never stopped spinning and the faster I ran, the harder it was to jump off and evaluate my current situation. Only through analyzing the patterns and trends that impact different social classes and technology did I realize that the disruption triangle will continue to close in on us.

So as you run on the wheel of life, will the amount of cheese you get for your efforts become smaller?

That in itself is the true meaning of the words 'live free or die hard'. They speak of a constant struggle and sometimes several failures in an attempt to live free, knowing that the flip side is a long hard life serving as a slave at the bottom of the pyramid.

This book, in a sense, is a personal checklist for survival and will become more true and relevant with every passing day. In the chapters ahead we will tear apart the fallacies around cultural norms so that we can determine what is truly vital for the future we desire. We must fight while we are young so that we do not get old and take our regrets to the grave.

"Death is nothing, but to live defeated and inglorious is to die daily."

-Napoleon Bonaparte

A Place For Future Generations

My research into the patterns of the human race has dropped me at the doorstep of our planet's future. Only by looking at our habits can we determine where we are going to end up as a society. I have uncovered material which is good for mankind and other material which is not so good. An interesting futuristic quote by Jonas Salk, who said, "If all the insects were to disappear from the Earth, within 50 years, all life on Earth would end. If all human beings disappeared from the Earth, within 50 years all forms of life would flourish."

Humans are a predatory species and we have to realize that once we get something we usually want more of it and it does not matter what it is. As the population continues to grow we will continue to put a larger strain on our infrastructure which eventually impacts you.

In the book Bold by Peter Diamandis he states that if everyone in the world wasted energy like the Europeans, we would need the resources for 3 planet Earths. If you switch from Europeans to Americans we would need 5 planet earths.

At times I have had the feeling of dread and doom that we are on the precipice of self annihilation. In the search for real world consequences and connections I ran across an excellent book Sapiens by historian Yuval Noah Harari, PHD. Sapiens links "facts" and "evidence" in an eye opening thought provoking way which gets the reader thinking. Next time you are at your garden center pickup and plant a tree to help our planet.

"The more that we remain in our comfort zone today, the more uncomfortable our future will be."

-Andrewzee

Chapter 2 Regret and Digging Yourself Out

"What will you regret by the age of 80 years old?"

-Jeff Bezos

Planes, Printing, and Progress

It doesn't matter if you are 18, 30, or 50 years old. You can always dream and you can always change course.

When I was young I wanted to be an Astronaut and I eventually talked myself out of it. Then I wanted to be a pilot, which I quickly lost focus on. The closest I got to an aircraft was when I attended a technical high school and I took an aeronautics class for a couple of years. The class was really cool because it was the first time I was able to use my hands and tools to disassemble aircraft parts like landing gears. The class required me to take an electrical course, which helped me understand electronics, as well as a year of machine shop, and I loved it.

As a kid, I was always amazed by planes. Intrigued with the mechanics of flight, their huge size, and their powerful sounding engines. I graduated from college with a computer science degree and thought I was ready for the world. A short time later, my uncle helped me land an interview with United Airlines at the San Francisco airport. With all the events leading up to this, I was as excited as a kid in a candy shop. During my interview, I was given a tour of a few areas in the hanger. I remember a little door opening to a huge airplane on the other side.

I can remember walking through that door like it was yesterday, it was amazing to stand side by side with a huge aircraft. I have always been fascinated with aviation, it's amazing to think that the Wright brothers made history with their first powered flight in 1907 at Kitty Hawk. What's even more fascinating is that this was their hobby when they weren't busy running their bicycle shop.

While I did not get a tour of the aircraft, I was stunned by the size of the landing gear which had tires 3 to 4 feet high and about 2 feet wide each. Ideas started going around in my mind about what this job could turn into.

After I wiped the excitement off my face I was led inside to another part of the building. In front of me were a few long metal tables and along the sides were what looked like buckets of multi-colored legos from afar. As I got closer I realized what I was looking at was multiple bins filled with thousands of colored wire connectors. The interviewer described what I would be doing. "Son, you will be working on upgrading the wiring harnesses on various parts of the aircraft. Sometimes the wiring will be worked on here in the shop at other times you will work on the aircraft."

As I drove away from United Airlines I got to thinking about what the job would entail. Replacing wires and connectors every single day. My appetite for the position had suddenly lessened.

I don't remember exactly what I said or I did, but I informed my uncle that I would not be pursuing the mechanic position because I could not see myself in a repetitive job for the rest of my life. So even while I was in my twenties, something inside of me made me think that any job that I would start would become a significant part of my life. Little did I know what promotions meant at the time and I failed to recognize that you have to start on the ground floor.

Right out of university I was able to get a position as a technician with a printing company in San Francisco that paid $26 dollars an hour. My advantages at the time were my field of study in electronics and I was young. I will never forget the operators of the printing machines, they were all around 50 years old and here I was coming in at half their age making around three times their salary. At the time an operator's job was to feed architecture drawings into these large machines to make copies for our clients like Skidmore Owings & Merrill (SOM) and Lucas Films. It was interesting to see some of the early Star Wars drawings by Lucas Films. SOM would send through designs on the Chase Tower in Dallas, and later they sent designs for megaprojects like the Burj Khalifa in Dubai, and One World Trade Center in New York.

I stayed with the company for four years and learned the different aspects of the job while coordinating my efforts with my seniors and making good relations. While about 30% of the job was troubleshooting electrical and image quality issues, the rest was maintenance. Sometimes while I was troubleshooting on service calls I would get an electrical shock due to electricity conducting over surfaces because of a short. It was a little dangerous, especially in the high voltage sections. Thankfully the machines had lockboxes over the power switches, preventing operators from coming around the side of the machine and turning on the power while I worked on the inner panels. An interesting point worth mentioning is that I eventually was talented enough to fix just about everything around me, a skill I am now thankful for. However, I drew a line when my boss pointed to the elevator and asked, "Can you see why the door won't close all the way?" As a tech, I learned shortcuts around problems, but a shortcut here could mean somebody's life. I said no thanks, call the professionals.

I started to track the parts for about 35 printing machines company-wide. There were around 5 machine models at the time, which printed blueprints and black and white copies from 42-inch wide paper roll stock.

We had a small shop where we stored all of the parts, as well as a single computer. On this computer, I developed a few simple dBase III screens to track our inventory. As the techs used the parts, they filled in the location, machine, and part number on the parts slips. When the techs visited San Francisco, all of the part slips would make their way to a box next to the parts computer. As I updated the inventory, ordered parts, and made updates to the screens, I realized it was more exciting to work on the computer with the data. I liked creating the screens and the data structure so much that I transitioned into programming afterward.

After a while, I began to realize there was no upward mobility with the printing company. The need for large 36-inch blueprints was going the way of the dinosaur as architecture firms began to use computers and plotters more frequently.

Eventually, I left my position at the printing company. It was worth it and I'm glad I did because, in the end, I quadrupled my salary, consulting for big brands.

I remember when I told the printing company that I would be leaving. They tried to use the only leverage they had on me and they told me I would have to relinquish my fuel card. It was a bummer because it felt like I was giving up something big. I even drove to Disneyland a few times on their fuel. However, I refused to let them intimidate me into staying. I gave up the card and moved on to greener pastures,

Create Your Own Job

After my printing company stretch, I switched careers towards programming and management but first had to take a support position with the United States Postal Service. When I took the job at the USPS I knew I didn't want to get into support, but I made the move to get into tech. This was the era when Netscape was just released onto the internet.

Before I could transition into programming, I had to take a step into a support role at the United States Postal data center in San Mateo, California. The position involved supporting two programs for every US post office branch. The job involved everything from taking support calls relating to printing issues, addressing hard disk errors, and configuring modems. I will never forget the time I had asked a user to insert the floppy disk and close the door. After a few seconds, I heard an office door slamming.

A few weeks into this position, I noticed a few process gaps. Support calls were taking twice as long to complete as they should have. We were not tracking solutions across calls.

We had a binder covering about two dozen scenarios on how to fix common situations, but that was it.

Yet everyone was taking a dozen or more calls a day without thinking about a solution. I found an opportunity to improve and suggested this:

- Create a searchable knowledge-based solution, so that technicians could apply solutions that worked in the past

- Track time per call

- Track calls per technician

- Track calls per incident type

- Track the history per USPS branch - who did what

- Basic reporting

During this time I subscribed to Dr. Dobbs Visual Programming magazine and started buying programming books. A month into my position at the USPS, I wound up going to Egghead software and purchased a copy of Visual Basic for about $300. This was a programming language that was easy to make sophisticated applications in no time at all.

Within seven weeks of purchasing the software, I was able to create a multi-user application with an MS Access backend with zero programming experience. The application was used by ten USPS employees. The motivation to solve a business need and learn multi-network programming got me very excited.

When I created this application I had only started to see programming examples in books. At the time of writing this application, I only knew two software developers, Derrick, a long time school buddy, and Andre, a soft-spoken Russian software developer.

Both Derrick and Andre worked at the USPS as software developers. Speaking with Andre felt a little like talking to a robot because I would ask him a question and he responded, but then he would not say another word. He would give me a stare with the look of blinking cursors in his eyes. Derrick and I were always researching the latest, greatest tech and chatting over a coffee or lunch. Both Derrick and Andre served as mentors in my early software development years. When you are getting started in something, you need to be able to ask questions and have an open mindset to the responses.

I could not believe that this little investment in a tool and my own self-learning could make such a difference at the time. Note: I created the application on my home computer, on my own time. As our team started to use the application, I wound up getting paid to work on the application for about 25% of my time at the USPS. The application tracked over 47,000 support tickets by the time I left.

What job or solution can you create while at your day job?

Who's Looking Out For Your Future

As the clock ticks away, we have fewer opportunities to change our future. The play button has been pressed and social norms don't want you to have the opportunity to pull out the disc and change the movie. When in fact the best decision you can make is changing the movie. If you have a conversation with someone that is stuck in their ways when it comes to new opportunities, you will most likely hear these excuses:

- I have no time

- I am too old to change things

- I am getting by. Why change?

- I've been here for five-plus years

- I do not know where to start

- I am worried about what others might say

The train of thought is that they must watch the movie they've started until they die. This is a repetitive pattern, especially for older folks. In this writing, I have peeled back the onion, exposing multiple layers of the good, the bad, and the ugly, so that you can take a close look at the various aspects of decisions which can lead to a future which might be a little better than what you have planned.

A CNBC article mentioned 1 in 3 Americans will have less than $5,000 available to them in retirement. What can you do with $5,000? Not much really. Experts recommend that the least amount you should accumulate for retirement is $1 million. People aren't putting aside as much as they should due to the rising costs of living and living paycheck to paycheck with little to spare.

Nobody wants to reach retirement age and realize that their cumulative lifetime decisions have dropped them off at the corner of Regret & I Cannot Do Anything Now Because I Am Too Old And Weak.

Retiring from a fulfilling, well-earned job at 60, and living from paycheck to paycheck are two completely different things. In the end, it will be a question of how much life you lived for your benefit. Were you constantly frustrated at the end of each day, feeling empty because the day's tasks were unfulfilling or did you live for yourself, truly enjoying life?

Imagine how it would feel to grow old and have done nothing on your bucket list. No scuba diving, no horseback riding, and no roller coasters, no desert safaris, nothing. Your desires will remain until the day you die. Why create a bucket list if you never plan on tackling it? What about the opera and art exhibitions you wanted to attend? What happened to that trip you promised your spouse years ago? Why didn't you make an effort to actually live your life? A life full of regrets is not a life to live.

How can you live a life that you won't regret at 65? A lot of it relies on the job you have. There is a major difference between working for a company and working for yourself. While many have biased opinions about both, there is a certain truth that cannot be denied when you consider both sides of the argument.

One-Armed Bandit

During my first month of training, Marv and I rode in the same car and visited blueprint shops while at other times, Marv would page me with a message like: 'Meet me at Broadway 9:30 am.'

Every time Marv came into work he'd have a cup of coffee in his hand. His toolbox must have weighed 30 pounds, but he never left his coffee behind. This is how I came to give him the nickname, the One-Armed Bandit.

During my first few weeks of training, we fell into a routine - arrive at a shop, place our tool boxes next to the machine that needed servicing, open up a few panels, turn the power off, and head out and get coffee. We would tell the shop manager that we needed to step out to get a part, but we always returned with a cup of coffee. Marv and I spent our time at the coffee shop chatting about movies we recently watched, what was going on in our personal lives, the weather, and so on.

Marv was assigned to work in the East Bay and I generally worked at the San Francisco locations at Broadway, 2nd Street, and Mission Street. When a technician would go on vacation I would respond to service calls in the East Bay in Oakland and San Ramon. While in the East Bay, I would sometimes run across Marv doing the exact same job I was doing. What struck me about this was Marv was 30 years my senior. It's as if I was seeing my future self. This got me thinking - is this going to be my future?

Marv continued to work for the printing company in the same position. We have stayed in touch over the years and I know of his struggles through our conversations and outings.

I will never forget the day when Marv purchased a brand new Mercedes for his 60th birthday, just five years before his retirement. Over the years, he managed to save up half the purchase price. We chatted about the car before he bought it. I told him to make sure that the loan didn't have a prepayment penalty so he could increase his payments and pay off the loan sooner. Why is it that we have to wait for the things we would like to have? He deserved a beautiful car for working hard his whole life, and if he had purchased the same car five years earlier he would have been paying more for the car than the rent on his apartment. It meant so much to him to drive that Mercedes into his reserved, manager parking spot, even if it meant being stuck in traffic every day.

He lived paycheck to paycheck but didn't have to. He could have made a move for the better, just as I did. What I find strange is the fact he built his life around work, as many do. We forget the truth in the words of Jim Collins, "Good is the enemy of great," settling for what we have and never aspiring or reaching for more.

Elephants raised in the circus think their mobility is limited by a small stake and chain. They grow up thinking that the restrictions imposed by the chain is just a way of life. Like circus elephants, humans can fall into a trap, never gathering the courage to change their situation or escape for a new opportunity. People become so bound to work that nothing else matters. They forget or are too tired to pursue personal goals or save and invest in the future. This kind of thinking shuts us out from the truth.

Marv worked until age 61 and then the company laid him off. He went from a six-figure job to unemployed and almost homeless in a stretch of six months. He planned on working until he was 70 years old and never thought much about saving for rainy days. Shortly afterward he was able to get SSI payments at about $900 a month which was right above the poverty line.

Ironically, Marv spent almost his entire savings on the Mercedes just a year before his layoff. During our conversations, I was shocked to hear he was more worried about keeping his car than earning income during his retirement years. I don't remember his exact words after the layoff but one of the first things Marv mentioned to me was his concern for how he was going to fill up the gas tank in his car. His next concern was if he would be able to continue making his car payments. Here I am thinking about Marv's future and well being, and Marv is thinking about his car. A lesson I hope that you take away is to pay yourself first, build a nest egg and anticipate what might come so that you are not blindsided by the actions of others.

He couldn't understand how the company he served for over 30 years could simply lay him off. We had this conversation several times and every time we did, the importance of having a long term plan that secured my future hit with a sad twist of reality. It goes without saying, he was upset with himself for not planning ahead.

Marv spent most of his time off watching football games. His knowledge of football was great for conversations. We shared many conversations about the days of Joe Montana, Ronnie Lott, and Roger Craig - some of the most valuable players for the San Francisco Forty-Niners football team at the time. He loved movies too. He would lend me just about any DVD title that you could name. His DVD collection was huge and it took up a complete wall in his apartment. I would generally have better success with borrowing movies from Marv than Blockbuster. I remember coming to work on a Monday and asking him about his weekend. He would tell me it was pretty good, that he was able to watch reruns of X, Y, and Z. I didn't think much about it at the time, but now realize how much time he actually spent watching football games, television shows, and movies - time he could never get back. When Marv would take a few days off work he would return with stories of old movies like *Gone with the Wind* and *Casablanca.* I guess the movies took the place of vacations for Marv because he never left his television screen. Years later I realized that as humans we can get locked into our patterns. We tend to live in a bubble of sorts and we may need help to pop the bubble.

The larger problem is that the concept of companies offering retirement fell to the wayside in the '90s. For Marv, living month to month with a regular paycheck was enough. There's no reason to plan ahead if your basic living needs are being met. For many, holding onto a regular job until retirement has become an illusion.

Eventually, Marv had to move downtown to a not-so-nice neighborhood where he was able to negotiate a long-term lease for a small hotel room. The room was 12 by 12 feet with a built-in kitchenette and a small bathroom. He had to downsize from a nice apartment with a fresh ocean breeze to a single room. When I found out about his move to the hotel, I couldn't help but think about how things should be getting easier for you as you get older. Looking out his hotel window, one would hope to see a beautiful grassy lawn with trees but his view revealed piles of trash. A dark musky area surrounded by other cheap hotels and run-down houses.

I will never forget the way that room made me feel. Marv's room was on the third floor and half of the times I visited, the elevator would be out of order. This meant we had to take the stairs which, in a way, felt safer. When the elevator worked, you would have to close a sliding metal, see-through gate and you could watch the floors pass as you rode up. On his floor, there must have been over ten doors on each side of the dark hallway. As I walked to the opposite end of the hallway, I paid particular attention to one of the two dim flickering lights. I felt uneasy being in a strange building in the dark with no lights. It reminded me of the creepy scenes from all the suspenseful movies I borrowed from Marv. Over time, we developed a father-son type relationship which kept our bond close throughout the years.

Just visiting and talking with Marv helped put a positive spin on his outlook on life. Back at the printing company, we often ate lunch together. On most days, we wound up going into the Mission district to eat at La Rondalla, a Mexican restaurant on 20th and Valencia Street in San Francisco. So, whenever I would drop in to visit him, I would make sure to stop by La Rondalla and pick up a burrito or tamales to bring him. The food always brightened his mood, giving him the energy to smile, sit up, and give me a hug. As you get older, life passes you by. The problem becomes compounded, as you are too tired to do anything about it. I feel an urge to share this story in hopes that the morals of it transfer into actions before you are too old to do anything to help your cause.

Marv has to use a walker now. His limited walking ability makes exploring the neighborhood and shopping difficult. Although, he did manage to get a few people on his floor to help out with his shopping. He likes to use Uber to get around which is fine for the first week of the month when he has some cash on hand. But by the second week, he's spent most of his allowance and he stays close to home, circling his block seeking a simple meal. Marv doesn't complain much, but he wishes for someone to drive him around and for a nicer place to live. His weekly exercise routine consisted of walking to the local church to pick up a bag of groceries provided by a food bank.

I think if we knew that one day we would depend on someone else to bring us our one meal for the day, we would fight a little harder before it's too late.

Live. Die. Repeat.

In the same movie *Live. Die. Repeat.* Tom Cruise and Emily Blunt are part of a special forces unit where Tom re-lives a series of airdrops onto a beach to fight against an alien invasion. Tom realizes that no matter how many times he re-lives the experience that he can only change a few minor details of the invasion.

With each beach landing, the commandos are slaughtered and Emily winds up dying every time.

The problem is that the aliens already know the humans' plans, which is why they are ready every time the commandos invade the beach. Eventually, Tom and Emily realize they need to change their focus on upstream activities and target the aliens' central command which will change the outcome of the war.

How can you beat the alien resistance and make your beach landing a success before it is too late?

I have played back Marv's story so many times and keep coming back to the idea that if we only do what is expected of us, reality speeds up and we won't be able to change.

One can achieve more than just a desk job at a company that doesn't value you and leaves you hanging after 30 years of employment. You probably know someone who had an experience similar to Marv's. So what are you doing differently? Shouldn't you be making an effort to jump off the merry-go-round?

The truth is that while we are helping companies get what they want, companies are sucking the life out of us. We devote huge amounts of time to companies that don't pay us what we're worth. And we're not only paying these companies with energy, but we're also paying them with our time. Time we could be spending with our families. The harder we work, the more separated we become from our loved ones. The more we work, the more stress we have, the worse our health gets. How long can this go on?

In the early years of a steady career, people unknowingly spend their energy putting all their effort into their job. Working 9 to 6, 9 to 7, and after a while, the overtime becomes a blur. They don't realize it, but their bodies start deteriorating inside. This internal discomfort reflects how they conduct themselves and on their personalities. They find themselves becoming irritable, stressed, and living on the edge. They put in long hours without counting the cost until they've retired and begin to question if those 50-hour weeks they poured themselves into were worth the health challenges they face.

Long hours don't only impact health, work strain can affect relationships. Weekends are consumed with thinking and worrying about work, rather than being present with loved ones.

People become so bound to work that nothing else matters. They forget or are too tired to pursue personal goals or save and invest in the future. Eventually, they regret all the soccer games they missed and wish they would have said 'no' more often.

Not only does this lifestyle bring regrets, but it is also very harmful to your mental health. Constant grueling work with limited time for yourself and family puts you into a constant state of anxiety and depression that is hard to shake off. Slowly, your personality changes but after a few years, you and your loved ones accept the new you. Remember those times when you were waiting for the clock to strike 5 pm so you could have a date night? Perhaps enjoy a game with your child? Slowly these excitements fade away and long hours become a way of life.

By repeating this pattern on a daily basis, we are robbed of the ability to focus our minds on topics that might be of better interest to us. Your destiny is a result of what you think and do on a daily basis.

"Your time is limited, so don't waste it living someone else's life. Don't be trapped by dogma - which is living with the results of other people's thinking. Don't let the noise of others' opinions drown out your own inner voice. And most important, have the courage to follow your heart and intuition."

--Steve Jobs

Are You Really Free?

Why do we keep seeing the same facial expressions on everyone as they make their way to their towers of labor? What you see on those faces is a resignation to fate and submission to the security of a desk job.

Ever get the feeling that just maybe you are part of the thousands who go through the motions every day?

During your next commute to work, take a few minutes to look at the facial expressions on everyone's face on the train, escalator, elevator or as they walk to work. Observe carefully and ask these questions; Are they smiling? Are their shoulders slumped? Are they dragging their feet when they walk?

As you watch, chances are that you'll find two classes of people - those who seem to have resigned to fate and those in a constant rush. The constant rush is not positive, rather an indication of fear. People are conscious that employers can drive massive layoffs, replacing them with cheaper labor. For them, every day is a bet against unemployment.

After studying the faces and the fears they hold, then it is time for a serious introspection. You must ask yourself the hard questions. If your company decides to downsize and lets you go, how will you pay your rent, feed your family, and survive?

Mt. Everest Or The Retirement Home

The problem with many of us is that we don't like to try new things. We prefer the safe path, no matter how boring or limited it is. The truth is, we are all capable of climbing the tallest peak Mount Everest at 29,000 ft. However, because of peer pressure and the old guidelines we are led down the common, well-trodden path that leads to the same fate as others. How can you step off the conveyor belt of life before you reach the end of the line?

We need to broaden our perspective and understand the multiple roles we can play in. Life is not limited to a simple desk job. There is so much out there for you to do! Focus on yourself and your comfort. Yes, there may be some harsh, hardworking years but it is far better to work hard for a few years and then enjoy the rest of your life rather than work until your last breath.

We have a choice about how we want to be remembered. We tend to live as though we have multiple lives to achieve our goals. Well, guess what? You only have one life. Act now before it is too late to make a difference.

It takes time and some planning to make the right moves. But the moves you make on the chessboard of life are by far the most important.

While some moves guide you towards Mt. Everest, others steer you into a senior care facility, which is where Marv finally ended up. His senior facility was over 200 miles away from his closest family member, solely chosen due to Marv's limited income.

I visited Marv at the retirement home every few weeks in the first year and then every couple of months afterward.

Walking into the place felt as if time had stopped and I was confronted with an 'old people smell'. After a few visits, I learned to place a tiny bit of Vicks vapor rub under my nose to help block the smell, just as morgue employees do.

The independence of every resident in the facility seemed to have been left outside as payment for entry. While some folks got around with walkers, others use wheelchairs. The remaining bunch were bedridden patients with their own set of complications.

Have you ever watched a movie where a character walks down a haunted hall and the eyes in the paintings are following them? As I passed the elderly residents in the hallway, they would all stare at me until I had gotten into Marv's room or out of sight. Rather than ignore them, I had decided to talk with a few of them. As we spoke, I could see happiness return to their faces. I could read their body language as we chatted and noticed their enthusiasm as they leaned towards me. As we spoke, their voices would rise and I would get the feeling that I was adding hours to their life simply by saying hello.

There was one woman who usually sat in a wheelchair in the dining room. Even though she was busy playing cards, surrounded by five friends, she still would catch up to me within a few feet of Marv's door and say, "Hi, Sunny. Is it time for our evening talk?" After a while, we got to know each other and I spent some time with her. During one of our short conversations, I found out that her previous job was to greet visitors at a museum and give tours. I asked her if she enjoyed the job. She told me it was interesting and she liked talking to all the people.

"How long did you work at the museum?" I asked

"Ever since I graduated from college."

"Is there anything you wanted to do but didn't."

She said, "Yes. I wanted to go on a two-week cruise, on one of those large ships."

"How come you never went?"

"I wanted to be there for the museum even when others called in sick," she said.

"What about your family? Are they close?"

"They live out of state and don't have space for me," she said.

I wish that I could've somehow given that sweet lady her cruise.

Every time I left the facility, I would think to myself, is this my future too? I would hope to be living with loved ones, or in a nice place, perhaps a personal assistant. My relationship with Marv was one of the reasons I took a closer look at my life and realized there must be a better way.

We have to take a step back, peek through the fog, and realize where we are heading. Companies will offer you a 401K, a gym membership, free rides to work, free drinks, and free food, but at the end of the day, it's all about WIFM (What's In It For Me) from the company's perspective. While you are doing your best for your company, it's yourself you need to look out for first.

"It is not death that a man should fear, but he should fear never beginning to live"

-Marcus Aurelius

Bronnie Ware, a hospice worker, writes there are five common regrets of those at the end of their lives. Her five points are numbered. I have added a few takeaways we should also be thinking about.

1. I wish I'd had the courage to live a life true to myself, not the life others expected of me.

    - Living a life that serves others merely for a paycheck, without ever taking pride in your work, cannot be rewarding.
    - Are you choosing a career because you want to defend the innocent and make a difference, or because your family thinks this is the best choice for you based on *their* experiences?
    - Which regrets are you taking to the grave? Realize it does not have to be this way.

2. I wish I didn't work so hard.

60

- Many of us prioritize work and when a deadline nears we work longer hours. We desire different results for our hard work but different results require different experiments and different work.
- Studies have shown that after working more than 40 hours in a week, productivity begins to diminish and mistakes go up.
- Life is short. Fast forward five years. Are you still in the same job and the same circumstances? Is the dollar amount that you are providing to the market going up or staying the same?
- Learn from the mistakes of others.

3. I wish I'd had the courage to express my feelings.

- Open, honest communication is the best instigator of productive conversations.
- If you hide your feelings, you are not being true to who you are.
- What conversations are you not having?

4. I wish I had stayed in touch with my friends.

- Happiness is the result of sharing great experiences with people you care about.
- Adjusting your circle of friends can help you grow and see different perspectives.
- Success is not achieved alone.

5. I wish that I had let myself be happier.

- Put yourself first and making yourself a priority
- Schedule your fun time or it never happens.
- Follow your passion projects or they never happen.
- If you are not happy with where you are at, switch something.

- Seek help if you feel stuck in a rut

"Remembering that you are going to die is the best way I know to avoid the trap of thinking you have something to lose. You are already naked. There is no reason not to follow your heart."

-Steve Jobs

A Cruise Ship Or A Boat

Have you ever tried to get all of your loved ones together for a two-week vacation? The excuses you'll hear are endless. I remember hearing everything from work schedules, not enough vacation days, to money problems. Then, when you finally arrive at your destination, you rush through the exhibits like you were in a timed competition. Were you actually able to relax, sit back, kick your legs up, and let the time melt by? Too often, we treat our vacations like we treat our work schedules, cramming so much in that we don't get a chance to catch our breath or fully enjoy ourselves.

One of my favorite memories I go back to is laying out on a lawn chair on the back of a cruise ship, sipping a nice drink, and watching the horizon teeter up and down, left to right, as the ship cruised the open ocean. I love that moment because time did not matter. I was on my own schedule, I was with my family, and everything was amazing.

Think about your last weekend trip. You packed your family into your car and drove to your destination with everyone else on the road too. All the while you think, 'This sucks, I'm wasting my Saturday.' Then Sunday evening, you jump back in your car and race home alongside everyone else. Why not flip things around so that you are in control of your time? Use the weekdays to commute to your vacations when the roads are less filled?

Why do we put so much effort into planning the perfect vacation, yet allow our lives to continue on autopilot, manipulated by the gods in the ivory towers? We seek new jobs every couple of years and expect that a new job will solve all our needs. It's like we are in a continuous line at the amusement park of life.

Regardless of how much money you make, one of the ultimate measurements of wealth is how much free time you can afford. While the majority of us may be in a similar boat. With just a few adjustments in our mindset and habits, we can start to turn our lives around.

Karoshi

A quick look into the Japanese work culture reveals that they use the term karoshi, which means death from overwork. This is no exaggeration, overworking is a major cause of untimely death in Japan, a country facing the reality of a steady population decline. In a survey conducted by the Japanese Family Planning Association, they found that close to half of the population ages 16 - 49 were not planning on having children. A major reason was work-related fatigue.

Most Japanese work more than 80 hours of overtime a week, unpaid. The idea of that probably sounds like exploitation to you, but to the average Japanese person, it isn't. Corporate culture in Japan is driven by the concept of the 'salaryman.' A salaryman is a person who spends their entire life working for a company and also spends their free time mingling with colleagues in after-work activities. So, you see, the life of an average Japanese worker is centered around whatever company they work for, not family.

Here in the US, many would say we're not faced with this kind of challenge, but the truth is that we are, just in a slightly different way. While the average Japanese worker spends extremely long hours at work, at times stretching into the next day, the average American worker might spend a few extra hours at work, but they are sure to take their work home with them. While Japan needs to work on ending its workday earlier and prioritizing individual welfare, America has to find a way to help people separate work life from family life

In December of 2015, the world was drawn to a grim example of the consequences of the extreme work ethic of Japan. Matsuri Takahashi was described as personable, diligent, and well-liked before she took a job with Dentsu, a major advertising company in Japan. In a span of eight months, she had transformed into a physical and mental wreck. She worked over 100 hours a week, getting just ten hours of sleep every week, and on top of that, her superiors were breathing down her neck. On Christmas Day of 2015, she decided she had had enough and took what probably seemed to be the only way out - she committed suicide by jumping from the top of the company dormitory where she lived.

Is there a possibility that we might see something like this in America's future? Is it already here?

Actually, it is, but luckily for us, we can identify it while it's still isolated and take steps to curb it. The one place in America where extreme work culture is gradually approaching the Japanese version is Silicon Valley. One company encouraging an extreme work culture is Uber. They recently changed their internal mantra from, 'work smarter, harder, and longer,' to 'work smarter and harder.' Arianna Huffington, an Uber board member, explained the change, saying they found that working longer actually negates working smarter. And she's right.

Despite having longer work hours, Japan is less productive than the USA, Sweden, UK, and several other nations. So working more hours doesn't necessarily mean that you're the most productive.

If Uber and other companies adopt this, it will be an about-face from the 'work till you drop' culture that the tech community exults. In 2016 Uber engineer Joseph Thomas committed suicide. His widow blamed his suicide on the extreme work culture of the company, long hours, and intense psychological pressure.

Fiverr, a popular platform that allows you to hire someone to do a job for you, recently launched an ad that glorified extreme work culture. The ad said, 'You eat coffee for lunch…Sleep deprivation is your drug of choice.' Before, these were messages that you kept to yourself. The fact that a brand is confidently saying this to the world shows that American culture is gradually accepting extreme work as a way of life.

"Working hard for something we don't care about is called stress; working hard for something we love is called passion."

-Simon Sinek

Prioritize Your Family

While helping one of my legal clients in Daly City, California, my wife got a call from my daughter's school. It turned out that my little one, who was 9 at the time, had fallen off a play structure on the playground and injured her arm. This seemed a little off since the structure was on top of a one-inch rubber mat. As soon as my wife got the message, she drove over to the school, picked her up, and called me to say that she would be bringing Sophia to the emergency room.

After the call I continued working with my client, hoping that not much was wrong. It was very distracting thinking of my injured little one on her way to the emergency room.

I was on the fence. On one side I kept thinking about what the doctors would discover, yet for some reason, I kept focusing on my client's needs.

A little while later, my wife messaged me that Sophia's arm was broken. The physicians determined she would receive better treatment at Children's Hospital in San Francisco and they arranged for ambulance transport. My wife was pissed off that I had not arrived at the hospital for our daughter and I couldn't blame her. A few minutes later I saw an ambulance get on the freeway without the normal lights and sirens blaring from my client's window. Based on the timing I knew my loved ones were on board. I should have told my client that I needed to leave for a family emergency.

People rarely wake up and decide they want to put their careers before family. Unfortunately, many of us wind up spending more time with our employer than our family. Your kids are young once and family events may not repeat. Have you ever worked so much you found yourself missing important family moments?

As you move up the corporate ladder constraints on your time can get tougher. I knew that I was not the only one having this experience. The book *Elon Musk* by Ashlee Vance states Elon Musk embraces work above family at all costs, while he condemns the thought of his employees taking time off for any reason. Elon did not want to hear about anything that would take focus away from his companies, including children and family matters. While I do envy what Elon has done to make the world a better place, we need to realize that we are in control of our choices and outcomes. For you to enjoy what you are doing at a much deeper level, you need to take a step back and realize that the decisions you make belong to you, not someone else.

After reading Elon's book, it helped spark ideas on both family values and productivity. To be successful we must be 100 percent aligned with our work. Yet if we work for someone, we must make sure to put our family first, regardless of our employer. Making lots of money for somebody else does pay the rent but we should not sacrifice our health for this. What's worse is that when we stop working, we don't get paid because a single employer is a single source of income. Stop spending your energy on others and care enough about your well being and the people around you.

"Put yourself first, you only live once."

-Andrewzee

Chapter 3 How To Get Free Time

"Time is more valuable than money. You can get more money, but you cannot get more time."

-Jim Rohn

How A Truck Repair Changed Everything

It's interesting how an emergency situation can force us to get our priorities right. For instance, your car breaks down unexpectedly. No matter what you had planned, you somehow find the time to call around for a mechanic, get estimates, schedule towing, and then get an alternative ride to work and back, you might even decide to work from home. One way or another, you get things done because you have no other choice.

One day, I got ready for my horrendous one and a half hour, one-way commute to Pleasanton, California. I packed my coffee, laptop, and sunglasses then got in my truck.

As I pulled out of the driveway, I noticed that my steering was almost impossible to turn. It felt like I was using all of my might to turn the truck, a classic man versus machine battle. After two turns, I pulled over and called a tow truck. The next thing I did was call my mechanic, David, and told him about the steering issue. David told me to send my truck over to the shop and he'd call me when it was ready to be picked up. Once the tow truck driver arrived, I gave him instructions to take my truck to the shop over in Half Moon Bay.

Since I didn't have to accompany my truck to the repair shop and I'd already called into work, I was left with a lot of free time I hadn't anticipated. As I walked back up the hill, the fact that I didn't have to deal with the commute to and from work sunk in. I was so excited.

A few hours later David called and told me that some of the gearings in my power steering setup broke. He explained that the lines would have to completely flushed because metal slivers were mixed with the power steering fluid, and then everything in the system would need to be replaced. He mentioned it was possible he would finish by the end of the day, and guaranteed that it would be ready the following afternoon at the latest. I urged him to take his time and call me when it was ready.

Working Remote, Day 1:

It was an incredible feeling to know that simply working from home would give me back three hours of my life.

It's interesting how this unfortunate event forced me to realign my thinking. I was able to aim at the stars instead of looking down at my feet. I was free to think of the endless possibilities rather than confining myself to the conventional box of thinking. Over the years I worked alone and with many teams to solve software and time management problems. I was doing good work. I was becoming something of an authority in the workplace and I was excelling. Too bad I couldn't say the same about my personal life. I was giving out a lot of value, but my personal development was increasingly pushed to the backburner. All my time and money was going towards helping others build legacies, but who was going to build mine?

The repair on my truck was godsent. It forced me to flip my thinking around. This train of thought laid the foundation for this book and got me thinking about better ways of doing everything. It was like my past life was under a spell of conformance. A feeling of being locked out of opportunities. To rebuild, I had to put pen to paper and develop a map of my future.

It all started with a one-page mind map where I wrote down techniques I had used in the past and the lessons I could share. A mind map is similar to a filing cabinet except, in this case, it's purely visual. This is what I came up with:

- **Regret:** More often than not, we regret the things we never dared to do, instead of the things we did. So never be shy about making your move.
- **Do what matters:** If you could only do one thing for as long as you live, what would it be? That's your calling and that's what really matters.

- **What do I want:** It's easy to confuse what you want with what society expects from you, but nothing is more frustrating than trying to fit people's expectations of you.
- **Life is short:** Depending on what part of the world you live in, life expectancy ranges from 40 to 80, not to mention there's a risk that anything could happen and cut it short unexpectedly. So why hold back on the things that matter?
- **Urbanization:** Cities are the settlements of the future, no matter what the nature lovers say. With the world population rapidly increasing and the demand for skilled labor on the rise, cities become increasingly attractive because of their ability to attract the best and most skilled people in one place.
- **Artificial intelligence:** This technology is going to change our lives in more ways than one. New jobs will be created while many jobs will be automated out of existence. We should all prepare for the coming storm.
- **Happiness:** Be happy, not because of what you have in your bank account, but because of what you carry inside of you.
- **Read more or get left behind:** The truism that readers are leaders has never been more true, especially in this information age. The difference between the next million-dollar opportunity could be determined by who refreshed his news feed the most.
- **You have one shot** at this thing called life, so don't waste it.
- **Focus on what matters** the most to you, not on what others say.

Working Remote, Day 2:

All the mind mapping of the previous day had lit a fire inside of me. I woke up two hours earlier than normal and figured out that if I could work on something for two hours every day, that will give me 14 hours a week, or 728 hours a year. I liked those numbers. Normally I would have hit the snooze button three to five times to steal a few more minutes of sleep, but my mind was fired up and ready to make the necessary changes.

Most days I would think about what else I could be doing versus crawling into my truck and spending three hours of my life on the highway. One of the many problems I experienced during this time on the road was slight headaches that got worse as I drove.

Was it the glare of the brake lights hitting me square in the face? Was it the feeling of being caged in? Was it the endless sounds of the road, speed bumps, honking, big semi-truck passing me by? At one point, I thought I was sensitive to gas fumes, but driving with the windows up or down didn't change a thing. The tediousness of driving to work made me feel like I was rooted in one spot, regardless of traffic flow.

At least once a week, I would find myself pulling over on the highway to think about the dichotomy in what I was doing and what I wanted to be doing with my life. The radio stations didn't make it any better, blaring bad news most of the time and telling you how bad the traffic was. It made me wonder why I was doing this to myself every day.

Despite all these thoughts, I kept up the miserable routine, afraid to try out the alternative. That is until my truck broke down. I felt better about not contributing to global warming and having my truck off the road. Imagine if 40% of the population worked from home worldwide. It would definitely help with greenhouse gasses. Imagine how much better the air quality would be, not to mention the reduced traffic gridlock.

That day, things would be different; it would be the first day of the rest of my life. I was given a new chance at life and I wasn't going to waste it. Picking up from where I left off on my mind-mapping exercise, I began organizing my thoughts according to the knowledge I had.

All of a sudden, I was enjoying a free-range lifestyle, with plenty of fresh air, sunshine, and open space that was all mine. I had been caged into a routine of commuting, giving the best of my time to an asphalt path. I wasn't giving the best service to my employer because most of my awakened moments were spent on the road, amongst thousands of other commuters. I got in my truck every day with the best ideas and life, but then I stepped out of the truck into the office parking lot feeling exsanguinated of my essence. Once I got home at the end of a long day, my physical and mental states were unhealthy. I literally fell apart every evening, leaving nothing but shards left for my loved ones. Sleep was simply a process by which I patched myself up for another day, just to repeat the entire process.

Day 3: Why Not Work Remote?

From feeling imprisoned with my hands and feet in shackles to being unstuck, the feeling was refreshing. By day 3, I used the well-worn line that I had an appointment with the doctor, to get an extra day out of the office, and it worked. The truck was running fine by this time, but I wasn't ready to let go of this taste of freedom. I wasn't tied to a job and the feeling lit me up like a Christmas tree from the inside. It then hit me like a ton of bricks, I could add more of what excited me and less of what demotivated me to my life. This is not to say that I didn't like my job. I was actually involved in a super important project that involved scanning resumes into a database. You can see how critical that is to world peace and security, can't you?

By the evening of the third day, I realized a few things:

- I slept better
- I felt relaxed
- I started taking deep 20-minute naps that left me feeling refreshed
- I focused on thoughts that mattered to me, on things that I found interesting. For the first time in a long time, my thoughts were about me instead of thoughts about my employer breathing down my neck.

More often than not, we are overloaded, trying to do too much at once and then we end up doing very little. We say 'yes' to working on projects we are not passionate about. We say 'yes' to other people's agendas to be nice. We live life not by planning it out, but by reacting. We spend our time responding to the needs of others rather than discerning and focusing on our own needs. How long can we truly function this way? Is there a vehicle break down in your future?

Life before my truck broke down was like a never-ending cyclone that kept sucking me away from important and necessary things. I barely had time to schedule an appointment to see the doctor. A few times I called in sick just so I could get checked out for recurring medical issues like lack of energy, back pain, and constant headaches. My doctor would ask when the symptoms started and the answer was always, "A month after I started my new position." He would then ask me to describe my average day. I described what it was like driving my full-size truck to work every day. He said that part of my back pain was coming from the bumps and rough patches I encountered on the road; the jarring motions reverberated through my body down to my lower back, something he saw often with truck drivers. He diagnosed me with sciatica, a condition caused by nerve damage, and he told me that the pain would gradually travel down my spine to my butt and eventually down to my left leg. At the peak of my Sciatica, I had to sit sideways to avoid the pain from shooting down my leg.

Something had to give, and it wasn't going to be me. In the coming weeks, I installed adjustable shocks onto my truck and started sitting on a two-inch-thick cushion, which made a huge difference.

The doctor also pointed out that my blood pressure was high and he gave me a few recommendations on how to correct it:

- Reduce weekly commute hours if possible, by working remotely or finding work closer to home. This piece of advice was like preaching to the choir. After the bliss of the past three days, I wasn't about to return to the status quo.

- Go visit a chiropractor to get a thorough check up on the state of my bones. This was necessary in order to know how best to manage my daily activities so as to not cause unnecessary stress to my body which was still recovering.
- Take a 30-minute nap every day. The period might be short, but it's powerful enough to power you through the rest of the day.
- Squeeze in time to get exercise. There's no rule about the perfect time to exercise, just get it done

To save my health, mental health, and family life, I had to quit my three-hour commute job. The next position I found was a project manager position. I was able to negotiate a 32-hour workweek, shaving off 8 hours for myself, and also getting two days a week to work remotely. The new job had challenges around every corner yet was flexible at the same time. All this was possible because I negotiated before putting my ink to the deal. The job also happened to be just a 25-minute drive from my home. Talk about convenience.

After I left the position in Pleasanton, I made a promise to myself that I would never cross a Bay Area bridge or commute longer than 35 minutes unless I could take BART (Bay Area Rapid Transit). On the train, at least I could work on a project on my laptop.

Another safety measure I put in place was to review the traffic patterns before applying for any job. For example, I could drive to Stanford in about 30 minutes, but commuting there during peak traffic hours could take over an hour. No thank you. I wound up limiting my search to within ten miles of my house. I even considered working out of Seattle, Las Vegas, Texas, and Florida. For the last three cities, the pay was about 20% less than San Francisco. To figure out the numbers, I drew a table with the cost of round-trip airfare, Airbnb for the week, and meals. The jobs would need to pay north of $60 an hour for this to be worthwhile. Would you rather take two flights a week or be stuck in traffic for three hours a day?

Before I started my new position, I took a well-deserved week off and recharged my battery. A few weeks into the new job, my back pain and headaches completely vanished. Had I stayed at my old job, I would still be suffering. No more chiropractor bills for me anymore, where before I was going in every month for readjustments

Unbox Yourself To See What Is Possible

After leaving my old job, I realized that I had to prioritize myself over everything otherwise I'd never get ahead. Some stagnating signs to watch out for are:

- Your income is staying the same. If it is, you should get out of the old job now. The truth is, your income might be the same on paper, but it is actually worth less than it was when you first started earning it, thanks to inflation. If your income isn't increasing by at least 10% on a yearly basis you're losing real income.
- Do you determine your schedule or is it controlled by your employer? We all have bosses one way or the other, but the amount of control you have and your ability to determine what your day looks like is important.
- Are your loved ones left to make do with scraps of your time? They deserve better, and you know it.
- Are you happy with how things are going? If you could go back in time and change the course of things, would you do so? If the answer is yes, you should probably give serious thought towards changing things in any way possible.
- Putting your trust in Social Security is going to become more of a risk as you near retirement. It's

estimated that by 2035, the <u>number of Americans 65 and older will increase</u> from about 48 million today to more than 79 million, as mentioned in Business Insider. In summary, more people will be taking money out of the system than they are putting in.

"If a man has not discovered something that he will die for, he isn't fit to live."

-Martin Luther King

Batching Your Time With Paul

Paul Graham, venture capitalist and founder of Y Combinator, has championed the maker's schedule, which is built on the assumption that different people thrive using different types of scheduling. A software developer might benefit most by setting aside chunks of silent time to work and dedicate to a problem.

Dedicate your mornings, when your mind is fresh, to your hardest or most creative work. Schedule your work in 30-90 minute blocks of time, and when you complete a block, stand up, walk around, and climb some stairs. By moving your body around, you create a mini reset that makes it easier to move from task to task. Try it, you will feel the difference.

Research shows that when a bug is found in software, a developer can resolve the issue in less than an hour if they've worked on that area of the code in the last 24 hours. But, if the developer has to come back to the code a week later, they can take three times longer to resolve that same bug.

You will become more grounded, focused, and productive if you dedicate time to a single task, rather than frantically switching back and forth between tasks.

Create a schedule that works for you and force everyone else to adjust to your timing. For example, publish a calendar with office hours and then schedule tasks in batches to keep your mind focused. Use a 'touch it once' mentality when you move it, respond to it, or delete it, and then you're done with it. Limit after-hour emails to urgent issues. If you find that you need some recharge time, you need to schedule it into your calendar.

Batch food preparation by cooking meals for two or three days at a time. Create sides that can be leveraged for multiple meals and freeze extra portions.

Batch your driving time by combining activities or only getting in your car when you have multiple destinations lined up.

By batching related tasks together we can turn randomness into productivity. Be selfish with your time, it's all you have, after all.

Rise And Shine

For busy people with no free time, waking up early can be an elusive productivity silver bullet. By dedicating some uninterrupted morning time to your most important task of the day, you will make progress while everyone else sleeps. This step alone can dramatically improve how much you get done in a day.

The only way I was able to accomplish writing this book was by waking up an hour and a half early every single day for over a year and putting in focused effort without interruption. Missing a day felt like sleeping in a cheap hotel, I felt like I cheated on myself by not working on my project.

If you want a different outcome in life, you have to stack patterns that will turn you into a new person.

If something isn't helping you advance, it might be pulling you back. This will be a new way of life for you. And once you're used to it, you'll wonder how you ever made it in the past living any other way

Your Super Power Is Saying "NO"

If Superman defended productivity, the symbol on his chest would be 'NO'.

- Say No to wasteful meetings before they start
- Say No to other people's agendas
- Say No to time-sucking activities

We've talked about how to eliminate wasteful activities and optimize the work we should be doing. But how do we decide which tasks and opportunities we should work on?

When Steve Jobs returned to Apple, the company was involved in dozens of projects that were causing the company to lose focus. They were working on mediocre products and burning through money without good returns. Steve Jobs grew Apple by saying no to the majority of potential projects so he could say yes to the few projects he believed would make an impact on society: iMac, iTunes, iPhone, and iPad.

The moral - Your ability to say no seriously affects how you spend your time. Stop working on things that waste your time and are not aligned with your long-term vision. As author Steven Pressfield wrote, 'The disease of our times is that we live on the surface. Were like the Platte river a mile wide and an inch deep.' Apple's success is the result of going deep. Steve Jobs chose the essentialist road, and today his legacy is one of the most profitable companies in the world.

"The difference between successful people and really successful people is that really successful people say no to almost everything."

-Warren Buffett

How To Say No

But how can you flex the power of 'NO'? If you need to say no to someone, but you're uncomfortable with saying the word, try saying 'let me think about it.' With this approach, you show compassion for the other person while guarding your time. Treat the word yes with scarcity, keep 'YES' close to your chest. Don't lead others to think you'll say yes, and try to avoid conversations that might force you to respond with 'No.' Avoid attending events that require long-term participation that ultimately fall out of alignment with your long-term goals. While it may be easy to schedule something on your calendar today, the time will come when you have to commit to this event. When saying no is tough, remind yourself that for every yes you give, you are saying no to your own agenda.

Compliance Is Expected

The more video content we consume, the more everything around us is tainted with a form of commercialization and the less we use our minds for more productive thoughts. Consider the hypnotic suggestion in the 1960s during television sign off. Subliminal messaging was displayed as the wording for the National Anthem was played such as:

- Trust the government

- God is real
- Believe in government god
- Rebellion is not tolerated
- Obey consume
- Buy believe
- Worship consume believe
- Do not question government god

This video can still be found on Youtube, and its black and white composition makes for an eerie viewing.

Back then, television commercials were very different after 1:00 am and the weirdest of the bunch would play between 3:00 and 5:00 am. They were repetitive. Remember, if the mind hears something over and over again it begins to accept it as true. This form of hypnosis, developed to capture your attention, works a lot like catching a fish. If the fisherman puts enough lines in the water, he's bound to catch something.

When I was a kid, my mother and I would watch the horror show *Creature Features* hosted by Bob Wilkins. At night we sat on wooden chairs in our small apartment and watched classics like *Creature from Black Lagoon*, *Night of the Living Dead* and *The Blob*. My mother's life revolved around broadcasted content. As she was slowly consumed by the evils of propaganda, portions of her life seemed to mirror the '80s movie *The Blob*. The Blob was a movie about an ever-growing, gelatin-like object that continuously consumed.

My mom didn't get out much and all of her conversations were related to what she saw on the news. I wish I had a dollar for every time she told me to be careful because of something that happened in another state. This upbringing jaded my feelings towards television and made me realize that if we don't have a focused agenda, the evilness of propaganda is waiting around every corner to hijack your time.

"Time well-spent results in more money to spend, more money to save, and more time to vacation."

Prora Germany

During the rise of Nazism, Germany sought to create compliant puppets in mass. The Strength Through Joy program targeted low wage workers to garner support for Hitler in the war effort.

In 1939, the Germans finished building a beach holiday camp on the island of Rugen in Germany. The enormous complex is more than two miles in length, six floors high, and was intended to be a premier vacation destination. But when the tourists arrived they were assigned bland rooms, they were woken up with loudspeakers, and they were given instructions on what to do and when to do it. They were forced to eat together, read propaganda material, and watch films that convey specific messages.

If we don't guard our minds, our thoughts and actions can be hijacked just like what happened with the Germans in this story.

In the 1982 movie *Blade Runner* starring Harrison Ford, every outside space is plastered with advertisements. At the time of the movie's release, this was considered absurd and dystopian. Now, perpetual advertising on every device and at every location is considered normal. Companies are in the business of attracting and holding your attention. Even if we think we are in control, even if we entertain their offer for only a few minutes, we still surrender our minds to their mission. If you watch standard cable programming, you're seeing an average of 16 to 20 minutes of advertisements per hour; so if you watch three hours of television a day, that's around 7 hours of advertisements a week, 28 hours a month, or a grand total of 336 hours a year.

If advertisements weren't effective, companies wouldn't use them. Companies are forever searching for better ways to influence and encourage you to buy and use their products. Major companies, including Ford, American Express, Apple, Nike, Coca Cola, and Samsung funded a seven million dollar project that employed neuroscientists to study how to influence buying desires via mind control. The experiments were reported by Martin Lindstrom and Jim Mc Calvert in their book *Stealing Fire*. If you're visiting a free website, keep in mind you are the product and the company's goal might be selling advertisements to control your future interests. Websites already have the ability to measure clicks and revisits.

Stores can use multiple wifi antennas to detect nearby smartphones and triangulate their locations. Should a user opt into certain apps, it would help make ad placement a little more appealing. Imagine you round the aisle of a store and either your phone buzzes in your pocket with an ad saying 'look at me', or a 3D ad displays in front of you. It's not hard to imagine a 3D ad that triangulates between your wifi signal and where you are standing while adjusting the viewing angle towards your eyes. You could be shopping with your child by your side while AI displays different ads for each of you.

Even if you did not buy anything in the store your anonymous digital footprint can be used to identify store traffic patterns. Every large ecommerce brand has a team of analysts looking for data patterns on what to place where. This is one reason milk is placed at the back of every store, so that you have to walk past all of the other items before reaching it. Airplane mode may be the safest way of remaining anonymous while shopping.

"How fortunate for governments that the people they administer don't think"

-Adolf Hitler

4 Scroll Rule

Too much internet surfing can make you unproductive and it scatters your brain's thought patterns. Just the other night, I got home early and took a well-deserved nap for about 45 minutes. I saved some accounts on Instagram that I wanted to examine. I like reviewing profiles to see what different or catchy things people are posting and gave myself five minutes to scroll through these accounts. During the first five minutes, I was generating ideas on developing similar content with my own twist. But after eight minutes of scrolling, brain fog hit me. I went into low energy, power-down mode and before I knew it fifteen minutes passed. Why did I drain myself with a non-productive task?

Instead of jumping into a few profiles and taking notes, I fell into the 'scroll of death', where you fall deep into the rabbit hole of a user's history. Next, you click their profile and you see they have 300 images and the scrolling continues. This can go on and on, like scrolling under the influence of distraction. This scrolling activity feeds the none focused mind like drugs feed an addict. The more information passing in front of our eyes, the more tired we become.

I remember another experience which resulted in my mind becoming tired fairly rapidly. When I was a kid, I often took the bus from San Francisco to Palo Alto to visit a trading card shop. The 40-mile trip was usually two and a half hours long. As I rode the bus, my eyes constantly read and processed the information I saw outside of the bus windows - people, houses, cars, businesses, and signs. I always arrived at the shop feeling drained, and when I returned home I would get headaches and the blood vessels in my eyes would be swollen. Returning from the five-hour bus trip, I would need to retreat to bed early. On a bus trip, you can look away and close your eyes but with internet access enabled everywhere, you have endless scrolling traps. Your personal energy supply will rapidly deplete if you allow your life to be controlled by endless scrolling. To avoid becoming part of the walking dead, I started a self-healing process I call the 4

Scroll Rule. I limited myself to swipe the screen or mouse four times and then I close the app. This rule helped me eliminate my wasted efforts.

Delayed Gratification

A famous study from the late 1960s known as the Marshmallow Experiment tracked willpower in children. Children who waited a short amount of time were given a single marshmallow, while children who waited for longer were given two marshmallows. Researchers found that the children who were able to wait longer for a reward tended to have better life outcomes. How many of us are also choosing a marshmallow now versus waiting for two marshmallows later?

Our lives are filled with opportunities to chase the next shiny object. Unfortunately, choosing instant gratification can limit our long term potential. Indulging on the 15th episode of your favorite show will not push you toward your goals. Dedicating time to continuous education is a wiser financial decision than binge-watching Netflix.

How often have you driven at night in the mountains and needed to trigger your high beams so you can see a little further? For a car, high beams are a safety feature that drivers use every now and then.

We need to trigger our personal high beams so we can see what's around the corner. However, unlike cars that only need high beams on sometimes, people need their high beams on all the time. Life is a series of blocks that we put together day by day. The more mindful we are with where we place our time in relation to these blocks the better our longer flow of events will happen with regard to where we will end up.

"Train yourself to let go of everything you fear to lose."

To Consume Or To Produce

Feel free to skip onto the next chapter if you have good habits at avoiding distractions and shiny objects.

Below I take a close look at the numbers related to distractions with respect to our lives which can be a reality check for some.

Many of us go to work, come home, have family dinner, watch some TV, read a story to our kids, go to bed, and repeat. We maintain multiple video subscriptions to accounts like Comcast, Netflix, Amazon Prime, and Hulu which keep us entertained but also distract us. As we're placated by this constant stream of entertainment, we don't realize we are feeding a sugar-like addiction to video programming. Like a drug addict, we may not think we have a bad habit, but we also can't stop once we start.

Looking back, I realize I was focused on short-term satisfaction. I would buy the latest movie, enjoy it, brag about it, then add the movie to my wall of DVDs. Little did I realize that this was a double negative, one where you paid for the movie with your hard-earned cash and then paid again with your free time.

While I had some great friends, a few relationships were built on conversations that began with, "Hey, did you get the latest *Batman* or *Avengers* movie? Did you see the scene in Spiderman?" etc. Little did I know that the patterns of my old life were holding me back and I didn't even realize it until I started to take a closer look at my progress over the years. As time passed, I switched my mindset to one that valued learning and growth over passive entertainment. I chose to eliminate Netflix, reduce Comcast to Internet only, cancel Hulu, and I began programming my mind for success. The passage of time that you spend paying homage to something created by someone else, is time that is lost forever.

Breaking News

Pointless information consumption and entertainment aren't limited to television and movies. What do you gain, what can you act upon after watching the news or reading the paper? Most news is negative and extremely repetitive. Watching daily news coverage sucks you into a doom and gloom mindset that siphons and constricts your creative energy. The more you watch, the more you tend to think life is based around the news. When you watch the news, whatever is broadcasted onto the screen becomes your reality. Your conversations and thoughts are consumed by the mind-numbing impact of it all. Remember that your focus ultimately becomes you. When the news is constantly distressing, you become distressed. When it's negative, you become pessimistic. When it's hopeless, you become hopeless.

Watching the news can waste an hour or more of your day. If something is actually important, you'll hear about it. People will tell you. How could you better spend this time?

Are you watching the news because 90% of the population is doing it? Are you doing this just to be the water cooler topic expert? If so, is that the best use of your time?

Flip your mindset. Drop news topics completely and instead try to hold conversations related to growth or how you will crush it this year. If the person you're talking to thinks you're crazy or doesn't share your optimism, find someone else who you can share growth conversations with. We either lead or follow.

What's next on the chopping block? Print media. Are you reading the paper or online news article for a particular reason?

Specific journals like Wired, Fortune, or Investing are targeted toward a particular niche. These journals may be a better use of your time, but even when reading these articles, you need to be hyper-focused on what you want to learn. The point is to manage your time wisely in everything you do and limit the time you spend in consuming space.

I Love It, It's Free, Are You Signing Your Life Away

Hold up, wait a minute. If it's free, what am I giving up? You are giving up:

- Your Data
- Your Time

The expression 'there is no free food' grows truer with each passing day. No one takes a loss so you can have free things, and if you got it for free, someone else paid for it. Sometimes, people don't have to pay for you to get something for free. Sometimes, you won't have to pay with cash. There are other ways you can pay for something in which you don't even realize you've given up a part of yourself. Take data and time for example. It could be data such as your address, email, or phone number - just about any data that should be yours for the keeping. Most marketers that entice people with freebies will try to get their hands on your personal information and along the way, they get you to pay for what you believed you got at no expense.

'In addition to any monetary payment for service, you agree to immediately assign your first-born child to NameDrop. If you do not have children yet, this agreement will be enforceable until the year 2050. All assigned children automatically become the property of NameDrop, Inc. No exceptions.' This quote is Paragraph 2.3.1 from the terms of service for NameDrop, an imaginary social network used to study whether or not people read and understand online terms of service. Don't be surprised to hear that all of the 543 collegiate candidates joined, despite the irrational provision.

Chances are that when signed up for free-service social media platforms like Facebook, Twitter, LinkedIn, Instagram, Snapchat, and others, you barely looked at the terms of service agreement that popped up on your screen. Not to worry, you aren't alone. Hardly anyone reads to understand terms of use. At the end of the Namedrop experiment, Jonathan Obar and Anne Oeldorf-Hirsch, communications professors at York University, Toronto, and the University of Connecticut said, "We say we understand with our repeated clicks on 'I Agree', but this is the biggest lie on the internet."

Contextually, Instagram's terms of use states: "…you hereby grant to Instagram a non-exclusive, fully paid and royalty-free, transferable, sub-licensable, worldwide license to use the content that you post on or through the Service," meaning in effect that you've vested them and similar corporations with such terms an expansive right to use your content without liability. So, if Instagram decides to furnish your cute profile pic to an adult-content company for advertisement, there's really nothing you can do because you signed off on it. Imagine the stigma you'd suffer! The same applies to Facebook which doesn't give third party applications or ad networks the right to use a user's name or picture in ads, but it does reserve the right to use a user's name and profile picture in advertisements on its own platform.

These platforms indirectly and secretly collect your data which includes your device location via GPS, Bluetooth or wifi signals, your mobile provider and internet service provider name, your language and time zone preference, and much more. Twitter and Facebook can sell your metadata to a phony firm that'll use it for nefarious activities, from tracking your approximate location to publishing/unveiling the adult-rated websites you've visited.

Even when you deactivate your account, Instagram's terms of service empowers them to keep your account data and history. So, if someone reposted a picture that you originally published, it would still come up on the platform. Facebook can take up to 90 days to erase your data after account deletion, and in that time they use your data and information as they please.

Facebook has over 29,000 data points on all of its users and has been careless with regards to privacy protection which is why Steve Wozniak, Apple co-founder decided to leave Facebook. With this many data points Facebook can understand your desires better than your friends. When is the last time you have heard of an investor writing a book against a company that they helped to fund? Well that book is called *Zucked: Waking Up to the Facebook Catastrophe* by Roger McNamee, an initial investor in Facebook. Reading this book will make you think twice before clicking the like button, (a.k.a., feed the algorithm).

Your Time

The time committed to getting and making use of free services is part of the price that you pay for having them in the first place. Take for instance a free eBook. No matter how lean the pages are, you are still going to use your free time to read them. Sometimes, the value they give may not be on par with the time you expended.

If our mind is occupied with X you cannot think of Y, where Y might be much more important.

Do you remember being a kid and staring at the wall of candy at your local corner store? Your eyes would light up and you'd smile cheek to cheek as you faced the display of sugary treats. It's the same concept now, but you're not a kid anymore and candy has evolved into digital bits that are displayed in the app store with fancy graphics and cute animations.

With every 'like' a small dose of dopamine is released in our minds. As our happiness meter goes up, the addiction becomes like nicotine to a smoker; Where one can't kick the habit of lighting up or in our case accumulating likes. While likes are not a significant achievement, we tend to feel empowered after flipping that digital bit from 0 to 1. These small actions cause serotonin to flow, impacting our moods and habits.

You are the product

Large corporations or the algorithm have a neutral position to put real or fake news on your feed to get you to spend more time on the site. This is known as clickbait - the more time you are on a site, the better. With AI learning, Facebook can target ads like a Navy Seal sniper can hit a target 100 yards out. Facebook does not even create the content that you consume. This allows them to get by as a platform company versus something like a newspaper media house that would have to pay writers, pick a position, and stand by it.

Facebook stays in the middle and enjoys the ride while everyone except them creates a never-ending stream of free content that circles the world 24 hours a day, 365 days a year.

With Facebook, you get to connect with people from your remote location, where you can message millions of people from across the world for free - all thanks to Mark Zuckerberg, but again, no thanks. You don't ever have to pay Mark to use Facebook but you pay the people that pay Mark, so indirectly, you are paying him. Like how whenever you buy a product from a Facebook ad, Mark gets a commission from your purchase.

Let us not forget that Google made Chrome so that they would have the best ability to sell you future services. It's the same reason the Android OS was made. In the end, free social sites will take your free time, your attention, and sometimes sell you a product. Can you be sure of yourself when you say you don't spend a dime while socializing on these apps?

Less Is More

That latest $1300 iPhone will allow more monitoring hooks in your pocket. They are always in a rush to advance their leverage on you and keep you under close quarters at all times. What do you spend your valuable time on when you surf the net? The system already knows and it will always be right in your face. You will always end up buying from them even when you have other plans.

Do you really need to update your status from the bathroom? It would be really weird if advertising started to become zone focused. If you are in your garage you see tool ads, if you are in your bathroom you see toothpaste ads. The more high tech your phone is, the more precise targeting is accomplished. They will always remind you of what you don't have, or they'll make you believe that what they have for you is better than what you presently have. A good copywriter will perform magic on your emotions and leave you begging to be sold to.

Put your phone down when you have a free moment to expend. Look around you, there are lots of fun things lying about. How about you actually communicate with the people around you?

According to Qui-Gon Jinn from *Star Wars*, "Your focus determines your reality."

Nobody will want to sell stuff to you if you're far away from their shop. Not Facebook, not Google, and not Apple.

"Once you start down the dark path, forever will it dominate your destiny, consume you it will."

-Yoda

From Time Suck To Time Lock

Time is the most important asset in our lives, far more important than money. We won't live forever, so why do we waste our efforts and hard-earned money on things and gadgets that take up space and won't help us move ahead, and worse, hold us back? We need to be honest with ourselves and eliminate all the time-sucking activities and energy wasters from our schedule so we can optimize the tasks that will move us ahead.

We are surrounded by distractions: new email notifications, text messages, phone calls, and visiting Facebook twenty times a day. Think about how much time you spend visiting social media sites or reviewing email links. If you spend around 15 minutes of your workday on three social media visits, and every time you switch from one task to another you have to pick up where you left off, you lose another 15 minutes (five minutes per social media visit) before you can get into a good flow state.

Let's do a little experiment, while 30 minutes a day may not seem like much, over a week it adds up to about two and a half hours of productivity; Over a month, that is 10 hours, over a year it's about 120 hours, and over the length of your career, say 33 years, that's nearly 4,000 hours, or two full working years, spent on social media. Think about that for a second. Is social media worth two years of your life? Do you think that the value, satisfaction, and fulfillment you receive from social media is worth two or more years of your life? Which would you rather multiply your app addiction or your success rate? When I would get the urge to flip over to social media or read the local news

93

website, I began asking myself, can I push through the urge? If I couldn't fight the urge, I found that thinking about or documenting the current time helped me focus. If the clock read 10:32 am, I would repeat '32' to myself every few seconds which wound up helping me be honest with my most important intentions.

On the flip side, let's consider video games for a moment. According to Jane McGonigal's book *SuperBetter: The Power of Living Gamefully,* by the age of 21, the average boy has spent 10,000 hours of his life playing video games. This adds up to 40 hours a week for 4 years. With that same 10,000 hours, you can earn a bachelor's degree.

Alternately, you have YouTuber Felix Kjellberg (aka PewDiePie) who has earned over $7.4 million making YouTube videos of himself playing video games. A point worth analyzing with PewDiePie is that he is transforming his input into leveraged output, which can be measured in the form of dollars. A jet engine uses blades to compress the air, adds fuel, and an electric spark, which then turns into thrust out the rear of the engine. For PewDiePie his thrust can be measured in dollars since he is leveraging his skill. What fuel can you leverage to increase your engine thrust?

Multiple studies have shown that playing games can relieve stress by focusing the mind on the game rather than stress. Jane McGonigal does a great job of giving specific steps that can help you in this area. Unless you think you can catch up to PewDiePie, you might want to try reading for twice the time you spend playing games. The more we consume, the less of an impact we leave on this planet, the more challenging our future might be.

Time Lock

I bounced around from shiny object to shiny object, moving forward but in no particular direction. With my newly gained discipline, I became better at switching events from the time-suck zone to the time-lock zone which helped me focus on my larger goals. All of a sudden, pockets of time started to appear. It was like the clock stopped and started spinning in reverse, I could not explain it. As time went on I realized that focusing on important tasks that can deliver the highest value to my future was the answer.

I loved the new me that was beginning to shape up. All of a sudden I became fully accountable for the future I desired and started to feel better day by day. It was like on one side of the mirror my old self sat in a chair gathering cobwebs, while on the other side the chair was gone, the TV was gone, and most of my thoughts switched to outcome goals. I decided that any spare moment would be tied to creating a product, learning, or helping others achieve their goals.

One thing that helped me was using a Time Timer. I love this little device because you set it to 20 minutes, 30 minutes, or 50 minutes, you grind away on your work, and you are done when your timer is done. One major advantage of this timer is that you don't need to be bound to your computer. It was used by Google Ventures and was the brainchild of a mother who had her son attend some of the meetings. It was created to solve the need for informing a child when a meeting would be over.

So how can you begin managing your time more effectively?

- Be the person creating the game instead of playing the game

- Be the person creating the movie instead of watching the movie

- Sit in the driver's seat and choose your own road

Turn your devices off or set to airplane mode. Close your email and only check it twice a day, once at the start of your day and once in the middle. Check your text messages once an hour. Do everything in batches. If you can disable app alerts it will help you focus instead of having the temptation to look at your phone for every little beep.

Start a journal and document everything you do for the week. Furthermore, document where you are and the quality of your work so that you can look back and find out what works for you. Record everything that takes more than 5 minutes. Ideally, you want a productivity log of how you work the best. If you put the results into a spreadsheet you can perform metrics on yourself. Review your results at the end of the week and ask yourself why you are doing every task in your journal.

If any of this resonates with you, share this book and information with those you care about. They have the right to take back their time too.

"Only by eliminating or optimizing the events that take our time can we find more time."

-Andrewzee

Chapter 4 Learning Patterns

"All children are artists. The problem is how to remain an artist once he grows up"

-Pablo Picasso

The Da Vinci Way Of Learning

'In the normal course of events many men and women are born with remarkable talents; but occasionally, in a way that transcends nature, a single person is marvelously endowed by Heaven with beauty, grace and talent in such abundance that he leaves other men far behind, all his actions seem inspired and indeed everything he does clearly comes from God rather than from human skill. Everyone acknowledged that this was true of Leonardo da Vinci, an artist of outstanding physical beauty, who displayed infinite grace in everything that he did and who cultivated his genius so brilliantly that all problems he studied he solved with ease."

-Giorgio Vasari

School is a step you take to get closer to your long term goals. No one should go to school simply to get a job. We are given one life and our decisions can impact us forever.

By applying the law of the vital few, we can take a look at our efforts and determine which specific actions return the highest value for our time. Life will always confront us with decisions about school, career choices, where to live, etc. We must constantly ask ourselves if we're spending our time on the most important tasks or if we're just staying busy.

Most know of Leonardo da Vinci for his famous paintings, but he was not just a painter. He was an inventor, sculptor, engineer, litterateur, anatomist, architect, scientist, mathematician, geologist, astronomer, botanist, writer, historian, and cartographer. He conceptualized the first flying machine, an armored fighting vehicle, solar energy, and much more. All of this happened in an age where electricity didn't exist.

He was born centuries before his time. We appreciate his mind and we are curious as to why there are so few like him. The answer to this may be what we'll call the Da Vinci Way of Education.

Leonardo Da Vinci never attended a conventional school. He was never boxed into a classroom and confined to a narrow, outdated curriculum. He was self-educated. Because of this, he was never exposed to an educational system that encouraged specialization. He was protected from these influences. His education took place in the studio of a renowned Florentine painter known as Andrea del Verrocchio whom he served for seven years. From there he proceeded to Ludovico il Moro of Milan and then he moved on to four other masters. The sum of these experiences gave him a wide berth of technical skills ranging from drafting, chemistry, metallurgy, metalworking, plaster casting, leatherworking, mechanics, carpentry, painting, drawing, sculpting, and modeling.

The basis of Da Vinci's education wasn't focused on getting a job; it focused on self-fulfillment and maximizing potential. Our current education system trains people to be tools for others, not innovators. It molds people to be efficient in a single role, without taking into consideration the possibility of automation one day assuming that role for us. A person with a wide berth of skills and experience can never be automated out of existence. We cannot depend on the educational system to secure our future, and it is our responsibility to self-educate.

According to Jim Rohn, "formal education will make you a living; self-education will make you a fortune."

Brian Tracy, a leading self-development consultant, conducted a survey and found that most people wanted to learn about health, as opposed to Pythagoras theorem. Have you ever attended a class where you were exposed to lessons on health, financial intelligence, public speaking, etc? These skills translate into the real world more than a grade on your certificate. A college education equips you with knowledge about what was done before, but they are inadequate when it comes to training you on how to take on the future. That is why Peter Thiel started the Thiel Fellowship. The fellowship offers $100,000 to people under 23 who are willing to drop out or skip school to chase their ideas in an environment that gives room for experimentation. In fact, the Wall Street Journal gave credence to this idea when it said, 'Not long ago, dropping out of school to start a company was considered risky. For this generation, it is a badge of honor, evidence of ambition and focus.'

Have you ever wondered why there are many business schools out there, but not that many successful businessmen? If the principles for business success can be taught from a textbook, why isn't the lecturer who teaches the same thing every year and is thus the most familiar a successful businessman?

"The real successful businessmen don't have the time to stay in class teaching others."

- 50 Cent

Our educational system applies techniques that were used when Henry Ford built the Model T a century ago. Who can imagine going to school today for an assembly plant job? What is so different about the jobs we get out of college today? We are educated in a way that conforms us to cubicle life and where we produce as many widgets as possible in a day. You may not think of your job this way but take a step back and look hard at what is going on.

This is not to disparage college education which has its benefits. The flexibility it affords should be treasured. It gives the opportunity to interact, build relationships with test ideas in a closed environment, and fail with minimal publicity. These opportunities should be maximized by undergraduates. The fringe benefits of a college education are more critical to life fulfillment than the actual purpose of a college education.

"Young people should ensure to explore all their options before making a commitment."

-Mark Zuckerberg

The purpose of a college education should be to equip you with the skills to survive in the real world because failure is a reality. A system that rewards you for getting A's does not exactly do you good. This is why the C students, the backbenchers who never seem to satisfy the lecturers, who turn assignments in late, who have their hands buried in many pies when they come out of school, usually have greater clarity about what they want from life. They've tested many things, they've gotten the excitement out of their systems, and they know exactly what works for them, enabling them to focus headlong. This is the Da Vinci Way of Education.

Explore your interests and potentials to the fullest. Don't pigeonhole yourself from the very beginning. Even if you eventually focus on one track, you will have the satisfaction of knowing what other choices had to offer. You will also have the satisfaction of knowing that the place you're in is your greatest chance of success because you've tried many things, failed at some, succeeded at others, and you'll know how to focus on your strengths. Self-education gives you space to discover what you're truly capable of by maximizing your creative potential. This approach to learning is the reason Da Vinci stands in a class of his own.

"College can be good for learning about what's been done before, but it can also discourage you from doing something new."

-Thiel Fellowship

You can have all of the fancy degrees imaginable, but at the end of the day, you still have to decide if you're happy. Are you satisfied with how you spend your days and weeks?

If you want to move up the corporate ladder, a focused degree will help. Many management positions honor a 4-year degree. One of the first lines of defense for companies is ignoring applicants who do not have a 4-year degree. So if you are going to climb that corporate ladder, you better get that degree. If you are going to develop web or mobile applications it's important that you know how to code with the latest technology such as Microsoft .Net, Java, MySQL, Angular, HTML 10, C++, etc.

"Going to an Ivy League school does not guarantee success at all. If you could hire Bill Gates, Mark Zuckerberg, etc, to work in your organization, wouldn't you?"

-Elon Musk

Sean Parker was 19 years old when he rolled up his sleeves and coded Napster. Within a year publishing the software on the internet, the music industry was forever changed. All of a sudden, anyone with an internet connection could download songs from anyone who had the song whether they had legally purchased it or not. The beauty of writing software is that your creativity is only limited to your thoughts.

So if you want to go after a developer job, code something that is worth putting on your resume and share it on the internet. Furthermore, you can pitch your application to venture capitalists.

Instagram had revenues north of 6 million dollars by 2018. Do you think anyone cares whether its developer has a 4-year degree or not? People are generally great at something if they do it over and over again. After all, practice makes perfect. If you have something to sell that people will enjoy, nobody will care about your educational background.

Henry Ford was once taken to court because he was an uneducated man running a successful business. At court, he was asked for answers to a few common history questions. He responded, "All I need to do is pick up the phone and call a member of my team, and I can get an answer to your question." Ford then asked, "Will you kindly tell me, *why* I should clutter up my mind with general knowledge?"

The sheer quantity of your knowledge is much less important than your ability to execute a set of focused tasks over a period of time. The deeper you dive and the more you understand a few key areas, the better. By focusing on a single area, you can get ahead of those in the pack who are still preoccupied with learning unnecessary things.

We cannot rely on a hope-and-pray education. This is simply not an option. We must be proactive with our long-term decisions and continuously educate ourselves.

Go to college, but don't expect to live the average student life of class-library-hostel and achieve great successes, it won't happen. Go beyond the course content; be commercially aware of the latest trends in your industry, so you can position yourself to take full advantage. You can't just learn things, you have to apply the things you learn for them to become a part of you. When you hit a brick wall in your learning curve, don't become academic and theorize about it, pursue a solution and make it a practical learning project to test your ideas. They might work, they might fail, but either way, you learn something new, ensuring your next attempt will have greater chances of success.

If you're lucky enough to read this before getting into college, ask yourself a few salient questions before making a final commitment. It's always better to know what you're getting into, instead of trying to bail out midway.

First of all, what is the profit value of the course you intend to study? In other words, how much do you stand to earn from this degree compared to the cost of acquiring it?

Another factor you should consider is the time value of that degree. In the next 10 or 20 years, what will be the value of your degree? Will it still be relevant in the coming years?

If you visit https://Trends.google.com and compare humanities or history to artificial intelligence from 2004 to today you will notice a steady decline in the first two topics. However, artificial intelligence is on the rise. A humanities position starts at about $55,000 a year versus an artificial intelligence engineer who would start anywhere from $175K to $250K per year.

While AI programming may not be your cup of tea, you might want to do analysis outside of your comfort zone in order to plan accordingly. If you can't give positive responses to the benefits of why you are taking a course, you need to stop and re-evaluate where you are.

Something else you should consider is the flexibility your degree or profession will afford you. It's estimated that by 2027, there will be more freelancers than employees. Before making a commitment, see if your degree can help you earn from multiple sources. you may even want to consider earning an additional certification for another job.

For instance, a psychology degree doesn't leave you stuck as an employee of the government or a health institution; you can work part-time as a sales representative or advertising agent. The interpersonal and persuasion skills that are an integral part of psychology can carry over into other fields.

Look for and reach out to those in your target industry sooner rather than later. Probe them for their thoughts on the future of their profession and ask what new entrants should expect and prepare themselves for.

Explore before making a commitment to specialize in a particular aspect of your profession. There is no guarantee that by the time you're ready for a master's degree or Ph.D., it will still be relevant. Furthermore, there is no guarantee that a master's degree is something you need to carve a niche in your field.

Finally, ask yourself if you're truly motivated to study this particular field or if you're just caving to societal and family expectations. Remember, you're the one that has to live with your decisions.

Not everyone can afford a college education, but anyone can afford the Da Vinci Way of Education. It costs next to nothing and it usually takes place at your convenience. The average college education for the 2017 - 2018 school year cost about $34,740 at private colleges, $9,970 for state residents at public colleges, and $25,620 for out-of-state residents attending public universities.

A 4-year degree costs between $20,000 and $40,000 a year, or $80,000 to $160,000 in total - about the same cost of a mortgage in many parts of the country. An article from Forbes stated that the average student debt for the class of 2016 is $37,172. What's more, a school loan is as heavy a burden as a mortgage and it's one of few types of loans that cannot be written off if you file for bankruptcy. Even though college is a massive investment (or liability), high school graduates are pressured to sign. They're made to believe that college is the only path to success.

Consumer Reports documented the case of Jackie Krowen, a student who racked up $152,000 in loans by simply searching the internet for loans and having checks mailed to her without the need to meet with anyone in person. How would you feel about paying $50,000 towards your loan and watching the balance drop by only $4,000? If you had a parent or relative cosign your loan, debt collectors will go after them if you decide you can't pay it off. With $152,000 in school loans, the American dream of buying a home is almost certainly not an option.

Here are some simple and easy steps for self-educating:

1. Set aside at least 30 minutes each day to read - novels, magazines, self-development, geography, anything that sparks curiosity. The essence of self-education is to expand boundaries. Set a goal to read a certain number of books every month or year. Fertilize diverse ideas with a variety of sources to deepen imagination.

2. Listen to audiobooks or podcasts when you can't read. It's easier to combine daily activities like jogging, walking to the bus station, or even taking a bath. Not to mention, when you become immersed, time flies.

3. Take online courses. In this day and age, we're spoiled with choices when it comes to online learning. Prized knowledge can be free of cost from sources like Massive Open Online Courses at MOOC.org or even the Massachusetts Institute of Technology at https://ocw.mit.edu/index.htm. The only skill you need is self-discipline which is a skill college won't teach you. Dedicate two or three hours a week to following up on online courses and don't make the mistake of taking more than one at a time. Finish one, then move on to the next. Consider blogging or vlogging to retain the information you've learned.

4. Convert TV time into NatGeo time. Instead of watching a mindless series, watch a documentary. New knowledge creates a natural thirst for more and you'll become a great conversationalist.

5. Redefine your circle. Jim Rohn says that you are the average of the five people you spend the most time with. Reflect on that. Who are the five people you spend the most time with? Talk the most with? The honest truth is, the people you associate with can make or break your future plans. Go to places where you can meet the type

of people you'd like to surround yourself with;
Conferences, meet-ups, etc.

What is the philosophy behind your educational pursuit? Is it to help someone else achieve their goals, or to advance your own goals? Are you seeking a career that stops earning once you've left the office, or keeps earning after the day is done? Focus on an education that liberates you, that gives you choices rather than restricts you. Focus on self-education; education tailored to your particular needs and interests. To have a better offensive position in the game of life we need to constantly learn and make adjustments along the way.

"The things that have been most valuable to me, I did not learn in school."

-Will Smith

Smarter Younger Kids – Monopoly

One thing that characterizes great achievers is the fact that they started early. Parents who expose their children to critical thinking skills early in life are giving them a winning edge. The seeds of productivity, creativity, and innovation start with your mind. One of the best ways to build this muscle is through the game of Monopoly.

Monopoly And Child Development

I played Monopoly as a kid but never took it seriously. That's the thing with kids; They play with toys and games that are exciting at the moment but then drop them as the fun wanes, usually without taking away any of the lessons. If you dedicate time to play Monopoly with your kids, they'll thank you as adults as the lessons prove useful in developing start-ups, scaling to profit, and pitching to venture capital for funding.

Monopoly helps kids learn how to build savings habits, as opposed to spending habits. You can't acquire property without a stash of cash in the bank. Investing in real estate, more often than not, is profitable. Real estate usually holds its price, unlike cars that start losing value the moment you drive off the lot. Later on in life, kids will be exposed to demands on their income – video games, movies, new clothes, etc. If they don't have the self-control to curb their spending, it will be tough for them to develop the habit. Saving money requires discipline, patience, and money management skills that Monopoly teaches.

The younger a person is when they get involved in real estate, the better. It's one of the best decisions a person could make in life. Just like in Monopoly, you can earn income from rent. You can rent rooms to friends and use the money to pay off your mortgage. 80% of millionaires use real estate to create their wealth. It could represent a forced savings account which you only get to cash out upon retirement. You can make $1,000/month from rent without ever having to do much. Once in a while, you'll have to answer the phone when tenants call and fix broken things, but by and large, you're not actively engaged in the income process - it's passive income. Everyone who eventually buys property wishes they had bought earlier when it was cheaper. Why not save your kids that regret later on in life?

In Monopoly, the winners are the rent collectors, the property owners. The losers pay rent. Every time you put money into someone else's hand for the roof over your head, you make them richer and make yourself poorer.

Generating passive income streams is very important for young entrepreneurs. At no time should the quest to make a living prevent us from actually living. Passive income gives the freedom to make the choices that build a life. It's one of the things that distinguish the rich from the poor. The poor have to actively work to earn a living, but the rich detach their earnings from their activities.

Passive income doesn't come automatically. It takes a lot of active participation in the beginning. You'll have to put in a lot of effort with little or no payoffs in the beginning. It will bring a lot of frustration but you'll learn a lot in the process. None of this sounds attractive, I know. So why should you do it? Because time will pass no matter what and in hindsight you'll wonder why you didn't put in the work when you were younger.

Building Your Child's Imagination

Take your children to museums. Help them understand how things work. Have them watch shows that explain how things are made. Have them apply their knowledge to make toys instead of buying new ones. Our future as a society depends on having a constant stream of dreamers, innovators, and people with great imaginations. Everything we enjoy today was created by someone who had the seeds of their imagination nurtured.

Kids who read are less likely to go to be locked up as an adult. In America, there's a lot of talk about private prisons becoming a booming industry. This is based on the number of 10 and 11-year olds who can't read. The more literate a person is, the less likely they are to engage in crime, especially crimes that involve time behind bars. The easiest way to raise literate children is to teach them how to read and help them find books they enjoy.

Reading fiction builds empathy. People who read visit places, past and present, using their imaginations. Empathy developed by reading would go a long way in helping us become selfless.

Some countries have discovered a link between reading and innovation, and their governments take steps to encourage it. China organized a government-supported science fiction fair in 2007. This was a huge step for a country that used to ban such topics. After some investigation, the Chinese found that they were quite good at developing or copying something that someone else had already created, but they lack in original creations. They sent a research delegation to tech giants in the US and they found that everyone creating and founding start-ups had one thing in common – they all read science fiction.

In a recent Stanford University survey involving 7,800 students from middle school through college, they found an alarming number of them had low levels of comprehension of online content. An average teenager was found to spend over ten hours a day on social media, from where they got most of their news. Unfortunately, most of them lacked the ability to differentiate between promotional content and a statement of fact; As well as the inability to separate fake news from real news.

Your child doesn't have to be another one of these statistics. Teach them early to question information on social media. Identify their interests and help them evaluate the best information sources. Model behavior by obtaining your information and news from a variety of sources.

Active Dreaming

Delay giving children phones. Give them a tablet pre-loaded with the best books and educational games you can find.

Instead of kids occupying time in front of the television or a handheld device, have them spend more time thinking about what they can create for others to enjoy. Get them involved in circles of people who are actively engaging their minds to create things that will shape our tomorrow. A good place to start is the Maker Faire. It's described as a 'family-friendly showcase of invention and creativity that gathers together tech enthusiasts, crafters, educators, tinkerers, food artisans, hobbyists, engineers, science clubs, artists, students, and commercial exhibitors. Makers come to show their creations. Attendees come to glimpse the future…and to learn to become makers.'

With the right kind of exposure, your kid could turn out like any of these young entrepreneurs:

- Hart Main (Age 13) – Invented the ManCan
  His business started out as a joke. He used to laugh at the scents his sister sold at fairs, telling her to try out manly scents. His parents overheard him and encouraged him to try it out himself. Hart used $100 he'd saved from his newspaper route to give it a try. He chose aromas like coffee, new mitt, bacon, and fresh-cut grass. In less than a year of starting, he had sold more than 25,000 cans of manly scent.

- Mihir Garimella (Age 15) – Builds Drones
  This Pittsburgh native wanted to build drones that could act as first responders to avoid putting human life at risk in search-and-rescue scenarios. He wanted to make drones smarter and better at navigating autonomously. To achieve this, he took inspiration from one of nature's creations – the fruit fly. His innovation won him accolades at the Google Science Fair.

Build Relationships

Spending too much time staring at electronic screens has negative consequences on children's eyesight, but staring into their parent's eyes won't do them any harm. Instead of sitting your kid in front of an electronic babysitter, build a relationship with them.

Reading is a great way to bond with children and lay foundation blocks for their future. Build a library collection at home or take them to visit the public library often. Take your kids to book signings so they can meet the people creating the works of art on your bookshelf.

Help your kids realize the long term benefits of books. Teach them how books are someone's life and visions are wrapped up in a small package. Talk with them about how long after we're gone, books will still be around for others to enjoy. An evergreen book remains timeless, these books are not based on subjects that will become irrelevant in the future.

Education doesn't only take place in schools and universities. A lot of it happens at home under parents' noses, giving children access to information, freedom to read, freedom of ideas, freedom of communication in an entertaining, relaxed setting.

It's one thing to be coached, but it's another to have everything handed to you on a silver platter.

Either way, children need to experience challenges early in life. The sooner they fail, the sooner they'll find success.

Mr. Brewster

One piece of advice I'll never forget came from my high school teacher, Mr. Brewster. He said, "If you want to do well in life, you need to be in sales."

At the time, I didn't think much of it. I wish I knew exactly why he decided to tell me this. He was my algebra teacher and I thought he liked working with numbers and teaching. Perhaps he regretted not going into sales. Regardless of the reason, the more I thought about his words, the more truth I saw in them. I realized I would need to be connected to sales one way or another. As time passes, I've reminded myself of this advice again and again.

Mr. Brewster must have been around 55 at the time. As many teachers guided my classroom work, it seemed that Mr. Brewster was looking out for my long term wellness. I wish Mr. Brewster could have enlightened me with the knowledge, experiences, and reasoning to understand and value his advice. I always wonder how things could have changed had I simply asked him why and ignited a conversation. Sometime later, I learned to be more observant of my mentors and realized that listening can be more important than speaking.

As Bruce Lee said, "if your cup is already full, then anything someone tells you spills over." You can only absorb and learn when you have an open mindset. You don't know what you don't know, and if you run across someone that has a 30-year advantage on you, don't be intimidated. Ask questions and listen. Seek knowledge. Many of us grow up thinking our cup is full, we think we know everything about everything. We want to appear smarter than we are, it's how our brains are wired.

I have seen the 'cup is full' attitude at work around senior management throughout my career. Believing we know it all is an anti-pattern that Blockbuster fell into when they thought they could copy Netflix. The better questions we ask of ourselves, the better our conclusions become. We are born into a bubble, yet to make better decisions we have to pop the bubble and see what is on the other side. Sometimes we need to forget what we know and start over with a younger, knowledge absorbing mindset which brings us to the OODA loop.

"Smart people learn from everything and everyone, average people from their experiences, stupid people already have all the answers."

- Socrates

OODA Loop - Fighting The Enemy We Cannot See

Enemies who operate from the shadows are more dangerous than the ones you can confront outright. Fighting enemies you can't see is at the heart of this topic.

'Do not swallow bait offered by the enemy,' this is a quote from Sun Tzu's book Art of War. The idea that your enemies are nonexistent once they're inactive or operating from the shadows. Cultural traditions are shadow enemies in their own way. They box you into certain roles and limit your growth, a fact that you may never realize. Traditional careers fall into this category. Unless you go out and seek habits that can leverage your skills and quadruple your income, you might wind up with the short end of the stick.

Leverage

Imagine someone is stuck on the side of the road with a flat tire and no cell service. They look in the trunk and see a jack, a tire iron, a spare tire, and another object.

Some people will be able to change the tire while others will not have enough strength to break the nuts loose that fasten the wheel to the car. If they don't have enough strength what should they do? They take a closer look in the trunk and realize there is a two-foot-long pipe. Could they use this to their advantage? They can amplify their capabilities by placing the pipe over the tire iron and increase their strength.

The longer the pipe is, the more leverage they have on the tire iron which will loosen the stubborn nuts.

What kinds of leverage can you use to get ahead?

- Can you pool your connections and create something?
- Can you leverage free time and work on one thing?
- Can you leverage a small available spot in a warehouse for your startup?
- Do you live near an airport where you can rent out cars via the Turo service?
- Do you have an extra car parking spot that you can rent?
- Can you negotiate your lease into a rent-to-own agreement and buy the building you live in?
- Can you leverage an office space and start a meetup?
- Can you leverage ten years of experience into a book, podcast, or YouTube channel?

Peter Thiel

Peter Thiel studied Philosophy at Stanford University, during which time he founded The Stanford Review. He then went on to attend Stanford's law school, graduated, and was on the path to being a lawyer. In 1998 Peter and several others cofounded Confinity, which was designed to take care of payments between Palm Pilots, the following year it merged with Elon Musk's X.com and PayPal was born. He was well on his way to having a 'perfectly respectable' career and taking his place in the rat race while sealing his fate as one of the millions with an unfulfilling job. What most of these jobs don't advertise is the fact that the owners of the companies depend on one thing; a steady influx of entry-level workers, therefore it is not in their best interests to let people rise through the ranks. This is why people often find themselves stuck in a rut when it comes to their work. Luckily for Peter, he took a detour from the path he was on.

Peter is also a board member of Facebook, a billionaire, and a philanthropist whose business savvy, revolutionary ideas have shaped the world. He found a way to live free by forming his exit strategy earlier than most. It is no surprise that the world's top 1% own half of the world's wealth. The focus of this section is to take a closer look at our internal patterns.

Can You Leverage An Exit Strategy For Your Profession?

For instance, you're a consultant in the telecommunications, media, and technology practice group of a major consulting firm. Everyone envies you. What they don't know is that perks aside, your job is more insecure than most. You face an uncertain future from one project to the next. When things go downhill for your clients, they also go downhill for your firm. When that happens, the firm has to let someone go and it might be you. What about the long hours? With ever-looming deadlines and meetings that never seem to cease. The only time you get to complete any real work is after work at the expense of personal and family time. These days, you spend two or three nights at home a week because you have to travel to places you'd rather not be, each day fleeting, giving you fewer chances to make meaning out of your life.

But that's not to say the job is without its plus sides. Every two years, you can smile on the way to the bank with a fatter paycheck and a promotion. You also get to build a powerful network of skilled and talented individuals. This network will come in handy for your future endeavors.

Either way, you want a change that gives you more time to spend with your family and puts you in charge of your employment status, not the budget of a client. Maybe ten years from now, you're hoping to be the CEO of your own tech consultancy firm, calling the shots at your own company, only servicing clients you're genuinely interested in. But why wait for ten years, or five, or even two? Who sets the rules for when you can be independent? Who do you need permission from? What is holding you back?

For example, you're in the service industry, like a coffee shop owner and you can only make so much money because you can only service a limited amount of customers. What if you focused on growing sales in your backend, meaning delivering goods to local businesses. Working on personal business is something many forget to do.To leverage your situation, you need more customers and you need to hire more people as you fully step into management. Only by developing systems for each job can you walk away as your business continues to work without your presence.

Systematizing doesn't just help you, it gives you the ability to sell your business. Doing everything yourself is not a business, it's a job. Imagine wanting to sell your future business one day? If the business runs itself, you're good to go. If you do

80% of the work, you cannot sell the business. You want to work on your business instead of working for your business.

The more items you can sell that are not tied to your time, the better. This is why so many people focus on information technology and specialize in programming. To get rich during the gold rush you needed to sell shovels and picks. To get rich today you need to sell an app, service, or something else that is not tied to your time. If you can create an app and it ranks in the top 100 in the app store you'll be a step closer to winning the passive income lottery.

The amount of work required to sell 100 or 10,000 items is pretty much the same once you have the proper systems in place. If you have a job installing 500 widgets a day you would have to delegate this task in order to play a different part of the game.

In both brick and mortar and online businesses, you need to leverage whatever it takes to bring in more sales. You can have the best coffee on the block but if you don't leverage your customers to recommend your coffee, growth may not occur at a sustainable rate. The best testimonial in business comes from your customers. Do you ask your customers what can we do better?

Software developers constantly chase the latest certification. People who work in an increasingly disruptive sector like technology have to stay ahead of the knowledge curve or they may get knocked out of the action. In 1991 Pierre Omidyar was an IT developer who seemed to have superhero powers. He could do things that no one else could. Pierre, like any developer, had the unique capability to control his fate and he chose to do exactly that. He turned his ideas into reality and still controlled everything from the ground up. He built apps, created features, and built technology. He doesn't need to find and convince a technical co-founder to build out an idea for him. Neither does he have to pay contractors outrageous amounts of money to build out basic features. Pierre eventually set up an exit strategy that developed into eBay. The very first item ever sold on eBay was a broken laser pointer. The same broken laser pointer is now showcased at 2025 Hamilton Avenue in San Jose, eBay's headquarters.

Luck often has no place in success. History is filled with examples of people who stumbled across great opportunities and failed to recognize them. For example, Ross Perot refused to buy into Microsoft. Marvel decided not to buy out DC Comics when they had the chance. Blockbuster Video Entertainment refused to buy Netflix. MySpace rejected Facebook's original offers.

How can we leverage what we are currently doing? If you've mastered a skill, you may want to consider writing a book or organizing an event where others will pay to learn from you.

Every teacher, instructor, and YouTube star started in a place not so different from you. As your skill level increases, you may realize that creating a YouTube channel is within your capability. Eventually, you may even gain a wider audience and potentially sell membership access to premier how-to videos.

If you are passionate about a topic, you might want to start a podcast from which you could reach thousands. You must figure out a way to get paid while you sleep or you will spend all your waking moments trying to earn income that matches your expenses.

To achieve this, we have to focus our efforts on what will amplify and maximize our time versus what will take it away. It is important to make a clear distinction between the two, as any mistakes at this point will render the whole exercise moot and leave you in the grip of time-wasting activities. The world is not kind or fair to people who refuse to act swiftly and decisively.

Unless you are running a company that is selling something, you are trading your time for dollars. This is how the system was designed and many people are okay with it; however, I think we all want more than being stuck in this pattern. If you aren't happy playing along with the system, let's take a look at the OODA loop, a military strategy that was designed to be the foundation of rational thinking in tense or high-risk situations. OODA stands for observe, orient, decide and act.

It was developed for fighter pilots by U.S Air Force Colonel John Boyd. However, it can be extended into other fields. Fighter pilots have to work fast under pressure and they have to make life or death decisions at the drop of a hat. Imagine being able to bypass unnecessary hassles and make smarter choices by applying a strategy that enhances your creativity and decision-making skills.

- **Observe** - Take a step back and take a look at your patterns - the habits and routines you've become accustomed to. Do these patterns entrap you like a hamster stuck running on a wheel? Or are they helping you break out of the mold that you have been placed in?
- **Orient** - You've identified your patterns and it's time to take advantage of your observations and adjust your mindset. Big changes start somewhere, an idea that's different from the others, something innovative.
- **Decide** - Have you ever thought about the new changes we see every day? These changes come from people who observe their surroundings and think about possible ways to make things better. Start asking yourself how can

you and what can you contribute to solve the problems around you.

Sara Blakely got the idea for Spanx one day when she was getting ready for a party and she realized that she didn't have the right undergarment. She experimented by cutting off the feet of her pantyhose and her idea was born. Not only did she have the idea, but she also spent two years and $5,000 on researching and developing her idea before pitching it to hosiery companies. She was rejected by many but eventually found a company willing to work with her. Willingness and perseverance matter.

- **Act** - Are your actions aligning you with your desired future? Decide what you want your future to look like and analyze your actions in that space. What needs to change? What needs to be adjusted? Is your vision achievable? Answer these questions and take the next steps.

Big actions and decisions are risky. The Wright brothers didn't learn to fly overnight. They believed in their mission and conducted hundreds of test flights at Kitty Hawk before becoming famous. They chose to practice their flying in Kitty Hawk, North Carolina because the winds were plentiful and the ground was covered with sand dunes that would help absorb impact from a crash. Everybody is a nobody until they succeed at something. There is so much to be achieved when people begin to see the bigger picture.

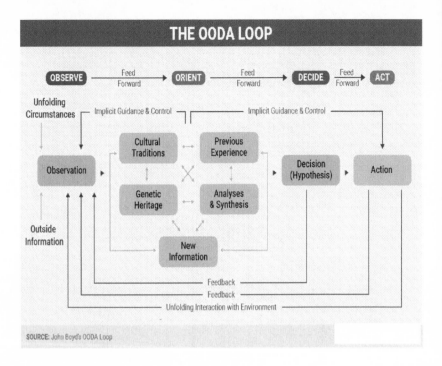

Focusing Your Energy

Only when you focus the sun's rays through a lens is there enough energy to leave a mark on an object. Without the focus of a lens, our habits are diffused as well.

The silence of meditation can help you better understand the problems you face by de-stressing your mind.

To achieve crystal clarity I sit quietly for about ten minutes every day and tune into my mind. The act of gently closing my eyes and thinking about what I want and why I want it helps prime my mind for the coming day or evening. Chanting the statement, "You can do this," helps me to keep external noise from hijacking my thoughts. The more I take time out with my thoughts the more that I can feel grounded and make progress. When I finish this 10-minute ritual I write down any additional thoughts which I may have had so that I can keep track of them somewhere.

Some people like to completely clear their minds of all thoughts. I find that thinking about a single thought can be just as effective. Maintaining this ritual at the same time every day helps create a natural rhythm that repeats like clockwork.

You can be in great physical shape but if you ignore your mind, your body will not follow. The mind and body must function as one. Pacifying the senses and overcoming wandering thoughts takes us a step closer to clarity.

The continuous act of leaning into your obstacles will help you with awareness and sharpen your focus in the following areas:

- Putting yourself first
- Inspiring your mission
- Discipline to make progress towards a single goal
- Belief that you can make an impact
- Staying grounded with purpose

My morning focus eventually became so strong I was able to ignore everything happening around me, regardless of my surroundings. If my environment happens to be noisy, it helps me to play rhythmic, non vocal music and chant the statement, "You can do this."

I have trained my body to see this as a flow state of happiness, something that psychologist Mihaly Csikszentmihalyi covered in his research.

Follow In Their Steps

Next, you must analyze people who have succeeded in their exit strategy, including those who failed or were too content with their situation to try. Figure out what they did right and wrong, then apply what you have learned to yourself. More importantly, you must use your feelings to help you, rather than hinder you. Know that you must care for yourself and take a hard look at your maneuvers; you must care for yourself enough to identify and make the right moves. It's not enough to wish that things were better, you need to make conscious moves towards your goals.

Focus on what you want, not on what others want for you. Others want us to keep afloat, but just barely. Some have said that it is in human nature to wish for our own prosperity and resent others'. Know that the goals you set for yourself shouldn't be derailed by the opinion of others, because others have planned their own goals for you which may not be in line with yours.

Your subconscious holds more power over your actions than you realize; therefore, it's important to be aware of it so you won't sabotage yourself. Know that your time and energy are too valuable to be wasted on activities that limit your worth.

Can You Jump Off The Hamster Wheel?

If we blindly follow the preset path, we will make progress; however, the progress will be limited and we will only be able to achieve what we are allowed to achieve. We should ask ourselves if we can escape the hamster wheel of life.

Many of us fail to recognize the amount of free time we have in a year. Our free time plays a partial role in how successful we are, but as time goes on, our free time is determined by our employer. As long as we exchange our time for money, we do not own our time.

Have you ever noticed at the zoo how animals pace in their cages? Pacing has become a way of life for them because it's all they know. People can fall into a similar type of pacing. Sometimes people accept certain ways of life because it's all they know. The only difference is that people have the advantage of freedom, yet some keep pacing the limitations of their minds.

What will change in the next five years?

- Your income may advance slightly every year
- Your job title might change
- Your responsibilities could change
- Your bills will follow you everywhere

If we have the same job for ten years, we wind up repeating one year of experience ten times. You can't keep doing the same thing over and over again and expect different results. If you are living paycheck to paycheck and you get sick, the house of cards will crumble.

What's the one thing you can do that you don't need anybody's help with? That ability is your superpower. It's the key to calling the shots in regards to your life. When you decide to 'Act' on it, you've hit the final stage of the OODA Loop.

We need to use the power of precognition. With all the fog around, it's no wonder we tend to get stuck in the loops of life. To see past the forest, we must rise above the tree line. Develop your superpowers so you can see the reality that awaits you in five years. Develop your superpower to see into the future you envision, seeing beyond the wall of obstacles you currently face. Where are you in the next five years? What do you see happening in your future that's worth looking forward to? Now start making those visions reality. The only thing standing between you and your future is the unseen enemy.

A Job Can Be Your Enemy

Conquering this enemy is nearly half the battle. If you don't free your mindset from the 'job' mentality, how can you envision things greater than yourself? An unleashed mindset creates a force field like the Invisible Woman from Marvel's *Fantastic Four*.

"The only thing worse than being blind, is having sight but no vision."

-Helen Keller

Most people will live in a particular pattern until it is too late to make a change. Some people may even die without ever realizing that change can be made. Others will choose to observe, orient, and pivot.

Let us look at Jen. She finished college at top of her class and got a job as an IT manager with a team all her own. Her firm is currently expanding, so things are really exciting. Her pay increases $5,000 every year and time flashes by. She hardly has time to take a break from her fast-paced life, except for her annual two-week vacation. Now she's in her fifth year and gets a three-week break. She's a Senior Manager now, but she still needs permission from higher up to get a day off. Even if she leaves the firm for another, the story would stay the same.

She doesn't have to stay stuck in the rat race. She could take her knowledge and experience and do something that works for her. When she does this, she's moved from the Observation stage of the OODA Loop to the Orientation stage.

Why can't she create an ebook, discussing everything that aspiring and current IT managers should know about the job to guarantee their success? She should know best, she was once in their shoes. She could also develop an app that helps companies build online databases and web applications. She could sell her skills as an IT consultant to different businesses instead of staying stuck with one company. Another alternative would be for her to create a course in project management or Oracle, which is within his competence as an IT manager. Whatever option she takes, the point is to create something big, so big it will outlast her; a single product produced only one time, but that can repeat itself multiple times for profit.

What about Stewart? He loves cooking but finds himself in the construction industry, switching companies and homes as the jobs change. His family has hardly any time to develop roots. If he keeps going at this rate, he'll have nothing tangible to his name by the time he hits 65.

He decides to quit his 9-5. In most towns he's lived in, there are restaurants competing against one another and they don't have loyal customers. He's a good cook and thinks this business is right up his lane. He knows just what to do when he opens up his own restaurant - he'll get every willing customer to become a brand ambassador for their favorite dish. In return, they get a discount the next time they come in. All they have to do is take pictures of the food, share it on Instagram, tag the restaurant, and if they get enough likes, Stewart might even throw in a dessert. This is an exciting promotion that customers jump on and they tell their friends all about it. The cycle continues and Stewart has a revolving door of old and new customers.

Stewart relied on his experience as a customer and his empathy as a cook, and was able to analyze a common business challenge to develop a unique solution. That's what formed the basis of his Decision, the third stage of the OODA Loop.

If we do not create the time to dream about the future we want we will always be living in somebody else's dream.

"Knowing others is intelligence,

Knowing yourself is true wisdom.

Mastering others is strength.

Mastering yourself is true power"

-Lao Tzu

Chapter 5 Believe You Can

If you believe in something, Fight for it. No one else will.

-Andrewzee

Be A Lion Among Mice

The more pampering we receive as children, the bigger the shock we are in for when we step into the real world. We must become the hunter. A hunter develops its own techniques and establishes patterns. They learn to work with what the land has to offer. Hunters climb mountains to get a better view of what is going on below them. From a perch, they can study the movements of prey and determine the best approach, angle, and strike to kill. Unlike hunters, we are raised with a mice mentality. We are taught to survive, not to thrive.

Lions are considered the king of the jungle because of their raw strength and power. In a way, we are like lions, constantly fighting to keep our positions and protecting our loved ones from danger. We feel the same pressure to be successful in life. We want to excel in our careers, foster healthy relationships, and still find quality time to relax and maintain our sanity.

Balance can be rather difficult and when things don't work out as they should, or when the progress is slower than expected, we sometimes label ourselves as failures. Lions constantly fight, no matter how many times they're attacked and that is how they stay on top. For us to stay on top, we need to be independent - be the hunter, not the hunted. Get out of the mouse mindset and put yourself in the mindset of a lion.

The power of positivity, starting with one's thoughts, can strongly influence one's everyday life. Wouldn't it be nice if you could be bold enough to join the table of lions? If you're a mouse, you will end up trading your time for money. Statistics show that 90% of individuals lead an average life because they shy away from taking calculated risks and making profitable decisions that can enhance their growth.

We are raised to be nice, fit in, play and communicate effectively with those around us, but this can make us mediocre. If you want to succeed in life, you need to transform your thinking from the stereotypical thought of a mouse to that of a lion. Why accept measly crumbs when you could be feasting? You need to possess the resilient spirit of the lion and teach your cubs that depending on a job is the shortcut to the endangered species list. Achieving this begins with thinking out of the box. Be wiser with your time, don't waste it basking in the temporal pleasure of frivolities. Join the hunt.

"A lion runs the fastest when he is hungry."

-Salman Khan

It Starts With A Dream

Dreams are the bedrock of our being. They lead to visions, visions lead to actions, and the right actions lead to success. In 1929, a man named Martin was born and when he grew up, he made American history.

32 years later, another great man was born. This man would build upon Martin's legacy, using non-violent strategies to tackle inequality. This man shattered preconceptions and fought to make inequality truly a thing of the past, this man's name is

Barack. Despite being born so many years apart, their ideologies were the same.

Both men had a dream, a very big dream for equal rights. A dream is not a wish; it's an idea that burns inside of you and you want nothing else but to see it become realized.

What is your dream? You can't achieve great success in life if you don't dream. All great leaders, including Barack and Martin, have a dream. Without one, you won't know which actions to take.

Act Now - Take Action And Believe You Can

You can be the best version of yourself but to do this, you need to take action. Martin took action and so did Barack, they did not stay in their comfort zones and hope for their dreams to be realized.

What steps are you taking right now to achieve your dreams?

Barack went to law school, became a community activist, and participated in the End Apartheid movement in South Africa.

Martin attended seminary and university. He became a Baptist minister during his final years at Boston University as a Ph.D. student.

Barack won a Nobel Peace prize, Martin is also a Nobel Peace Prize winner. What is your accomplishment? You must take deliberate actions if you desire to see change.

"It might seem like you have all the time in the world but the hour is late. And the clock of destiny is ticking out. We must act now before it is too late."

Time waits for no one and procrastinating will get you nowhere. You may be scared of challenges, but they are unavoidable.

"If you can't fly then run, if you can't run then walk, if you can't walk then crawl, but whatever you do you have to keep moving forward."

-Martin Luther King Jr.

Be bold enough to press on towards your goal. There will be challenges but you should press on anyway.

Challenges are what make us human. Know that you are not alone, many people have gone through the same or worse than what you are currently experiencing. You may think you can't do it, but you are underestimating your potential. If others doubt you, so what? Our struggles are part of our destiny and they only make us stronger.

Barack was a bi-racial kid who only met his biological father once before he passed on. His mother remarried and moved the family to Indonesia where he struggled to fit in. He returned to Hawaii to live with his grandparents at age ten. Barack struggled with his identity; his dreams and reality were not always aligned. But his struggles and diverse background became the very means through which his personality was shaped. He understood the power of diversity, his speeches later in his career connected people from all over the world with his ideologies of life.

136

Failure is only a phase in life. It doesn't matter how many times you fail, what's important is that you learn. There will be times when you'll do everything right and still fail but don't be deterred. Reevaluate yourself and keep moving. You are valuable, stronger than your adversaries and the world needs your greatness.

Martin suffered through domestic violence as a kid. He rebelled against his father and turned to alcohol. Eventually, he realized that violence was not a way to deal with his challenges and he used that message to change the world.

Moving forward is the ultimate goal. You will become the best version of yourself so long as you make deliberate efforts to work towards your goals. There will be times when using the best strategies will not work, but remain hopeful, patience will make all the difference.

There will be people who will tell you that you can't do it. Ignore them. They don't see the vision that you do. Imagine if Barack had listened to the people who told him he couldn't achieve his goal. What if Martin gave up when people said he was a worthless liar? You need to find the courage to move on despite the setbacks.

Winners are losers who never gave up. Try, learn, and try again.

Never Lose Focus

The biggest mistake of most dreamers is that they lose their focus easily. Focus is what separates a winner from a dreamer. Keep your mind on what you want to do and not what you want to be.

Becoming rich is not a valid goal. "I want to make social change in the lives of disadvantaged families and communities" was Barack's goal. Martin's goal was to see a desegregated world where people would be judged by their actions alone.

You need to envision the end game. Twenty years from now, will you still be connected to your goal? A purposeful life's goal is an enduring commitment.

Bill Gates' goal was never to be the richest man on the planet, he just wanted everyone to have access to computers.

The path to success is paved with unforeseen changes, you need to be able to adjust while keeping your eyes on the prize. To stay focused, you need to see the world differently and change how you confront the challenges that come your way. When you find yourself in a situation where you doubt your actions, stop and ask yourself, why you started this in the first place. Focusing on what you want to do rather than what you want to be will keep you going even when no one else believes.

Not every battle is worth fighting and the excuse of 'the end justifies the means' doesn't apply when you keep your mind on your goal. Learn how to deal with the things you can't change and change the things you can.

What drives you? Don't just strive to get by, make a difference.

Be decisive. Barack decided that he wanted to be a politician and he made his move. Martin decided that no matter what, he would not resort to violence to achieve his goal of equality. Even when the very people he was fighting for questioned his tactics and wanted to use violence, he refused and focused on his original purpose.

You can't achieve success without first making a decision about what you stand for. Keep your principles and stay focused because distractions will test you. Without strong moral principles and a strong focus on a goal, you will not have the conviction to continue.

Have you noticed that most successful people sleep less and do more than others? Barack only slept for five hours every night and Martin was the same. We all have 24 hours in a day and great achievers spend less time sleeping and more time working towards their goals.

Find Strength In Others

A life of success is a life of learning and one of the most valuable resources at your disposal is learning from others. Barack learned from Martin, and both of them learned from Gandhi. They learned patience, the use of non-violence in achieving one's goals, and best of all, they learned to use vision to connect people.

Barack looked up to Martin for courage, he learned to be fearless and to shun self-doubt. Giants stand on the shoulders of other giants who came before them. Use your time wisely, learn about those who have walked similar paths, and succeeded at what you dream of.

Barack continued reading about historical figures even after he achieved one of his greatest goals. He needed books to get him through lonely nights.

The journey to success is a path of solidarity, and you will find yourself alone at times. You should read and connect with people who have been in your shoes.

How many books have you read this month? Being busy is not an excuse. Barack's schedule was fully booked but he still found time to read. If you want to succeed, you must read.

If you can't find inspiration in the stories of others, you can always find hope in the stories of others.

Finally

You can step out of your comfort zone, learn something new, and make a difference in the world today.

Barack was the first black president of the Harvard law review and he became the first black president in American history. His bravery came from the victories of others including Martin and Nelson Mandela. He read, he learned, and he wrote. He valued people's struggles and he had empathy for those who were less fortunate than him. Barack's actions as a politician showed that bravery and beliefs in one's self are paramount to achieving the impossible.

You need to believe in yourself, even if no one else does. You are the best resource and ally you have.

Martin was the prominent leader of the American civil rights movement from 1954 to 1968. His passion, confidence, and powerful words still inspire people to become their best selves today. Martin's "I have a dream" speech continues to inspire people to believe in themselves and to never give up.

My dream is to inspire you to think 'yes I can.' You can become the best version of yourself. You can face challenges. You can overcome your past and press forward. Yes, you can! If you believe you will achieve, no matter what.

The following are some of the characteristics you'll need to mold your thinking.

- Have one large ambitious goal rather than many small, less impactful goals.
- Believe in your mission like your life depends on it.
- Work towards your goal every day, a little at a time.
- Put in the work while you still can.
- Think 'how can I' instead of 'why I cannot'.
- Believe you can make a difference.
- Giving up is not an option.

"A dream doesn't become reality through magic; it takes sweat, determination, and hard work."

-Colin Powell

The Magic Of Harry Potter

Hogwarts, a dream school where wands cast spells at the speed of light, magic potions bring divine healing, and the feverish thrill of the game Quidditch. These are elements that we have not only fallen in love with but which lie at the very center of the alternate universe that the Harry Potter brand and stories have come to represent.

Behind these elements is an absolutely brilliant mind. Quietly spinning wheels for years, book after book, J.K. Rowling's gift is the truest magic of all, ensuring that this galaxy of wizardry continues to thrive.

Her story is not just a story of one of the most accomplished writers of our time, or a story about one of the world's richest women. It's an enduring story of how circumstances and challenges cost us an English teacher and interpreter, but through trials, failures, and sheer impossibility gave us a world-famous writer.

In a journey to greatness that was no brief sprint, J.K. Rowling is proof that sometimes the road to success is littered with grueling 9-5 jobs, divorce, foreign lands, and pain.

Gloucestershire England

Joanne Kathleen Rowling was born on July 31st, 1965. Her father, Peter James Rowling was a Rolls Royce Aircraft engineer, and her mother, Anne Rowling, was a science technician.

Growing up, her life was less than picture-perfect. Her teenage years were painfully colored with her mother's struggle with multiple sclerosis. She took solace in Jessica Mitford, communist and civil rights activist that served as an inspiration. Rowling also took comfort in reading Jane Austen novels.

She later graduated from the University of Exeter with a BA in French and Classics, a quiet and somewhat unremarkable start to a life destined for greatness.

London, Manchester And The Birth Of A Dream

After graduation, her pursuit of the Golden Fleece took her to London. While in London, she found work as a researcher and bilingual secretary at Amnesty International.

From London, she moved to Manchester to work in the Chamber of Commerce. During a delayed train trip from

Manchester to London, the Harry Potter series began to take shape in her mind. Taking advantage of the four-hour delay, she took notes, crafting the intricate tale of the experiences of a young wizard in an exciting school of wizardry.

It was at this point that life would throw the first of many curve balls at her. A few months after she started writing, she was informed of her mother's death, ending her mother's long battle with multiple sclerosis. One of Rowling's regrets is that she was never able to share the body of work that became Harry Potter with her mother.

Porto Portugal

Following her mother's death, Rowling followed her dreams to Porto, Portugal. She applied for a teaching position she found in a newspaper and was employed as an English language teacher. At night, she taught, but during the day, she continued writing her novel about wizards.

In the midst of balancing her teaching role and her writing, she met Jorge Arantes. Arantes was a Portuguese television journalist and they quickly bonded over their love for Jane Austen. They were married and a few months later they welcomed a daughter.

A few months later in a devastating turn of events, Rowling fled the country and took their daughter with her, claiming her husband was physically abusive.

Edinburgh

An unemployed, single mother fleeing an abusive marriage hardly seems successful. Yet, it was these challenges that characterized Rowling's life as she rebuilt her life.

She moved with her daughter to Edinburgh, Scotland where her sister lived. Rowling has said many times that she felt like a failure at this point in her life. She came close to the brink, fighting depression and suicidal thoughts, but she kept fighting.

Arantes attempted to locate her and obtain custody of their daughter. Rowling obtained an order of restraint that forced him to return to Portugal, she eventually divorced him.

With a child to care for and a writing passion to pursue, Rowling signed up for state benefits and completed her first novel. Her dedication was unhindered by motherhood as she took long walks and wrote in cafes, savoring peace, clarity, and coffee while her daughter slept.

Stone To Gold

Rowling searched for someone to publish her first novel. After dozens of rejection letters from publishing houses, her big break came when the eight-year-old daughter of the Chairman of Bloomsbury, a publishing house based in London delightedly read the first chapter and she demanded the next installment. Rowling had turned stone turned to gold.

Barry Cunningham, the editor at Bloomsbury urged her to get a job to support herself as the revenue from a children's book is traditionally low, but Rowling continued writing aided by a timely grant from the Scottish Arts Council. When her book was finally released, it became a success, garnering plaudits and awards every step of the way. Months later, Rowling won the Nestle Smarties Book Prize, the British Book Award for the children's book of the year, and many more.

True commercial success came a year later when the book crossed the seas to America. Scholastic Inc. obtained the rights to publish the novel for over $100,000. This deal was all the magic Rowling needed to start a new life. She has described this first payout as unbelievable. It allowed her to move into a comfortable flat and focus on writing.

Harry Potter

After her first novel, the floodgates opened and there was no stopping her. She went on to write six other novels in the series and they all proved commercial successes.

In 2017, Forbes attempted to put figures to the power of magic and valued the Harry Potter brand at $25 billion with over 450 million books sold in 79 languages and box office earnings of $7.7 billion from film adaptations of the novels.

Creating Magic

J.K. Rowling is enthusiastic about interacting with readers and sharing tips with writers who are struggling with the creative process.

The story of Rowling writing in cafes is now an anecdote but it still holds a certain lesson for writers. For Rowling, food is important in the writing process and cafe writing spots are perfect for grabbing coffee and snacks. Creativity cannot be bullied into submission, remember to give in to your urges and grab something to eat while you work.

While her books appear free-flowing, she actually draws out detailed plans for her plots, characters, and settings.

She's surprisingly old fashioned when it comes to her medium of expression. Using an old typewriter for her first novel, she now prefers to write down her thoughts on paper and transfer them to a laptop.

Perhaps the most important lesson from Rowling's writing habits is to always keep the mind open to new ideas and projects despite trying to meet a deadline or finish existing work. Stay disciplined to your goals but don't close your mind to fresh ideas.

No Excuses

There are no excuses for not following through with your dream. Rowling had to teach at night and write in the day. This was a tremendous sacrifice for someone trying to earn a living in a foreign country. In Edinburgh, she took long walks to tire her baby out and settled down to write in cafes as the first Harry Potter novel came together.

No matter what you face, a 9-5 job, kids, bad working conditions, decide there will be no excuses.

J.K. Rowling is a synonym for uncommon determination. Her story leaves you feeling that even in darkest times, there is a band in the silence urging you into the light with inspiring lyrics of civil rights anthem, 'We shall overcome...swing low, sweet chariot.'

"There's a world out there. Open a window, and it's there."

-Robin Williams

Powerful Women

Everything you've ever wanted is on the other side of fear. You've probably heard this saying somewhere. Maybe you've thought about how true it really was.

Here are stories of three women who have broken boundaries, achieved great personal success, and broke through glass ceilings. These women are an inspiration. They didn't follow the herd mentality. They are perfect models for the forward-looking mindset. They never let their failures stand in the way of their endeavors. They are paving roads for others to follow. They are the Power Women of America.

-   Written with my daughter Sophia in mind. Love dad

Marissa Mayer

The simple interface of the Google search engine may not have come into being, if not for Marissa Mayer, former CEO of Yahoo and Vice President in charge of search products and user experience for five years at Google. Her father was an environmental engineer who worked for water treatment plants, and her mother was an art teacher who decorated their Wausau home with Marimekko prints. This design esthetic greatly influenced Mayer's design choices at Google.

"I always did something I was a little not ready to do. I think that's how you grow. When there's that moment of 'Wow, I'm not really sure I can do this,' and you push through those moments, that's when you have a breakthrough."

Growing up, Mayer had several hobbies - ice skating, ballet, piano, embroidery, cake decorating, and others. The one that she really took to was dancing. By junior high, she was dancing 35 hours a week. She learned how to absorb criticism and develop self-discipline, poise, and confidence.

Growing up, she wanted to become a pediatric neurosurgeon, but later she didn't find it to be challenging enough. At the same time, she began picking an interest in symbolic systems, cognitive psychology, linguistics, philosophy, and computer science. Making the switch wasn't easy, but she did it, and all that interest laid the foundation for her in-depth knowledge of interface design and artificial intelligence.

After graduating from Stanford University, Marissa received 14 job offers, including a teaching position at Carnegie Mellon University and a consulting job at McKinsey & Company. She had arrived, more or less. She turned down prestigious offers and took a leap of faith and she joined Google as its 20th employee. At the time, Google was a company with barely any revenue and they were attempting to achieve gender balance. Within a short time, Marrisa began overseeing teams of male engineers, writing code, and developing and designing for Google's most profitable functions. For instance, she was the only woman on the three-man team that developed Google AdWords, an advertising platform that allows businesses to show their product to relevant, potential customers based on their search terms. AdWords helped deliver 96% of the company's revenue in the first quarter of 2011.

Don't assume it was a smooth ride for her; she hit a lot of rough patches.

She was hired as a coder for Google and her first big project was to build Google's advertising system. It took her months to make progress. Eventually, Google hired star coder

Jeff Dean and he finished it in weeks. This was a real blow to her in a male-dominated work environment. But did she pack her bags and go? No. She had plenty of other job offers but she chose to stick to it. She loved her job at Google and was determined to make her mark as a coder.

Google was still a startup with a thousand and one problems. Solving them required more than coding skills. She got involved in marketing, PR, and even rigged servers. She ran staff meetings for CEO Larry Page. She went as far as deciding whether new Google products had user interfaces that lived up to Google's standards. This was the role that she eventually settled into and made her mark.

Sheryl Sandberg

Sheryl Sandberg was born to Jewish parents who struggled for the right to emigrate from the Soviet Union to Israel during the '70s. In 1975, they were arrested in Kishinev, the capital of Soviet Moldova and they were expelled from the country. They included their children in demonstrations for Jewish rights. The sum of these experiences helped Sheryl write a book to inspire other women, encouraging them to believe they could achieve more than they dreamed.

One habit that has stayed with her since childhood was her voracious appetite for books. In a New York Times interview, she said that the number of dog-eared pages in a book were a good measure of how much she enjoyed it. Her favorite book growing up was *A Wrinkle in Time* by Madeleine L'Engle. She identified with Meg Murry, the geeky heroine of the book who worked with others to fight against an unjust system and save her family. The book was her first exposure to time travel. She reportedly asked Facebook's engineers to build her a tesseract that could fold the fabric of time and space, but no one was up to the task.

By 2007, Sandberg was in a comfortable position with Google as Vice President of global online sales and operations. But she wanted more of a challenge. That same year, she met Mark Zuckerberg, CEO of Facebook at a Christmas Party. By February 2008, she was the COO of Facebook. Facebook was barely a year old. It had no profit or company culture. It was more or less the basics of Zuckerberg's original idea. She gave up the opportunity to become Google's Chief Financial Officer to join Facebook.

Her morale was tested in 2015 when she lost her husband. Feeling alone and isolated, she confided in her boss about how her relationships were gone because no one knew the right things to say. Towards the end of her grieving period, she wrote and posted an unfiltered, grief-stricken account of her experience at Facebook. She second-guessed the idea, slept on it, woke up, decided that things could not get any worse, and hit the post button. Her post had garnered 74,000 comments. People from all over the world shared their stories of grief. Later, she said that she no longer felt alone.

Today she is praised for her decision. She's a billionaire now and one of the most powerful women in the world. But would people have encouraged or shamed her ten years ago?

The enemy of greater success is success itself. When you're in a position that seems so enviable it's easy to just sit back and enjoy the ride. Keep pushing. Moving against the current. Keep swimming to the mouth of the river.

Michelle Obama

Do what you say you're going to do, be honest and true, and treat people with dignity and respect - these words from Marian and Fraser Robinson, parents of Michelle Obama, guide her every waking moment. They're the reason she chose to marry Barack. He reminded her of her father's decency, honesty, and compassion.

Growing up, her favorite book was *Olivia* by Ian Falconer. She credits the book with helping her learn to love reading. Before this book, reading was a chore; something she did because she had to. *Olivia* grabbed her by the scruff and pulled her in, making reading one of her new hobbies. In an interview conducted by Carla Hayden, a librarian from the Library of Congress, Michelle said how good it felt to get her first library ID card at age four. From then on, she looked forward to the day she could 'graduate' from the children's section and read the 'serious books' from the adult section.

She also exhibited a great flair for the piano and played every day. She played so much she had to be told to stop. She was also a great athlete in high school but shied away from competitive sports because she hated losing.

Training to become a lawyer with her parents' values of tenacity, she quickly rose through the ranks, gaining considerable experience in public service and non-profits. By 2005, she was Vice President for community and external affairs for the University of Chicago hospitals. Less than three years later, she put her career on hold to support her husband on the campaign trail. She wrote her own speeches and attracted crowds of a 1,000-plus. Obama won the Presidency two times in a row and she brought a lot to the office of First Lady. But what if it hadn't worked out? She risked a stable career, not for her personal gain, but for the ambition of her husband which also stood to affect their family life.

A Final Word

These three women all have something in common. Whether it was taking a job with a startup that had a funny-sounding name, leaving a comfortable position in an established company to join a startup with no cash flow, or putting your career on the line to support a candidate that no one expected to win; they went for the scariest option. They took the road less traveled. They went against the normative way of thinking. They swam against the current.

Their parents played a large part in shaping their habits and principles. A love for literature helped them become successful. They also had multiple interests in diverse subjects. Multiple interests helped build their intelligence and gave them tenacity to face challenges.

At times, you'll have to make sacrifices, not for your own future gain, but for someone you care about. You'll have doubts. What if it all backfires? What if the person doesn't appreciate a single thing I've done for them? But what if they do? You'll never know if you don't take the plunge.

Marissa Mayer, Sheryl Sandberg, Michelle Obama; these three women have had successful careers and created legacies that will outlive them. One such way is the books they've written and the books that have been written about them.

They have words worth documenting because they took a chance to think differently. They've left the world significantly changed.

Instead of spending your life trying to climb up the corporate ladder, think of your life as a series of small adventures where you try swimming up different, less crowded streams to the top.

How To Swim Against The Current

When the movie *Finding Nemo* came out in 2003, it was Dory, the plucky, forgetful blue fish that taught us to just keep swimming in the face of adversity. This phrase has a deeper meaning for many of us, especially for Ellen DeGeneres, the woman who voiced Dory. Ellen came out as a lesbian in 1997 while she was starring in *Ellen*, a popular sitcom. Ratings dropped, the show was canceled, and she was without a job. For more than three years, she was without a consistent job and attacked for being gay until Andrew Stanton found the perfect role for her in his movie. Thanks to her voice and her style of stand-up comedy.

The road will not be a walk in the park. At times you wonder if you made the right decision. You'll need a clearly defined purpose in regards to why you're going against the trend. If there's no compelling 'why', you won't last long and you might as well just stay where you are.

Make it a goal to intentionally practice little acts of courage; talk to someone new at the office, asking for help from someone you've never spoken to. Speak up about what agitates you. Speaking about what worries you the most creates a stronger commitment to deliver.

"The most important thing in life is to stop saying 'I wish' and start saying 'I will.' Consider nothing impossible, then treat possibilities as probabilities."

-Charles Dickens

Your Mindset Determines Your Future

There are several factors that influence your daily habits and the way you handle distractions. Among them are your confidence and your state of mind.

Go for a walk through the forest or a park and daydream. Take yourself away from the distractions of the city. Develop your thoughts, let go of your undesired thoughts, and retain the ones you wish.

To build your confidence you need is setting realistic goals. This involves creating a list of things you want to achieve. You can determine the extent of your success by writing your achievements and their dates on small cards. Place the cards in a jar and label it 'success jar'. The fuller the jar gets, the closer you are to your goal.

Our belief system is reinforced by assertions. It does this by making ourselves think about the actions we wish to demonstrate. We make our assertions and beliefs clear whenever we say them aloud.

Our habits are shaped by our daily routines. Scott Adams, the creator of Dilbert, wanted to become a comic writer. He began to write down his dream every day, repeating 'I, Scott Adams, will be a famous comic writer,' and eventually, it came true.

You can do the same by writing down your goals every day. When a process is repeated, it eventually becomes natural. The words we repeat to ourselves are powerful; hence, the mind believes them. With constant repetition, we are able to gain a deep sense of reassurance.

Apart from a constant repetition of words, it's important to speak positive words to yourself. There is power in positive speech. Here are some examples of positive utterances:

- As I continue to learn, I will possess every required quality to attain extraordinary success.
- I will strive hard today to become better than yesterday.
- I have a superhero in me that will guide me to perform extraordinarily.
- Like water, my divergent thinking will flow around any obstacle that stands my way.
- I will shun my former negative habits and substitute them with positive ones.

What's That In Your Wallet?

Jim Carry is a renowned actor, no doubt. Before he achieved this fame, he wrote himself a check for 10 million dollars which would be paid to him in two years for rendered acting services.

Today, Jim has achieved fame for movies like *Ace Ventura*, *Pet Detective*, and *The Mask*. How did this check make a difference? It is important to note that Jim placed the check in his wallet. He did this so that whenever he made any payment, he would be reminded of it. Looking at Jim's mindset challenge, what can you do to broaden the check concept?

- Every day, write your goal on a piece of paper and tape it to your wall
- Write yourself notes and place them inside your refrigerator, your car, and the bathroom. You can even make a custom screensaver or display.
- Make a voice recording in which you talk about your goal and set it as a daily alarm on your phone.

- Customize a T-shirt with your goal and wear it around town. This will cause others to ask you about your vision. When you make your plans public, you feel an urgency to complete them.

Millions of people are served by Disneyland parks on a yearly basis. It all began with an idea, an imagination, and three little circles that became Mickey Mouse. Many concepts presented by Walt Disney have become huge in the eyes of the public. If you ever get a chance, visit San Francisco's Walt Disney Family Museum located in the Presidio. The museum is filled with rich history, going all the way back to when Walt started drawing cartoons for a living. Because Walt chose to follow his plan all of us can now enjoy the Disney experience.

Decide and make a promise today that you will live and act out your idea every day. It is only when you do this that your idea will manifest itself.

"Without reflection, we go blindly on our way, creating more unintended consequences, and failing to achieve anything useful."

-Margaret J. Wheatley

One of Thomas Edison's most famous lines is, "I didn't fail. I just found 2,000 ways not to make a light bulb." Edison was awarded over 1,000 patents because he developed a system for generating patentable ideas. Why do the same teams win championships year after year, even though all their players change? They win because they have developed a proven system or a process that can create repeatable results. Reading this book is only the first step to better develop your own systems for success. If you reach a conclusion, even if it's wrong, you can use what you've learned from that failure to create a better hypothesis and run a new test that's more likely to succeed and help you evolve.

Free Your Mind

You have to let go of fear, doubt, and disbelief. Close your eyes and repeat the phrase, "Free Your Mind." The repetition of these words is almost like a meditation practice. Whenever I doubt myself, fear something, or my thoughts begin to spiral I come back to this phrase. Let go of the thoughts that are holding you back.

To reset your mind, close your eyes and repeat the word, "Reset," and picture a blank wall. Thinking about a blank wall gives you a clean slate, allowing you to rest easy and free your previous thoughts.

The Chain Calendar Method And A Double Identity

Goals are not built on hopes and wishful thinking. If you're serious about achieving a goal, you need to work toward it every day. You need to schedule it into your calendar and track your progress at the end of the week. You will need to mold your life around your goal and avoid distractions at all costs. Days come and go and you either grow or you don't.

Try recording your progress on an old fashioned calendar by marking down the number of hours you've worked on a project every day. Use a thick marker so that you can see your progress from across the room. If you have a full-time day job, visually seeing the numbers will motivate and commit you to your goal.

As you begin this process, you'll probably write a lot of ones and twos and sometimes threes. When I practiced this method I noticed that the more determined I became, the higher the numbers I wrote in each calendar square. In addition to motivating you, this exercise is a great way to track the time you spend on long projects. What gets measured gets done.

When you're on a mission to improve yourself or get a product out the door, no one can tell you that you have to stop because you work for them.

Corporate interests are aligned with growing the bottom line, so if you are working on a personal product, you might need to be selective about the information you share. Living a double life online and offline is a must. While you're at your day job do your best to achieve your tasks. When the clock strikes 5:00 pm, tear through the door and switch into a superhuman mode.

This is not the time to run and meet your friends for drinks and gossip. It's the start of your second shift and not everyone is built for this. Many times during the writing process I felt alone but I realized that only I control where I end up. The more I shared my ideas with my close friends, the more I realized that I was onto something and my motivation stayed strong.

Next time you leave work, step into that phone booth and transform from Clark Kent to Superman. For me, it took some of the following steps.

- Play motivation music

- Find a spot with lighting that works for you. Very bright lighting is bothersome to me, the more natural the lighting, the better I feel
- Have coffee or tea
- Put on noise-canceling headphones

Doom And Gloom

I once worked with someone named Bob. Bob could put a negative spin on just about anything, from work to traffic, from neighbors to family.

When Bob would mention his kids he would say things like, 'My son is struggling to get ahead in his job after working there for ten years.' He would go into detail about why his son could not move forward. Then, Bob would bring up his wife and mention how she was having turf wars with the other moms at volunteer events.

I cannot remember a single positive, fulfilling conversation I had with him. The more you're exposed to the Bobs of the world, the more you allow your mind to process negative thoughts, and the more like Bob you become. Doom & Gloom effects will rub off on you.

Negative people are like the Peanuts character Pigpen, wherever they go, a proverbial dirt cloud of negativity follows, infecting everyone in their path. When you run across these types of individuals, change the topic to something positive as soon as possible, and if that doesn't work, come up with an excuse to leave. If you want to maintain their friendship, tell them you prefer to have positive conversations on other topics.

"Positive thinking will let you do everything better than negative thinking will"

Pigpen Mindset

Procrastination is one of the worst side-effects of a fixed, Pigpen mindset. Our brain naturally finds ways to keep us away from the things we fear.

Instead of facing our fears, however trivial, unfounded, and self-sabotaging they may be, we turn to distractions. How many times have you gone to Netflix and spent five minutes searching for something to watch, but found nothing? How many times do we start a process that takes away five minutes because we are unfocused?

These time-wasters placate us. They allow us to feel busy and important without doing the more challenging and scary things we should be doing. The most challenging road is the one filled with opportunities.

To help crystallize your vision, take a picture of yourself with a background of a couple of places you would like to visit. Print these photos out and write a date on it for when you would like to visit each place.

Then, tape the photos on the bottom half of your wall. Use index cards to label the photos i.e. 'My trip to Paris'. Next, fill out more index cards with specific, actionable steps that you need to take in order to visit your chosen destinations. Tape the index cards around the photos and use them as a path to get you where you want to go. Notice I used the word 'path', not trail. A path gets you to your destination in the shortest amount of time without distractions along the way.

If we go back in time to Kitty Hawk in 1903, think of what it took for the Wright brothers to achieve their success as they invented flight. They invented a system that allowed a pilot to maintain control of the airplane through the air which is the basis for what all aircraft still use today. They had the vision and went from a glider to a motorized flying machine. If we were to outline the process the Wright brothers took the index cards might read something like the following:

- Develop a reliable method for controlling an airplane through the wind that can carry a man into the air for over 30 seconds
- Use the profits from the bicycle repair business to fund their project
- Find a safe place to practice flight with lots of wind
- Become friendly with the locals to get their support
- Build or rent a shack so that you have a work area to build your flying machine
- Make this your life mission
- Achieve safe reliable flight control

Now write down your 7 steps to achieve a single goal.

_____

_____

_____

_____

You control your confidence and taking small steps is better than taking none at all.

Expire By Date

In order to live our best lives and truly live free, perhaps it is time for us to start putting expiry dates on jobs, habits and situations that drain us, clog our creativity and hold us back.

Put your label on that job, situation or relationship that is feeding you with negative energy. Create a timeline of when you want to quit and what you aspire to move on to. Put a label in places that used to bring you negative energy before. Give it time and you will observe that this will help you focus on the things that you want to become.

Accomplished author and perhaps one of the most inspiring people to have ever lived; J.K Rowling notes In her commencement speech; 'The Fringe Benefits of Failure, and the Importance of Imagination' at Harvard in 2008 that; 'There is an expiry date for blaming your parents for steering you in the wrong direction'. She continues very importantly that; 'The moment you are old enough to take the wheel, responsibility lies with you'.

This is a truth that you must hold dear and begin to live every day. Stop blaming your background and life circumstances. Take control today by labelling all the things you are uncomfortable with. Put an expiry date on them and take responsibility for moving yourself from where you are to where you want to be.

Like J.K Rowling notes at the tail end of her commencement speech; 'We do not need magic to transform our world. We carry all the power we need inside ourselves. We have the power to imagine better' .

"You can't depend on your eyes when your imagination is out of focus."

-Mark Twain

Chapter 6 Chess Mindset

"Life is a chess game and you are given the board of life to make the right combination of moves which impact your one game."

-Andrewzee

Queen vs Pawn

Every day we are given the opportunity to make decisions that will impact our lives. If a day goes by and you don't make a move, you have lost your advantage for the day. If you are playing on someone else's board they will reap the benefits of your labor. You have to realize that you are in a game and the clock is ticking away. Plan your moves wisely.

A queen can move in any direction while pawns' moves are very limited. Do you want to call the shots or do you want someone else calling the shots? Can you plan three or four moves ahead or are you always making short term, single move decisions? In chess, the whole point of the game is to capture your opponent's king in the least number of moves.

We need to work smarter not harder. However, students are funneled into a system that creates pawns instead of queens, forcing us to think in a single move mentality. While there is nothing wrong with being a pawn, winning a game of chess is the result of strategically coordinating multiple pieces to attack a particular target. Unfortunately, we generally play single move games with short term focus.

Education is used to get a job. If we look at life through the job lens, our actions are limited to that of a single pawn. While we may love our job, are we prepared to do the exact same thing for another ten years?

We must elevate our level of thinking to use the full board and multiple pieces in our quest for success.

While a queen or castle can make an attack on the other side of the board, these pieces need a line of sight prepared for them, just like we need to plan ahead. Everyone is born a pawn. It is up to us to get good at the game of life. If we can master it, it will return significant rewards. Life is like a game of chess. To win you have to make a move. Knowing which move to make comes with insight and knowledge, and by learning the lessons that are accumulated along the way.

We become each and every piece within the game called life!"

-Allan Rufus

Anyone who is familiar with chess has no doubt been inspired by how exciting, invigorating, and challenging it is. Many have discovered that chess is capable of teaching valuable lessons in forethought, planning, awareness, and defense tactics that can also be applied in real life. How these lessons can help stimulate growth and give you a strategic advantage in your respective careers is what this book is all about.

Just like the game of chess, if we visualize where we want to be we can take the steps to get there and create win-win situations. Life often creates a series of patterns which to the enterprising person can be identified as clearly defined lines of success. Learning how to spot these patterns, knowing when they occur, and taking full advantage of them will most certainly yield success.

Anyone making strides in their careers today is able to spot significant trends and patterns as they occur. They can use it as a guide to enable them to accurately envision where they want to be in their respective careers at a particular point in time, allowing them to plan out necessary steps needed to get there.

Why It's Important To Act Like A Leader And Speak Up

Some people I've worked with don't know how to behave like leaders when it is needed. The majority of them found it difficult to comply when asked to take up roles where they were expected to lead others because they didn't feel entitled to do so. I observed this pattern at work and found it interesting to read about it in the book *Nice Girls Don't Get the Corner Office* by Lois P. Frankel.

It is very important for you to know when to act like a leader and speak up. For example, when in a meeting, don't allow yourself to be boxed-in. Free things up and don't allow people to interrupt you because that would be a clear sign that what the other person has to say is more meaningful than whatever it is you have to say.

It takes courage to be able to do this but once you're able to pull it off, the easier it gets and you ultimately mark yourself as a leader.

Avoid Small Talk

Like in the game of chess, where you need to remove a trivial piece out of the way so a more cherished piece can be brought into play, you also need to shuffle the people you surround yourself with. You have to be firm in your decision to avoid people who want to engage you in unimportant and unnecessary small talk that does not support your vision.

The goal here is to make every effort to get into the game. Don't allow people who don't share your vision to pin you down. It's important that you try as much as possible to have good mentors and leaders in your inner circle, people who are brilliant and can support you with your vision. This will help you stay focused on your goals and enable you to get to your desired destination faster.

Steps To Break Through Your Future

One step at a time, like the game of chess where you look at the big picture when deciding on a move, decisions made with too narrow a focus often turn out bad.

Learn to take charge. As mentioned earlier, you have to know when to act like a leader and speak up. Don't hesitate to take on responsibilities and let your superiors know that you're interested in working in top-level positions. Listen to their advice, find out what skills you need to develop, figure out what needs to be done before being told, and work hard to make it happen.

Learn to take risks. Like Mark Zuckerberg said, "The biggest risk is not taking any risk... In a world that is changing really quickly, the only strategy that is guaranteed to fail is not taking risks." These days opportunities don't just come your way, you need to step out of your comfort zone to grab them. This involves taking risks and overcoming your fear of failure.

Work on your emotional intelligence. Before you can lead and motivate others, you need to have firm control of your emotions because the higher you go, your job becomes less about you and more about others. Listen before reacting. Seek first to understand, and then to be understood.

Anticipation

Just as the queen can move in any direction, the knight can leap, but you need to plan three moves ahead of time. You need to anticipate what the other person will do in a particular situation.

Just like in the game of chess, before making any drastic decision - especially when moving in for a checkmate, you have to be able to anticipate what could go wrong and plan accordingly. In any given situation, it is important to always have a backup plan and a second backup plan, in case the first fails.

Most of the problems you will likely encounter in your career will require a gentle, cerebral approach. You may get stuck in a position known in chess as zugzwang: where any move you make is a bad one. It happens like that sometimes, in chess and in life, but making sacrifices may result in a winning position later on. It's important not to lose hope and keep your head in the game.

There are so many lessons that can be learned from playing chess. They can keep you feeling alive, vibrant, polished and motivated. You don't have to be a conniving cheater to win… you just have to be better.

The Queen of Pop - How Having A Little Lady Gaga In Us Can Accelerate Our Advancement

Just Dance. Bad Romance. God Bless America. Born This Way. These were just some of the classics that Lady Gaga belted out at the Pepsi Zero Sugar Super Bowl LI Halftime Show on February 5th, 2017. After her performance, she was compared to Effie Trinket from the *Hunger Games* movie, because of their strikingly similar looks and ensembles, but that didn't stop her from generating the bulk of the 27 million tweets that characterized Super Bowl XLIV.

In the movie Hunger Games, characters that did not advance were eventually terminated. Lady Gaga's career followed a similar trajectory. At several stages of her music career, Gaga could have called it quits, but she plodded on. She evolved with each challenge that came her way, leaving behind a trail of successes. In life, though we may not be terminated like in the movie, we all encounter certain challenges that give us the choice to either stay rooted in self-pity or to just keep moving forward.

The Definition Of Gaga - Consistent

Gaga grew up in the Upper West Side of Manhattan as Stefani Joanne Angelina Germanotta. She developed an early reputation for her work ethic and studiousness. By age four, when most of her peers were still doodling in kindergarten, she played the piano like a pro. She was bullied in school for her eccentric fashion sense - big Evita brows and a deep orange tan. In a chat with Yahoo CEO Marissa Mayer, Gaga credits her drive to the bullying she endured. With time she developed a thick skin, which would prove vital for her future struggles on the way to the top.

By age eleven, she decided to stretch beyond the piano. She started taking vocal lessons with Don Lawrence. He coached her every day for six months as a build-up to her *Sound of Music* tribute performance. He was also her vocal instructor for the jazz album, *Cheek to Cheek,* a collaborative work with Tony Bennett. In an interview with the Telegraph, Gaga stated that working with Bennett was liberating and she admitted to being controlled for years.

From mastering the piano to weekly acting classes, one thing has always defined Gaga - consistent and intentional study. What defines you?

Gaga: A Life On The Offensive

Gaga never allowed life to happen to her, it was always the other way around; she happened to live. She dropped out of the music program at NYU Tisch School of the Arts in 2006 to pursue a career as a rockstar. She worked three day-jobs at a time; one of them being a go-go dancing gig. She was signed to Def Jam records in 2007 at the age of nineteen. At that point, it looked like she was set for the stars. But three months later, they dropped her. Her unusual style wasn't what they were looking for. Did she drop her head in resignation? No. She moved to the Lower East Side of Manhattan where she sang and danced at burlesque bars. She went back to the drawing board, experimenting with new performers and new music influencers. She also had a band known as the Stefani Germanotta Band aka SGBand. She was the lead singer and they performed throughout New York where she developed her stage presence and unique style.

In 2008 she got a job with Interscope Records as a songwriter where she waxed lyrics for Fergie, Britney Spears, New Kids on the Block, and the PussyCat Dolls. It was on the job that she got her big break. Akon heard her singing a song she wrote and he signed her to his record label. The same talent that Def Jam couldn't handle, found its voice two years later with Interscope. That year she released her first album, *The Fame,* which didn't only receive wide acclaim but sold over 4 million units. But there's more to this album than meets the eye.

Just Dance

The Fame was described by Gaga as a 'happy record' but it wasn't written in happy circumstances. *Just Dance,* one of the album's singles, was written in less than by Gaga, Akon and her producer, RedOne, in under ten minutes. It was a last-ditch attempt to prove her worth to Akon and RedOne who had given her another shot at fame. In an interview with *Heat,* she described how she felt at the time. "That record saved my life. I was in such a dark space in New York. I was so depressed, always in a bar. I got on a plane to LA to do my music and was given one shot to write the song that would change my life and I did. I never went back. I left behind my boyfriend, my apartment. I still haven't been back. My mother went in and cleared it for me."

The gamble paid off. The song hit number one in Australia, the UK, Canada, Ireland, and the Netherlands. It made the top five in Hungary, Czech Republic, New Zealand, Sweden, Spain, Norway, and Scotland. Back home in the US, the song entered the Billboard chart at No. 76 on August 16th, 2008 and by January 2009, it sat at number one. As of February 2018, it reached over 10 million digital downloads globally, with 7.2 million coming from the US alone. Clearly, Gaga was here to stay.

But the story doesn't end there. Seven years down the line, Gaga was once again at the end of her career. Fans were too familiar with her act and her album *Artpop* flopped. But she proved to us that there was more to her than elaborate costumes and stage performances. She went back to her jazz roots, releasing the album *Cheek to Cheek* in collaboration with Tony Bennett. It went on to win a Grammy and in the words of Jon Dolan from Rolling Stone, it proved 'she could be a sophisticated lady.'

She didn't stop there. She kept pushing for a new victory, refusing to be boxed in, expanding her hall of fame. What is in your hall of fame?

From singing in bars to entertaining audiences exceeding 100 million, Gaga continually advanced, taking charge of her career, never letting others define and mold her reaction.

How many times have you thrown in the towel when things went south; how many times did you throw in the towel when you could have discovered new strengths, catapulting you to greater relevance? Every time Gaga sank, she learned lessons, reinvented herself, and soared. If you're going to achieve your goals, you need to get on the offensive side of life.

What Makes Her Gaga?

Mention of those who shaped and are still shaping the music career of Lady Gaga would not be complete without mention of Don Lawrence. Not only was he her first voice coach but he has remained her voice coach since then, guiding her through her daily 30-minute vocal warmup exercises. The lesson we can take from this is the importance of mentors outside our immediate family circle. These dispassionate people have fewer qualms about bringing our flaws to our attention. Gaga also received great inspiration from jazz singer Amy Winehouse, especially when she was working on, especially when she was working on her *Cheek to Cheek* album with Tony Bennett. Gaga also gives credit to Madonna, Michael Jackson and Beyoncé for inspiring her to want to pursue a musical career.

173

She's now toned down on the eccentricity of her fashion sense, admitting that she dressed certain ways to maintain her personality in an industry that was known for molding people into something else.

Gaga is frank about the experiences that shaped her. For instance, she admitted to using cocaine and drinking heavily to get inspiration for her music. After realizing how much it affected her physical and mental health, she quit and has remained sober ever since. She also admitted that her song *Swine* was inspired by the time she was raped.

She writes or at least co-writes all of her songs. She says that she doesn't feel connected to a song if she doesn't take part in developing it.

We all could take a page from Lady Gaga's book about openness. The key principle here is developing the ability to take the rocks that life throws at you and use them as the building blocks for the future you envision.

Take Branding Lessons From Lady Gaga

How many of us would wear clothing made from meat? Like actual red meat. Gaga pulled it off at the MTV Video Music Awards in 2010. What about arriving at an event in an egg-shaped costume, carried by your crew? Or a dress made of purple hair? No way, right? That is exactly why Gaga is so unique. Google her and one of the first suggestions will relate to her fashion sense. When people think about your brand, what comes to mind? If you have to sit back and think about it, then clearly your brand stands for nothing. It should just pop into your mind. Your product is average; just like every other thing on the shelf.

This same thought process also applies to those of us who are planning start-ups. Don't leave it to chance that your company will carve a niche by itself. You have to decide what you want to stand for and implement it, or get submerged in all the noise.

What You Should Take Away From Gaga's Story

Gaga was bullied in high school, which helped her develop a thick skin to criticisms and confidently carve her niche without caring what others said or thought. This and the entire sum of her experiences make her the pop icon she is today. In the same vein, you gain nothing in denying your past. To define your future, you have to look back on the road you've tread. If you launched a product into the market or your relationship failed, it wouldn't make sense to relaunch or just plunge into a new one without first taking stock of what went wrong.

Rejection doesn't mean your idea is invalid. Usually, people are just not ready for it, the same way Def Jam wasn't ready for Gaga, but two years down the line they must have regretted not holding on to her. If they're not ready for you, it means you are way ahead of them. Sooner or later, they will be playing catch up. It's like what Bernard Shaw once said, 'The reasonable man adapts himself to the conditions that surround him. The unreasonable man adapts surrounding conditions to himself. Therefore, all progress depends on the unreasonable man.'

"I had a boyfriend who told me I'd never succeed, never be nominated for a Grammy, never have a hit song, and that he hoped I'd fail. I said to him, 'Someday, when we're not together, you won't be able to order a cup of coffee at the fucking deli without hearing or seeing me."

-Lady Gaga

Who's On Your Team?

The 'mastermind' is the collective mental power of all your team members. It will allow you to achieve goals in a fraction of the time by leveraging a common vision, teamwork, team enthusiasm, and better budgeting.

One of the best ways to manage your growth is by using a community approach. Attend weekly meetups and work towards a set of fixed goals. While you may be a solopreneur on the inside, it helps to have a radar seeking the best, smartest people around you at all times.

Masterminds are beneficial because they allow everyone to bring experience and expertise to the table, effectively making your group or company a superpower in financial, technical, scientific, or mechanics, regardless of the trade.

The members of a good mastermind agree on a purpose and continuously work together to achieve it. They meet every few days, every week, or every month, and do whatever it takes to achieve a goal. Accountability is a key component of a mastermind. As a team, they must create, recognize, and act upon opportunities. It is important to prioritize face to face communication over email whenever possible. Speaking over the phone is okay but a Skype session is even better.

Masterminds can take advantage of opportunities that an individual cannot face or even recognize. By introducing a third mind, you will always have a third opinion that provides better traction than two minds. Potential grows exponentially as you continue to add members to the mastermind.

All startups have highs and lows, but the lows are much easier to survive when you have more than one founder. A mastermind is important because it can leverage time, support, courage, and dedication through the ups and downs of building your empire.

Getting input from all available sources can increase the chance of finding a brilliant idea centered around new solutions, similar to crowdsourcing. If you are in management, consider using a star model management style which initiates company growth in all directions versus top-down. If there are quiet people on your team you may need to call on them so that they can make their opinions heard or set up a voting system in private.

Candor: The Golden Ticket For Productive Teams

The movie *Toy Story* was created by the brain trust at Pixar (their internal mastermind). This brain trust exercised extreme candor when it came to expressing their thoughts and opinions of a storyline related to the movie. Pixar used honest discussions to argue points and there was no top-down chain of command. Pixar even went so far as to remove their long slim table as you would see in the movies with two people seated at opposite ends of the table. They also removed the name tags at the table so that everyone involved in the discussions would be seen as an equal and given a fair opportunity to speak their mind. The end product speaks for itself: a movie that won the hearts of millions and many awards. The mastermind at Pixar included John Lasseter, Ed Catmull, Andrew Stanton, Pete Doctor, Lee Unkrich, and Joe Ranfit, but the key ingredient to their project, and yours, is candor.

When Walt Disney recommended something to his team and everyone agreed to it, he immediately dismissed the idea. Ideas that are argued and debated over, even when they seem impossible, can become better over time, producing magic that only Disney can deliver. Disney encourages employees to think outside of the box and deliver 'Mickey Mouse' breakthroughs of imagination and enjoyment. Some people call this 'delivering the Disney experience.' Walt earned the trust, commitment, and respect of his followers. His positive motivational force was absorbed by all of his employees and everyone he touched. By empowering others, he inspired his mastermind members to create the magic which then fed the Disney imagination machine.

The Declaration of Independence was started by 56 men who formed one of the most famous masterminds in history. Together, these men achieved what no single man could have achieved. The commitment of these 56 men towards a single goal of independence and unprecedented democracy leveraged each man's unique capabilities and skills. The famous signatures of these legendary minds speak for themselves, including John Hancock, Benjamin Franklin, Thomas Jefferson, Samuel Chase, John Adams, Samuel Adams, and many more.

With a pool of diverse knowledge in your mastermind, you too can have a network that will leverage to inspiration, change, and define the future.

Amplify Your Success By Keeping A Young Mindset

If you watch children play and see their interaction with other schoolmates, you will notice they don't fear judgment. Kids say what's on their minds without regard for others' opinions. The older we get, the opposite takes hold and we worry about being judged by others. To change our future, we need to re-enter our younger mindset.

Doing More With Less

In Daymond John's book *The Power of Broke,* he writes about the lessons he learned from his younger self creating Fubu, an American hip hop apparel company worth over $6 billion. Daymond created his company while living at his mother's house in Hollis, Queens, a southeast section of New York City back in the 1990s.

As a youngster, Daymond's friends tried to look cool by driving hot cars but Daymond purchased a used 15 passenger van. He initially purchased the van to aid him in moving inventory. Do you want to look cool or do you want to make money? If you are on a mission, you cannot let anything stand in your way. Daymond John has been a Shark on *Shark Tank*, a TV series where people pitch their business ideas to potential investors.

So what makes a Shark hungry?

- You have 70% margins and are profitable
- Your idea is unique
- Your idea is hard to replicate
- Your product is selling in Walmart
- You have revenue with minimal outstanding bills
- You own the patent and have sales

What makes a Shark lose its appetite?

- You have a "me too" product that is easy to copy
- You cannot prove a demand for your product
- You have no paying customers besides your family and friends
- You say you are going to talk to Walmart, Target, Macy's.

Sharks can smell the blood in the water-based on what you have done, not what you are going to do.

What can you do with what you have today? Do you really need to pay $2,000 for a class or can you find the same information in a couple of days online through YouTube videos? Can you read a few blogs and come up with a better way of accomplishing a task?

When Elon Musk and his brother were starting their first company, Zip2, instead of getting an apartment, they slept in their office space. This simplified expenses and allowed them to spend more time at the office.

Can you use freeware like Google Docs instead of paying for Microsoft Office? A Google Doc can be shared to any email address and scales well with large companies. How can you achieve your goals without spending additional money, without getting additional outside help, or paying consultants? In the startup world this is called bootstrapping. How can you do a test for $100 versus a large scale test at $10,000? Bootstrapping is another topic altogether.

To extend on the Power of Broke concept I would highly recommend the book *The Billionaire Next Door* by Thomas J. Stanley and William D. Danko. The studies included in this book look at what financially separates different classes of people.

"Everyone has an idea, but it's taking those first steps toward turning that idea into a reality that are always the toughest."

-Daymond John

Movies On The Cheap

Mad Max. Blair Witch Project. Paranormal Activity. What do these three movies have in common? They all had budgets less than $300,000 but raked in as much as $248 million. *Paranormal Activity* had a budget of $15,000 and was shot with a handheld camera at the director's house, but it grossed over $149 million. That's a profit of $9,933 for every dollar spent.

Another movie, although not with a budget as low as these three, is *Star Wars* by George Lucas. With a budget of $11 million, the movie went on to gross $775 million at the box office. Lucas pulled this off by ensuring that his production company, Lucasfilm Ltd, was in charge of the production process so that he could control the budget. He also preferred using fresh-faced actors, as they were cheaper.

You might say, "Lucas had a reputation and all of that, I'm just an upcoming movie producer. I don't even have the funds to push a low-budget movie, how do I go about it?"

Have you heard about platforms like Slated? They help connect filmmakers to top-notch big money investors and all the talent needed to pull off a Blockbuster. It has 22,000 producers, 18,000 writers, 15,000 directors, 12,000 actors, 1,900 investors and 1,700 sales agents and distributors. 68% of Sundance 2018 movies and 58% of Oscar 2018 films were made by Slated members.

Extremely low budget movies like the ones mentioned earlier were able to lift off the ground thanks to doing away with expensive equipment. *Paranormal Activity* was shot with a handheld camera and it wasn't the only movie that worked with that hack. *Blair Witch Project* was also shot with a handheld camera. These low budget movies also did away with large shooting crews. For instance, *Paranormal Activity* was co-produced, directed, written, edited and shot by Oren Peli. The only major thing he didn't do was act in the movie.

When shooting Mad Max, the crew closed roads in Melbourne, Australia without a filming permit. You'd think they would have gotten in trouble for that, but as filming progressed, the people who lived in Victoria became so interested in the production that they started helping the crew close the roads and escorting their vehicles.

These movies were mostly shot in one location. *Paranormal Activity* was shot in a house, while *Blair Witch Project* was shot in Seneca State Park in Montgomery County, Maryland. The producers made sure to use natural people in shooting their movie. They interviewed a lot of people who didn't even know that the footage was going to be part of a movie. They didn't even know how to use a camera before shooting the movie and had to take a crash course in handling a camera.

Another thing all these movies had in common was that they were tested at small movie festivals to see the audience's perception. It was at such a festival that the movie, *Blair Witch Project* was discovered and shot into the limelight.

So, what's holding you back from that project? You don't have the necessary skills and can't afford to hire those with the competence? Then why not learn those skills for yourself. Becoming an all in one is one of the easiest ways to cut cost for whatever project you might have planned.

What if you don't have the skills to maneuver popular video editing apps like Adobe Photoshop or Final Cut Pro. There's a creative way around it with iMovie, a free, popular software that comes with every Mac laptop. It's super easy to use without previous video editing experience. For instance, the latest iMovie app allows users to edit audio which was impossible before. Under every video clip, there's a bar for the corresponding audio waveform where you can select any part you want to modify.

For around $30 dollars a month you can subscribe to unlimited learning on Linda.com which has been combined with Linkedin.com/learning. Not only can you find training videos on how to use movie effects software, but you can find topics on business, creativity, and technology.

A lot of times, we shoot videos with our smartphones and digital still cameras. The problem is we're not pros, there's bound to be some shakiness. iMovie also takes care of this. It allows you to import the shaky video clip to a section that reduces motion distortion.

Now, what's your excuse for still having cold feet about that movie project?

You may doubt the success of your movie projects. So why not test yourself with something like short commercials on YouTube?

To succeed at this, you have to ensure that your content is driven by ideas, not expensive equipment. If you have to sit down with a pen and paper to jot down ideas for your videos, do it. Don't just stumble into it and hope it will work out. From the very beginning, you have to decide what the title of the videos will be. Type that into YouTube's search box to see what your competition is doing. You also need to pay attention to the thumbnail, meta tags, and filename before you submit to the YouTube search engine. Don't get lazy and think that a single video published on YouTube will also work on Instagram. You need to cater the video to match the platform along with all of the relatable metadata.

You also have to decide what the goal of your video is and make sure that at all times, your video hits the nail on the head. If you're giving advice, it better be clear. If you're doing a review, it better be informative.

Once you get the hang of managing a winning YouTube channel, you should be strong enough to launch your movie project.

You can beat the queue. You can put the noise of the crowd behind you. All you have to do is think differently. See things in new ways. Unleash your inner genius, and make lemonade out of your lemons.

How The Amish Get So Much Done

Humans have never been as busy as we are today. Our schedules are so tightly planned that most of us can't find time for ourselves, our loved ones, or do the things we truly want. You'd expect that our output is increasing, right? The opposite is happening.

According to the News Observer, falling productivity is the greatest obstacle to economic growth. This is true both in the US and the UK. National productivity levels are below 2% and this does not just affect the economy, it affects you too.

Our productivity as a nation has plunged except in one group of people, the Amish. They are the only bunch who are managing to get things done.

For most of us, the battle against procrastination is daily. We need to dig deep and find out what the Amish people are doing right so we can learn from them.

Despite the numerous tech gadgets available today, we are struggling to get things done while the Amish traditional lifestyle still triumphs. Some people might be surprised by this fact and wonder why this is happening because we are all very busy. So why are the Amish more productive than the rest of us? There two simple reasons for this -

1. We are busy doing the wrong things.
2. Many of us don't realize that we are not actually being productive. Because we are so busy, our brains confuse these activities for major achievements and then we are too exhausted for difficult tasks that lead to true productivity.

Some people try to use willpower to force themselves to get things done, but willpower has a limit. There is so much that you can do with your willpower before you get exhausted. For the Amish community, being productive is a lifestyle and they don't need willpower to carry out their daily tasks.

The traditional advice of 'finding motivation' doesn't work, this is why we keep spending our money and time in self-help seminars. After two weeks we are exhausted and can't continue. From losing weight to studying, learning a new language to completing projects at work, there is so much advice available that doesn't actually work.

So, are we doomed to just procrastinate and become lazier by the day? No, we can do something about it. We can learn from the Amish people, understand what they are doing right, and figure out how to apply it to our modern lifestyle.

The Amish community business success rates stand at 90%. Half of all new startups fail in their first five years. Not the Amish, they are thriving. The average Amish person wakes up at 4:30 am. Before noon, they have completed tasks that would take most of us three days to finish.

You don't have to join the Amish community, or wake up at 4 am. There are some fundamental ideologies you can learn from them and incorporate into your daily life that will increase your productivity.

The first ideology you need to understand is that the Amish do deep work. When an Amish person is sewing a cloth, there's no email message to check or a Facebook post to comment on. It's not just about social media; modern life is filled with distractions. The internet just makes it worse. Becoming distracted from important tasks is so easy.

Keeping up with the latest gossip, tech gadgets, and doomsday news consumes a lot of time. This is why the media is one of the most successful industries and it is still expanding. Most of us are too busy keeping up with the world and we forget to do the things that are most important to us. It is not surprising that even at work, people can't go without their smartphones.

These interferences are absent in the Amish community. We can't change how the world works but we can alter our immediate environment. Our workspace, bedroom, and study areas should be distraction-free. For example, the idea of "the Amish hour" where you read a book or switch off all gadgets to focus on a task for one hour before bed has proven to be effective at improving focus.

The idea of uninterrupted focus while working is emphasized by author Cal Newport in his book *Deep Work*. Multitasking is a myth, humans can't do more than one thing at a time. What we refer to as multitasking is actually our brains quickly switching between various tasks, but we're not doing them simultaneously.

Research has shown that multitasking reduces our productivity and can cause long-term, irreversible damage to our brain. Being focused is the key to being productive.

A clear and extreme example is the life of the renowned physicist Albert Einstein. His entire life was focused on understanding and solving physics-related mysteries. Einstein was known for his obsession. He could not focus on building a stable relationship. He even rejected an offer to become Israel's president in 1952, just so he can focus on his work.

You don't have to become obsessed like Einstein, but you do need to focus on what is important at specific times. Sadly, the media confuses research which shows that taking breaks improves productivity while actually focusing on a task.

Taking short breaks while working can improve your overall productivity, but it does not mean doing something unrelated to the original task.

Einstein played the violin whenever he needed to brainstorm or take a mental break. By doing this, he gave his brain a break to think about what he was trying to accomplish. He didn't switch to something different that required deep focus. Playing the violin was just a means for him to focus on solving physics problems.

The lesson here is when you are trying to complete a challenging task, take short mental breaks. Distractions are not the same as taking mental breaks. Surfing through social media is not a break for your brain because it demands your attention.

So, how can you focus and attain deep work while living a balanced life?

Cal suggests we use routines to achieve true focus. He mentions four different ways we can implement routines into our daily lives. Two of them are for nomads or professional mind managers: the bimodal and rhythmic philosophy is ideal for most of us.

With the bimodal method, you divide your time into time blocks. You could set three hours for the gym, two hours to check social media, and maybe seven hours to sleep. By doing this, you are enabling your mind to focus on a task, then you complete it and move on to the next. Switching back and forth is harmful.

The second method is the rhythmic method. This method involves doing something for a designated period every day or weekly. It does not have to be a particular time of the day but it's important that you do it for the same length of time. For example, Jerry Seinfeld credits his success as a comedian to writing one joke every day.

For most of us, building a rhythmic work routine is easier than the bimodal method. You'll find out that allocating time slots to complete a task will make you aware of timing and you'll automatically start trying to be more effective.

Secondly, the Amish do what they know best. During an interview, Einstein was asked why he chose to be a physicist instead of a doctor or an engineer. He replied that he would have been terrible in those fields.

Many people still believe the 'follow your passion advice' and we think it's how people succeed, but it is the complete opposite. Cal Newport in his book *So good that they can't ignore you*, argues that passion is the result of years spent developing a skill.

You don't become passionate then do the tasks. You do what you have to do and as your skill level increases and you get rewarded, you develop passion.

For Steve Jobs, building tech gadgets was never his passion. He cared about helping people improve their lives and Apple was just a side project that became successful.

The Amish don't follow their passion, especially when they decide what business they want to start. They offer the world what they are best at. Restaurants, bakeries, and local farm shops are a common business that Amish people like to venture into because they are good at it.

Kate Stolz, a famous model who left the Amish community when she was twenty years old, admits that she wanted to become a model because of her passion for making clothes. Here is the secret lesson, Kate was not passionate about making clothes when she started learning at the age of nine. She started doing it, then realized she was passionate about it.

This is the narrative mainstream media won't tell you. If you are a student, learn to study. If you want to run, then learn to run (yeah, there is a technique for that). It doesn't matter what the task is, there is always someone who has figured out how to do it better in less time.

Devote time to learn about the things you want to accomplish and it will make you more productive when you start doing it. Plus, you'll enjoy it more.

The Amish find passion in the skills that they've built over the years through deep work. You too can quickly improve your productivity if you implement these ideologies in your life.

"Without change, there is no innovation, creativity, or incentive for improvement. Those who initiate change will have a better opportunity to manage the change that is inevitable."

-William Pollard

Chapter 7 Different

"If you do not find a way to make money while you sleep, you'll work until you die."

-Warren Buffet

Being Different Can Set You Free

Many people fear to be different because of what society might think or say about them. This hinders them from following their dreams and doing what they believe in. Great ideas are lost in the process of trying to please society while living a life that's uncomfortable to avoid judgment. Making mistakes is a part of life, and people can change their situations when they let positivity in. Environment is also an important factor that people need to consider when they need self-discipline and want to be successful. People who are seen as crazy always turn out to be geniuses because they believe in what they are doing.

Being different means that we have to do away with the 9-5 mindset and think about doing something that will benefit society and create employment opportunities. Steve Jobs, CFO of Pixar Animation and Apple, talks about doing something different to change the world. He says to himself, "If today was my last day on earth, would I want to do what I am about to do today?" He argues that death is the only destination we share and people, even those who believe they'll go to heaven, fear death. Every time he asks himself the above question and answers for several days in a row he knows he needs to change something. Positive thinking can greatly impact your life, unlike draining, negative energy.

Steve Jobs did not graduate from college. He dropped out of college six months after he enrolled. His biological parents placed him for adoption, but they asked that his adoptive parents be university graduates. When his biological mother realized his adoptive parents were not graduates, she refused to sign the final adoption papers. Steve Jobs managed to enroll in a college that was as expensive as Stanford University. All of his adoptive parents' money went towards his education. Steve had a hard time finding comfort in his college experience and decided to drop out. He loved working with his friend and building something that he believed in. He now advises Stanford graduates to connect to their future and make a difference, to trust and believe in something, to gain confidence and follow their hearts.

He also believes in love and loss. He started working with his friend in his garage at the age of twenty. Ten years later, he was fired from Apple, the company he started in his garage. He became a public failure. He felt confused and lost for a period of time but this didn't change his love for what he did and believed in. His creative side came to the surface and he gave himself another chance. After five years, he started a company known as NEXT, then PIXAR animation. The best animation company in the world came to be and it was during this time he met a beautiful lady, Laureen, whom he believed would become his wife. Apple bought NEXT and he returned to his original company. Everything happens for a reason. The real message behind his presentation is that people should do what they love to get great results. He once said, "Sometimes life is going to hit you on the head with a brick, but never lose faith." He advised that no situation should make anyone lose hope in life because a while later, he was diagnosed with pancreatic cancer and was cured with surgery.

Steve tells Stanford graduates that people who are perceived to be too unwise to make a difference in the world are the ones who do. He says people should be motivated by the fact that they will be dead one day. This is the most critical tool that they will ever encounter to help them make significant choices in life. He says, "Your time is limited, so do not waste it living someone else's life." He advises not to be trapped by what other people think, instead, believe in intuition and follow your heart because hearts already have an idea of who they want to become.

We need to break free from the chains of other people's opinions and believe in our intuitions. Forgo immediate pleasures in exchange for long-term love and self-respect. Great minds come from people who society thinks are crazy. It's these individuals who change the nation.

Great ideas and success come from individuals who society see as let-downs because they don't work well with directions and don't bother following societal guidelines. People who are foolish enough to think they are capable of changing the world end up changing the world. Don't fill your mind with what people expect of you because you have limited time in this world. Make better use of the time you have. Following your intuition is crucial because it already knows what you want.

Through The Lens Of Y Combinator With Paul Graham

In a cramped college apartment, three students crowd over the future of the world and technology. Oblivious to the rain pouring outside, they ponder over how their product fits into the grand scheme of things in a saturated market.

They ask the hard questions. They look at the failures of the past and the people already defining a future they so desperately want to be part of.

What are these three students staring at? The holy grail of startups - the Y Combinator.

What is the Y Combinator? How has this venture capital firm become such an important part of the conversation about how technology and innovation will change the world?

This story is particularly important if you are a United States immigrant. The odds, statistics, and opportunities to start something special are in your favor. This is what makes the unique insight into Paul Graham and the Y Combinator so important.

Finding Y

Y Combinator is one of the most prestigious funding avenues for startups. Since its 2005 inception, the American startup accelerator and seed capital firm has consistently ranked at the top. Y Combinator is revered for its unique approach in picking the startups it funds. Every year, startups from diverse backgrounds try to earn a spot in the two batches that Y Combinator funds. Successful startups get access to seed money, advice, and connections for only 7% equity. Popular alumni from the program include Airbnb, Stripe, Dropbox, Reddit, Docker, Gusto, and Stripe.

Behind the glamour of a successful demo day with plenty of investors who have the capital to invest in your business is a carefully curated process defined by thought-provoking questions. Leading the questions is the multi-talented Paul Graham, who has made it his life's work to find the people behind solving the most interesting problems.

Being Paul Graham

A man of many parts with each part as interesting as the next, Paul Graham is a computer scientist, venture capitalist, essayist, and author. His association with the startup community starts with Viaweb, a company he co-founded with Robert Morris. Viaweb allowed users to create internet stores. Yahoo was attracted to the success of the product, purchased it in 1998 and it became Yahoo Stores after the acquisition.

In a bid to walk the talk, Paul Graham joined forces with Trevor Blackwell, Jessica Livingston, and Robert Morris in 2005 to start Y Combinator. Y Combinator continues to lead the drive for the most effective startup execution.

Brilliant with the most unusual perspectives, Paul Graham continues to steer conversations around the most important issues from nerd culture to hardcore programming on his website www.paulgraham.com.

Even more engaging than the startups he so passionately lends advice to are the thoughts and key principles that have consistently him. In his widely read interview with www.theinformation.com, Paul offers insight into the habits and beliefs that make him stand out.

Building For The Market

'Who really wants this' is a question that Paul Graham pauses to ask before making a move. This question is a critical response to the behavior of several startups who craft a product that suits their own tastes or problems and then go out to foist it on an unwilling market.

Ultimately, to succeed, you must listen to your potential customers. They should constantly be at the back of your mind as you plan and strategize.

Tweaking It

Too many times we emphasize doggedness, perseverance, and outright stubbornness instead of simply reflecting on the idea we have then trying to see how we can tweak and redesign to overcome our challenges.

For Paul, a key principle that ensures success and keeps him relevant is his clear understanding of the need for people to constantly tweak or replace their ideas. This means that whether you are an individual or a leader of a team, you must take time to question the direction and implication of your actions.

The ideas that have redefined the future are simple tweaks that have brought solutions to everyday experiences.

Here are some examples:

- Average photos and filters turned into Instagram
- A flea market with an auction site turned into eBay
- Banks and internet selling turned into PayPal
- A taxi service and crowdsourcing turned into Uber
- Wind tunnel and sky diving turned into IFly
- The US postal service and DVD disks turned into Netflix
- Renewable energy and automobiles turned into SolarCity and Tesla
- Bed and Breakfasts and an online directory turned into Airbnb
- A USB storage device connected to the cloud turned into Dropbox
- Conventional banking services plus internet payments turned into Stripe
- Your neighborhood pharmacy plus doorstep delivery turned into Pill Pack
- Your music playlist and digital streaming turned into Spotify
- Your mega store turned into Amazon
- Your favorite news site plus uninhibited user contribution turned into Reddit.

Good Is Not Enough

The words 'pretty good' are music to the ears of a founder. They signify that the person who took a chance on the product finds it interesting or they'll be inquisitive enough to try it again.

For Paul Graham, these same words sound the death knell. Don't focus on the preliminary comments, the pats on the back, the glowing reviews, and become too comfortable.

The Y: Questions as building blocks.

We start this experience by looking at the questions that ultimately determine the fate of startups at Y Combinator. For ten minutes, startups have to provide answers to questions that test their knowledge in the area they are working in and the problem they aim to solve.

The questions outlined below test your understanding of your purpose, product, problem, and market advantage. There are life lessons that you can take away from these questions.

- What do you understand that others don't?
- What are you going to do next?
- What have you learned so far from working on it?
- What's an impressive thing you have done?
- What is new about what you make?
- How are you meeting customers' needs?
- What resistance will customers have to trying you and how will you overcome it?
- What is the conversion rate?
- Why did your team get together?
- How do you know your customers need what you are making?
- Who would use your product?
- Why will you succeed?
- Six months from now, what will be your biggest problem?

- If your startup succeeds, what additional areas might you be able to expand into?

Lose Your Jargon

The first question often asked at a Y Combinator is what problem are you trying to solve. While it might seem straightforward, a lot of people struggle with it and at the end of the interview, both parties lack a clear understanding of what problem is going to be solved and how that will be achieved.

Most times, the challenge lies in our fear to let go of the jargon, the technical jargon, and the marketing jargon for our idea. All of this jargon sounds impressive so we hide behind it to derive confidence. When it is stripped away and people are asked to describe what they're doing in plain English, they come up short with no flowery or technical language to fill in the gaps.

Essentially, to succeed in life and in a Y Combinator interview you must know your why and how in the simplest terms. No one wants to hear marketing buzzwords and technical language, they want to hear you.

What's My Problem?

At the center of every great startup or industry revolution is a problem that needs solving. Know your problem like the back of your hand. Know how your customers are affected. Present your thoughts on how you can change the status quo and what is wrong with everything that is on the market trying to solve that same problem.

Your idea, your technology, and the tiny details that surround it might change but one thing that should remain constant is your knowledge and the energy you wrap around your problem.

If you know what your problem is you'll understand what kind of people you should work with and what you should focus on.

Energy Is Everything

Your energy and enthusiasm guide your audience in decision making, whether it's a venture capital firm or a new group of users you are trying to convince.

You can't fake energy and passion for your idea, people will feel it and within a few minutes they'll close off from the conversation. This is important because a lot of times what seals the deal is not your idea or tech itself, but your passion and personal stories.

Brian Chesky, Joe Gebbia, and Nathan Blecharezyk used their positive energy to get Airbnb up and running. Before they met with Paul Graham, they were struggling. To raise money for their company they sold two different types of cereal for $40 a box, Captain McCain's and Obama O's. It was that passion and relentless energy that ultimately convinced Paul Graham to bring them into the Y Combinator. This innovation and drive to succeed won Graham over even when he was not entirely sure if their idea would fly. He said, "If you can convince people to pay forty dollars for a four-dollar box of cereal, you can probably convince people to sleep in other people's airbeds."

Tell Your People Stories

Your interactions with consumers are a very powerful sales tool. Share the honest experiences of users who have taken a chance on the beta version of your product. Point out how the feedback they share is helping you tweak and reshape your idea.

People ultimately respond better to an idea that has been tested aggressively against users. Don't just keep sitting at your table trying to refine your product, go into the market to find out what works and what doesn't. You can expect a significant learning experience that will provide powerful stories that will help to sell your brand.

Patrick and John Collison of the popular startup Stripe revolutionized payment over the internet. They spread their business by word of mouth. Even though Stripe was geared towards top-level investors, they recognized that everyday people struggled with payments and they offered their solution to friends and family as they sought to build a business.

Be Honest

If you had it all figured out, chances are you won't be reading this book. Resist every temptation to lie when you are asked about what the possible challenges would be in making your idea work.

What investors want to see is your ability to anticipate likely challenges and recognize them for what they are.

Sit yourself (and your team) down and ask the hard questions. This process makes you appealing and convincing when pitching your idea to people who can help make it happen.

Run through these questions until you know your answers, problems, and processes by heart.

- Can it eliminate a step and save time?
- Can it be run without humans?
- Can it be used instead of money?

- Can it save traveling time?
- Can it reduce costs?
- Can it outlast the competition?
- Will it make people feel better?
- Can it make you feel smarter or look better
- Is it stronger or lighter?
- Is the service way better at something, think taxi cabs and Uber?
- Can you take an existing concept and add your unique twist to the equation?
- Can you make something twice more fun?

The biggest mistake is thinking that this conversation does not involve you. You might not be a high tech worker, you might not even make $50,000 a year, but the future of work and technology will change the way we live our lives.

First mover advantage is awarded to those that have the right information and can act upon it.

"Find out what you like and what you hate about life. Start doing more of what you love, less of what you hate."

-Mihaly Csikszentmihalyi

Change The Playing Field

For us to disrupt our own thinking we have to think bigger. This is the way industries are disrupted, by challenging the status quo of each sector. Peter Thiel wrote in his book *Zero to One* that 90% of companies are striving innovation challenges by making a product or feature better by a mere 10%.

Airbnb

Sergey Brin and Larry Page went deep and placed a high value on backlink tracking, something no one else was doing at the time. They took a first principle approach towards a solution that turned into Google. While everyone else was searching simply on a title to obtain search results, Google focused on PageRank. An algorithm that went from the bottom up, one which used over a hundred web page attributes to help assign page-level authority and better to serve you. Google uses these PageRank attributes to provide you with the best experience possible, similarly, the aircraft industries' efforts to eliminate disasters have resulted in one of the safest ways to travel by air. Extreme attention to detail can make something ten to fifty times better than what previously existed.

Napster

Napster was an app that revolutionized the music industry and created the world of media streaming we know today. Before Napster, people had to go to the store to buy music. For many years, the music industry deliberately refused to move ahead. Sean Parker alongside Sean Fanning, two 19-year-old boys, thought differently to create a program that forced the music industry to innovate. The idea of Napster was allowing peer-to-peer audio file sharing between computers for free. It seems obvious now, but back in 1999 people were shocked that this was possible.

Parker was already involved in the world of computer programming. He found an opportunity and took a different approach. He could have tried to convince record labels to buy his product. Instead, he let young people who loved music drive the change. When Napster was first introduced, the music industry didn't care because they couldn't see its potential. In just one-year , record label CEOs regretted not paying attention. Napster became so popular, college campuses had to block it because it congested their already slow network. At the height of Napster's success, it had over 80 million members before it was forcefully shut down due to multiple lawsuits citing copyright infringement. Two young minds refused to follow the status quo because big record labels stalled the music industry for personal gain. They could not see beyond themselves and the industry was almost destroyed. The original Napster may have been shut down but its legacy lives on. Roxio bought the company for $5.3 million, making Parker an instant millionaire. Thinking differently changed his mindset forever, as he moved on to co-found Facebook and Spotify.

What Parker did not predict was the rise of Apple's iTunes store. When you push yourself to do something different, you create a ripple effect that changes other aspects of your life. Over 35 billion songs were sold on iTunes by 2013 and Apple created iPods to help contain its success. iPods became a huge success, selling over 300 million pieces before the company pulled the plug. Have you ever heard the phrase, one success leads to another? It's true. People misjudge the underdog because they are used to thinking the same way. Minds are unique in their ability to refocus attention depending on how a problem is approached.

To think and do things differently, you need to strip the problem to its core. The brain loves simplicity. When you think only of the big problems, you deny yourself the opportunity to see a different approach. The world favors visionaries who can think in non-conforming ways. Sean Parker is worth over $2.6 billion and Elon Musk is the 54th richest person in the world with $19.9 billion to his name. Achieving great success is something we all want, we desire wealth and comfort but only a few people understand the power of disruptive thinking.

You cannot get ahead if you're doing what everyone else is doing. Just like the record labels, you cannot relax and expect things to stay the way they've always been. The world is hungry for change and you need to position yourself to be the one that delivers. Napster is still a popular streaming service in Europe. iTunes is still topping the sales chart. The early bird gets the biggest worms. When the Elon Musk Mars colony becomes a reality, it will change human history forever. He's not just waiting for the competition. Musk is also building the biggest battery factory ever known to man. What achievement is inside of you? No one makes it to the top by being just like everybody else.

Sean Parker is now a happily married family man and he's giving big to charitable causes through the Parker foundation. Even though he won't admit it, Parker is a rebel who's always thinking of next-level ideas. There will always be things that we are not supposed to do, you should be brave enough to rebel against the system. Imagine the courage Parker and Fanning had to summon to face the media conglomerates and their army of lawyers. They could have been jailed but they took the risk because they saw it necessary to shake things up. Playing it safe is not always the best option. You will face opposition and challenges but with courage and a mindset of change, you too can shake up your life in a positive direction. Open your mind to possibilities, focus on solving simple problems first, and stay restless for success.

Solving A Pain By Being Different

Ideas happen when pain points exist. Back in the day people were slapped with $9/day late fees from Blockbuster. There was a problem waiting for a solution.

Reid Hastings had the idea to start Netflix when Andrew Tanenbaum wrote out a computer problem on a blackboard and asked students how much time and data it would take if you filled up a station wagon with tapes and drove the car to a particular destination. Reid thought of capacity, delivery, and timeliness - all major Netflix functions. Netflix's solved the following problems:

- Eliminated late fees

- Eliminated charges for lost or stolen DVDs

To do so they had to:

- Made customers commit to a monthly payment plan

- Leverage the US postal service

Blockbuster did everything in its power to copy the Netflix model, but the company couldn't catch up and its dominance eroded in front of America's eyes. In the battle for customers, Blockbuster was at a disadvantage because they copied ideas from Netflix, whereas Netflix applied scientific methods to launch their business.

On the surface, both companies had an online presence. Netflix offered $1 million to entrants who could make a 10% improvement in the movie suggestion algorithm.

A deeper look under the hood reveals Netflix hired 1st principle thinkers, a key ingredient in Elon Musk's success. The thought pattern is just because things have been executed a certain way doesn't mean that it's the only way.

The 1st principle thinking should exist in new employees before they start. Here are some of the key aspects of Netflix's work model:

- Giving ownership to the individual and team versus a top-down command and control.
- Making the employee feel like they make an impact on the company versus being a cog in a machine.
- Identifying the root cause of a problem versus treating the symptoms.
- Challenging authority with better ideas
- Hiring people smarter than yourself
- Part of their hiring process is having applicants review the Netflix culture deck. Simply by doing this Netflix gets a higher concentration of applicants which matches the company culture. The Netflix culture deck is available online for anyone to view.

Netflix treats their employees like a football team, where everyone fights to maintain their spot on a 52 man roster. Employees must go above and beyond to stay on the team. Average performance leads to a severance package. They want the right people on the bus as much as they need to keep the wrong people off the bus.

Whether you are part of a company or an individual working alone, you cannot sit by as the threats from younger, hungrier, skilled workers increase every day. Reinvent yourself and look under every stone for opportunities.

Elon Musk

He is the foremost entrepreneur, described as a combination of Steve Jobs and Henry Ford - someone who is at the forefront of changing the way we live. Never one to allow any setback to dent his ambitions, he is relentless in his quest to leave a positive mark in this world, pushing the boundaries of science and innovation. He will change the way we live our lives, whatever the personal cost to him.

Elon Musk: In His Mother's Words

'When you were a baby, I told people you were a genius. Maybe now they believe me' - Maye Musk, in a tweet to her son, Elon Musk

In an interview with Natasha Lader for The Economist's 1843 magazine, Maye gave insights into how she raised an entrepreneur like Elon Musk. Maye ran a private dietetic practice out of her home and her children, Elon, Kimbal, and Tosca did clerical work, such as writing letters and answering the phone. Early work exposure gave the children a sense of independence and a strong work ethic. Kimbal and Tosca have gone on to create powerful brands in their own right. While Kimbal is pioneering a sustainable food movement, Tosca is making moves in the film industry with her streaming platform PassionFlix, the Netflix for romance movies. Maye was also a part-time model and has been on the cover of Time magazine. To save money, she gave her kids haircuts, manicures, and pedicures. The Musk children didn't eat out or go to the movies. When you consider his upbringing, it's less strange that Elon kept his food spending to $1 a day in college.

Maye raised her children to be independent and create their own opportunities, rather than waiting on others. In 2015, she told Vanity Fair that her children grew up knowing the harder they worked, the better they'd do and the luckier they'd get.

This is not to say that Maye never harbored fear for Elon's future. Compared to his siblings, he was very introverted to the point of making her fear he was deaf.

Elon Musk: In His Own Words

In an interview posted on the Grunge YouTube channel, Elon admitted to having an abusive childhood. His poor relationship with his father may also have been a result of his parents' divorce when he was ten. His father, Errol, was reportedly tough with his children to the point of abuse, often lecturing them for hours. Errol failed to believe that anything can be achieved.

Elon was bullied by bigger kids so much that he described his school years as 'lonely and brutal'. His only escape was technology. Some kids have dreams of flying airplanes; others want to build rockets to travel to Mars. These are very exciting dreams. The only problem here is that a rocket costs over $65 million to build, and even if you can raise the money, you can't park it in your parents' garage.

Elon Musk had big dreams as he played with homemade rockets, but he started small. He developed coding and programming skills via the Commodore VIC-20, an inexpensive home computer. At thirteen he created his first video game and sold the code for $500 to a magazine called PC and Office Technology, instantly making him a prodigy.

Not all great inventors are necessarily great businessmen. So how is Elon Musk able to combine both? Simple. He started early. In Pretoria, South Africa, Elon and his younger brother Kimbal sold candy door-to-door, but not just to anyone; they targeted wealthy neighborhoods and sold homemade chocolate Easter eggs. Making the eggs cost 50 cents, but they sold them for $10 apiece. When customers asked why the eggs cost so much, he would say something like, "Well, you're supporting a young capitalist. And the reality is if you don't buy it from me, you're not going to get one - and I know you can afford $10."

Elon used to read for five hours a day, and not just school or pleasure reading. He read with the mindset of solving problems. He had a fear of darkness as a child, so to cure it, he read books on physics until he learned that darkness was simply the absence of photons, and thus, it was quite silly to be afraid of photons. Later, he admitted that physics had a great influence on his way of thinking. You had to boil things down to their fundamental truths and then reason up from there.

Since a young age, Elon wanted to solve exponential challenges such as energy generation, space travel, and the Internet.

In researching Elon I realized that as a child one of his favorite books was *The Hitchhiker's Guide to the Galaxy* by Douglas Adams. The book is hilarious, weird, and you won't understand why some parts are even in there, but it's interesting. The story starts out with an interstate highway being built right through the galaxy with planet Earth standing in the way of the construction.

Douglas Adams really let his imagination run wild in writing the book:

- Character's names like Prestegnic-Volgongelt or Now-Goalian Sun Tiger
- Volgons lay panting and thieving on the galactic shores
- The volgons would speak in a Beetle Juician galactic dialect
- Gazelle like creatures with silky skin and gui eyes

What thoughts can be planted in your mind from the experiences and imaginations of the authors?

As I finished reading *The Hitchhiker's Guide to the Galaxy*, I got to thinking about how our futures might be different if we were instructed to write creative essays anticipating what the future would look like. What if we did this every year starting at the age of ten?

What if we were assigned to find the most creative authors and read a few of their books. We would jump-start our imaginations. Elon thinks differently, similar to Steve Jobs, where anything they can think of, they can create. How can reading forty books a year impact you?

Elon moved to Canada when he turned seventeen to avoid serving in the South African military whose main duty then was to enforce apartheid in Canada.

He admitted that he's unable to stay single for long. This has led him through a zig-zag of relationships as reported by the Independent. He divorced his first wife in 2008. His second wife, Tallula Riley, admitted that she was initially attracted to his forlorn outlook. The charm, however, didn't last. They came close to divorce twice in their four-year marriage until she finally ended things. Later that same year, he started dating actress Amber Herd, but they didn't make it till the end of the next year.

None of this takes away from the energy revolution. He plays a major part in Tesla. He carries a humble approach towards his work, and he believes that no matter what, even if Tesla never existed, sustainable energy would still be achieved. The logic he gives for this is quite simple; the alternative to sustainable energy is unsustainable energy, and that won't last long. In the video, *There are Two Futures* by Elon Musk, he sets the maximum expiry date for unsustainable energy for 2040. For him, what Tesla does is ensure we get to the future faster than we otherwise would.

While in college, he lived on less than a dollar a day. It wasn't because he came from a poor background. He showed an aptitude for business quite early, and not in the tech industry, but with nightclubs. He and his friend would rent an empty house and organize a house party which would be open to anyone for $5. While his friend ensured that things stayed interesting, he stayed sober and kept things in check throughout the night.

After school, he tried to get a job with Netscape Communications, the company that created the first web browser, Netscape Navigator. This was at the height of the Internet boom when Netscape was hiring up to 50 engineers a month. Musk wasn't really sure what he wanted to do. He knew that he liked inventing things, but he wasn't sure if he wanted to start a company or work for someone else.

Netscape was not impressed with the scrawny college graduate who had a funny name and two college degrees in Physics and Economics. At one point, Elon actually hung around the lobby, probably hoping someone would notice him, but no one did and he was too shy to talk to anyone he saw. So, he left. Maybe if he had gotten that job, we would have never had Tesla, Solar City, or SpaceX.

Elon Musk The True Iron Man

Fans of Marvel's Iron Man character will be interested to know that the Tony Stark character was based on Elon Musk, with a bit of embellishment. If you compare them closely you'll find the two characters actually have a lot in common. They were both estranged from their fathers, they both had an early affinity for technology, and they both have a strong belief in the social purpose of their companies. Their age and weight are even roughly the same. Musk is 41 and weighs 220lbs, while Stark is 42 and weighs 225lbs. No wonder he earned a cameo in *Iron Man 2*. Furthermore, Elon's accomplishments make him this century's closest being to the Iron Man character.

At Tesla, robots used to make cars are named after superheroes:

- Xavier - Stands at the entrance to the trim line, lifting cars down to the floor from an electrified rail.
- Iceman, Wolverine, and Beast - Responsible for heavy lifting.
- Storm and Colossus - At the end of the chassis line.
- Vulcan and Havok - A team that lifts cars back onto the rail.

However, Elon didn't plunge into the energy industry in his first entrepreneurial attempt.

In 1996 he and his brother re-ignited their childhood partnership and they went into the business of media. They set up a company known as Zip2, which helped companies like the New York Times make an online transition and develop city guides. Elon Musk wanted to be the company's CEO but the board decided he was too young and inexperienced. Instead, they gave the job to Rich Sorkin, a serial entrepreneur with over $1 billion in net profits today. Compaq bought the company in 1999 for an estimated $300 million.

One of the first industries he disrupted was the banking industry. He did this through the company X.com. This company rivaled PayPal, a name we're all familiar with, until both companies merged into Paypal which revolutionized sending money to email addresses.

Elon was appointed CEO, a role he occupied until 2000 when he was removed due to leadership disagreements. Musk wanted the company to abandon its Unix platform in favor of Windows, a move which the Board of Directors rejected. This disagreement led to Musk being fired and he was replaced with Peter Thiel. When the company was sold for $1.5 billion in stock, Elon's cut was $165 million. Many of those he worked with in Paypal, just like him, moved on to setup bigger companies. Three of them created YouTube. One of them created LinkedIn. This just goes to show that your current enterprise may not be what defines your future greatness.

After leaving PayPal, Musk went through what some call a 'Moksha Moment', something most successful entrepreneurs go through. This is the point where entrepreneurs go all in, with no reservations whatsoever. At that point, it's win or lose, with no option to fall back on.

Moksha Moment

After Musk left PayPal he had $180 million in total and this is how he invested it; $100 million in SpaceX, $70 million in Tesla, and $10 million in SolarCity. At that point, he had to borrow money just to pay his rent. Tesla wasn't actually his original company. He discovered the company and bought into it. After disagreements with the CEO, he fired him and took his place. Today, Tesla cars occupy two spots in the world's top 10 most expensive cars. It all started with a $70 million investment and the risk of losing everything. Since 2002, SpaceX has grown into the only private company in the world capable of returning a spacecraft from low Earth orbit, rather than blowing it up in space, a feat it achieved in 2010. In 2012, it launched the first commercial spacecraft to deliver cargo to and from the International Space Station. One of the interesting things Elon did to achieve this was he recruited top graduates who were more interested in working for a worthy cause than a paycheck, thus reducing the cost of payroll. In other words, while NASA would hire a great engineer for $140,000 and half the productivity, SpaceX would get the same person for $70,000 and double the productivity. From its headquarters in Hawthorne, California, it has more than 6,000 employees with suppliers in all 50 states.

Have you ever given yourself so fully to something that if it failed, you would go down with it? That's what differentiates rock star entrepreneurs from the stragglers; the ability to single-mindedly pursue one goal as if their life depends on it because, in actuality, it does.

Elon Musk: What Are His First Principles?

In a life span of less than 45 years, he has disrupted four industries: Financial services (X.com became PayPal), automotive (Tesla Motors), aerospace (SpaceX), and energy (SolarCity). It's easy to assume he was able to do this because of his amazing genius and his work ethic. If you did, you wouldn't be far from the truth. In fact, for 15 years, Elon Musk worked for 100 hours a week, multitasking, eating during meetings, and responding to emails. Only recently did he scale down to 85 hours.

If his success was only due to extremely hard work and genius, there should be a lot of Elon Musk's out there, right?

The dividing line between accelerated success and hard work is what Elon calls 'First Principles' which he revealed in a one-on-one interview with Chris Anderson. The First Principles Reasoning Rule is essentially this: boil things down to their fundamental truths and reason up from there, as opposed to reasoning by analogy. Reasoning by analogy is what most of us do, which largely involves copying what other people do with slight variations. First Principles thinking demands that you take everything and question it, then create new knowledge and solutions from scratch. Most people, regardless of how proficient and hardworking they are, apply reasoning by analogy and follow the best practices, because that's what everybody else is doing. This is not to disparage popular methods that work. But the thing with wagons is, the more people on them, the slower they get. For some people, the best practices initially worked really well. Best practices were the result of first principle thinking at some point. But as more people use them, their efficacy drops until they become outdated and outmoded.

First Principle catapulted Elon into starting his companies. He does not think about a problem the way everyone else does. Forcing yourself to look at the facts of a situation can help you develop your own perspective on how to solve problems. Just because it's always been done that way doesn't mean everyone has to follow that path. Question your assumptions about a given problem or scenario and create a new knowledge framework from scratch. PayPal became successful by challenging every assumption of how a financial company should work. When we solve real-world problems we use root cause analysis to go deep.

First Principle Reasoning follows three steps:

Step 1: Identify And Define Your Current Assumptions

Spend more time thinking about the problem than the solution. This goes against the grain of popular wisdom. It's common to be solution-oriented, think about solving problems all the time. If you don't fully understand the problem, how are you going to develop a comprehensive solution to it? Also, how are you going to fully understand the problem if you don't devote sufficient time and energy to understanding it?

"If I had an hour to solve a problem, I'd spend 55 minutes thinking about the problem and 5 minutes thinking about solutions."

-Albert Einstein

Step 2: Break Down The Problem Into Its Fundamental Principles

Problems are like wrapped gifts. You have to open them up to get to the root, to discover the treasure that lies within. It is in this treasure that your solution lies. In an interview with Kevin Rose, Musk explained how this step might be applied with respect to making batteries cheaper. The current challenge now is how expensive batteries are, which explains the high cost of electric cars and battery-powered devices. To understand this battery problem, we literally break down a battery into its component parts; cobalt, nickel, aluminum, carbon, and some other components. If you bought the components individually, you would get it at a cheaper rate, and the cost of making batteries could be brought down significantly.

"It is important to view knowledge as a sort of semantic tree. Make sure you understand the fundamental principles, i.e. the trunk and big branches, before you get into the leaves/details or there is nothing for them to hang on to."

-Elon Musk

STEP 3: Create New Solutions From Scratch

Once you've identified the problems and broken them down into component parts, the next thing is for you to build innovative solutions from scratch, just like the batteries.

The First Principle way of thinking is the key to breaking out of the herd mentality and charting your own course. If you were to present this principle to a classroom of students, it could be taught within the context of schoolwork and academics. For instance, a student having challenges with their school work would have to consider why they consistently fail, despite their effort (or lack of effort), and their study methods. They could go further and break it down by subject. Was there a particular subject they did well in? Why was that different? By applying this method to every aspect of their academic program, they would be able to figure out their strengths and weaknesses, and properly leverage them to create new study habits that are uniquely theirs and work.

SpaceX

Elon was very interested in finding a backup planet for the human race as well as making space travel affordable. The problem lies with the cost per pound to leave the atmosphere.

The movie *2012* tells of a heroic struggle of survivors who are challenged by rising sea levels that almost top Mt. Everest as Earth's core overheats. The end of the world is near and a few who are part of the elite class obtain tickets to board futuristic-looking vessels AKA Noah's Ark.

If the end of days comes near in the next 50 years and space colonization is a reality, we might see the wealthy scrambling to pay exorbitant amounts of money to be the first to leave our planet.

Until recently, Elon Musk's SpaceX was the only company with a mission to make space travel accessible to everyone. That was until Jeff Bezos of Amazon got into the aerospace industry through another company known as Blue Origin. In what seems like a subtle reference to SpaceX, the mission statement of Blue Origin, states partly that 'We are not in a race, and there will be many players in this human endeavor to go to space to benefit Earth...We will go about this step by step because it is an illusion that skipping steps gets us there faster. Slow is smooth, and smooth is fast.'

Whichever way the wind blows, it's interesting to see someone with the caliber of Bezos stepping up to Elon Musk, a man who has consistently operated without rivals. We believe Musk is up to the challenge. He was the one to realize the cost of space travel could be cut in half if rockets could be reused, something the bureaucracy at NASA struggled to develop. He also cut costs by creating parts of his rocket in house rather than outsourcing. While NASA takes a long time and incurs high costs to execute its projects due to its Waterfall Production method, SpaceX preferred the Agile Production method.

A Fresh Install Of Your Personal Software

If you have ever owned a Windows computer or a smartphone you will notice that over time the machine tends to get slower. This decrease in speed is caused by software updates that have been installed and your personal installations. One of the best ways for the device to regain speed is to erase everything and do a fresh install of the original software. Let's walk down this path for just a bit.

- Removing apps frees up disk space which also removes background services. Think of this as removing unnecessary tasks from your to-do list. If a task does not bring you value, stop doing it. If you completely stop a task it can be removed from your mind.
- Reinstall only the apps that you use. Only do things that move you ahead.

Let's say you are doing a remodel of your house and have the walls opened up to add a window. If you attach two additional electrical outlets to an existing wall outlet designed for a microwave oven, you may cause the circuit breaker to blow or cause a fire. You may have success if you use one appliance at a time; however, if you try to take advantage of all three outlets at the same time, things will stop working. The correct way to do this is by pulling a building permit, adding two new circuit breakers in your electrical box and then running dedicated wiring to each outlet. In the end, you will have three circuit breakers and three sets of wiring connected to three outlets.

The takeaway is that our existing physical capacity cannot take the overload. While we may think we can multitask, we are not wired for it. What will occur is limited momentum and frustration. To achieve additional tasks we have to scale outward - assign the work to someone else or take something off our plate.

While replacing your computer or smartphone is an option, replacing yourself is not. If we start doing more, we will fall in a rut and we won't see performance gains. This is the main reason old habits are hard to replace. If you want to get more done, ignore what is not important.

Door #1 Or Door #2

How can you create value not tied to your time and become the captain of your ship? Every time we hear about someone successful, we see the end result. We do not see the hard work they put in. We don't know how they bridged the gap between where they are today, and where they were five years ago. If we don't know how they bridged that gap, we don't know how we can either. The problem is, the system guided us to build small boats which are subject to the weather and economic swings. This deception has forced our hand in picking a lifelong career. Most careers are fine; however, there is a common problem with them. They are tied to your time and disguised as a job. If you stop working, you don't get paid.

Look at the descriptions of both doors below. Now which one do you think has a line around the block, and why is that?

- Door #1 - Stable weekly income with two weeks off per year until you die or retire at 70 years old.
- Door #2 - Work hard now for a few years, afterward live free and control your life based on your desires.

Let's pause the program and think about this for a moment.

Repeating the same job 1,000 times is a sign that we are stuck behind Door #1. If your purpose is to create a widget for someone else's boat, you will get paid but the corporation is profiting the most from your labor. It doesn't matter if you create 10, 50, or 100 widgets, or how fast you can create the widgets. Ironically, the harder you work, the less the people above you have to work.

If you are at the top of your food chain and have a skill in creating a certain type of complex widget, you can package up your skills and teach them to someone else, which will help grow your position, causing Door #2 to open.

What widget could we make and sell that might make owning a boat a little more comfortable so that we can leverage our time?

If we switch our mindset to selling millions of widgets, wouldn't this be a more interesting problem to have? This thought alone can help you leave the herd that's stuck behind Door #1.

The next chapter covers dozens of scenarios on how to move from the bottom of the pyramid to the top. Only by questioning authority and not accepting what people tell you at face value will walking through Door #2 be achieved.

"Live as if you were to die tomorrow. Learn as if you were to live forever."

-Mahatma Gandhi

Chapter 8 Black Swans

"A surgeon is paid a high dollar amount based on the value he provides to the market.

What value can you deliver that separates you?"

-Andrewzee

Black swans are as rare as white tigers, making the study of these creatures a difficult effort. The following people are black swans who started their lives just like you and me.

Their talents vary but they accomplished their missions, they persevered against all odds, and they knew deep down that fitting in was not an option.

By studying the black swans of our society, we can learn useful lessons about their knowledge and tactics.

The following stories give ambitious young individuals a peek into the creative lives of people who've created works of art that have impacted millions.

We can all have a dream, we can all focus our energies on that dream, and make our own Acropolis just like the two famous architects Iktinos and Callicrates did in Athens.

Steven Spielberg And George Lucas

Movies - who doesn't love them? They take us to a world that we never believed could exist. They have become a part of our history. Movies are not just for entertainment, they are means to which we perceive the world around us.

Movie plots inspire and connect us with characters. Cinematography has shone a light on our struggles, our aspirations, and our deepest desires.

However, the stories behind the people who make movies and how they do it is more instigating than any film plot.

Making movies is hard work. Nowadays many of us watch movies and don't appreciate the effort that goes into making them. The entire process of creating movies is a journey filled with tears, persistence, determination, and a genuine obsession with bringing ideas to life.

I want to share with you some of the most inspiring Hollywood stories of all time. Steve and George are Hollywood directors who disrupted the American movie industry and became the standard of excellence.

In the early years, Hollywood was not very accepting of newcomers, especially people who were not influential. Some great men had to push the doors of creativity wide open for us to enjoy the movies we have today.

George Lucas and Steven Spielberg are two of the most amazing movie makers of all time. Both Steven and George are movie directors worth billions of dollars according to Forbes magazine. They have been around since the 1960s, continually bringing their genius to the silver screen.

George Lucas is the founder of the Star Wars franchise and the owner of Lucas film. He struggled to find himself and he wandered for years in search of his creative genius. From photography to anthropology to art illustration, before he accidentally found cinematography.

The amazing mind behind Star Wars discovered his passion by chance. This happened when he wrote a USC test because his friend did not want to be alone. He passed the test and after some encouragement from his friend, he decided to accept the admission.

In college, he passed a camera test for a one-minute animation. Everyone was impressed by his skills and creativity, George finally had his defining moment. He knew that of all the things he had tried, movie making was going to be his breakthrough. The one-minute animation won him his first prize in the National Student Film Festival. For a boy who grew up in a small town with only one cinema, and who only got to see movies when he went to film school, that was an incredible achievement.

You may be like George, confused and wondering what direction you should take. Unfortunately, life does not come with a map to success - things can get tricky.

You may have to go through the circles before you arrive at your destination. What matters the most is that you discover your true passion.

While it takes some a long time to find themselves, others just listen to their inner voice. If you find your passion early, you are among the lucky ones. It does not mean the road to success will be easy, you still need diligence and persistence.

Steven Spielberg, the creator of *E. T.*, *BFG*, and *Indiana Jones*, knew at 18 years old that he wanted to make movies.

As a kid, Steven Spielberg's dad helped him discover cinematography when he took him to see *The Greatest Show on Earth*. Back in 1952, this was an amazing piece of art starring Charlton Heston. Steven was captured by the train crash scene and months later all he wanted was to see that moment again and again. He begged his father to buy him Lionel trains just so he could crash them into each other. His father eventually got tired of repairing the trains and told Steven that if he crashed them again, that would be it, no more trains.

Steven was scared to lose his trains, but on the other hand, he was eager to see the collision again. This was the moment Steven had a life-changing idea. He decided to use his father's home movie camera to capture the trains crashing. He was able to film the crash and keep his trains because they were not destroyed. He made his first movie then went on to explore the world and tell stories through the lens of a camera.

George and Steven took different paths to self-discovery but they have a lot in common, more than just movies.

Both men are willing to share the experiences of others and connect with them through cinematography. It starts with you being able to connect with your inner genius, your characters, and your viewers. Being compassionate is the secret to telling good stories. You must understand what characters see and feel. Making movies is not just about the glitz and the glamour, it takes more than that.

Another commonality they share is their fathers never believed in them. George's dad asked him to pay for his own degree because he wanted him to be an office salesman instead. Steven's father told him to major in English so he could become a teacher just in case the movie thing did not work out. Their fathers did not believe in their dreams, but it didn't stop them - they both persevered.

People will doubt you, even those closest to you. Don't expect others to always be there for you. Focus on your goals and trust yourself. The more focused and passionate you are, the fewer things will stand in your way. Ironically the harder the life we live when we are young the better we can turn out.

Steven Spielberg and George Lucas are dreamers, men from small beginnings with big ideas. Through persistence and commitment, they manage to become great directors in Hollywood even though they were outsiders.

Dreams worth achieving come with challenges, it is impossible to succeed without learning how to overcome tough times. Challenges are a part of life and we can't avoid them.

It took George four years to write the first *Star Wars* script and every studio rejected it except 20th Century Fox. Sometimes it just takes one special person to believe in you. Don't give up is not just a popular saying. I know you've heard it many times before but never forget it. Patience is the secret ingredient of every success story.

During the shooting of *Star Wars*, George faced and conquered the odds. The budget was tight, staff members were fainting, and the whole project looked like a failure, but he persisted.

Steven used his challenges as inspiration for his movie scripts. *E.T.* was inspired by his parents' divorce - a story about a child losing what he holds precious. He added an alien to create an emotional dilemma of loving something unworthy.

You too turn your struggles into something positive for others. If you've failed, try to teach people how to avoid the same mistakes. Challenges add a personal touch to whatever you are doing. In the creative world, vulnerability matters, it helps people connect with your work. Let your guard down - allow your intuition to guide you. Teach yourself how to listen to your gut.

People may tell you what you should do, but in the end, you are the director of your life. You make the decisions. You are the main character and the scriptwriter. Don't take a backseat in your own life, be proactive. Let your creativity shine and don't be deterred by the world.

"The future belongs to those who believe in the beauty of their dreams."

-Eleanor Roosevelt

Ready Player One

Ernest Cline's recent success reads more like a fairytale than the science fiction he is known and cherished for. A self-confessed nerd watched his words jump from the pages of his book to the big screen. Ernest Cline is an inspiration to a generation immersed in pop culture and comic franchises.

How does a Star Wars fan and aspiring screenwriter make that leap? What drove him to jump? How does he plan to hang in there for the next books?

Ernest Cline's story is a lesson in perseverance, self-belief, and the irresistible blessing of passion touched by talent.

The Journey To Bestseller

Ready Player One took an incredible amount of time and work to finish. Spanning close to ten years, Ernest Cline poured childhood fantasies of video games and movies into a story that represented all of his life's pleasure.

The characters in *Ready Player One* included Godzilla, Robocop, Spiderman, Batman, Halo, Chucky and many more. A school parking lot filled with vehicles like TIE fighters, X Wings, the Millennium Falcon from Star Wars, Nasa's space shuttle, and the DeLorean from *Back to The Future*.

Ready Player One shone the limelight on Ernest Cline as a writer but he had a different life before then. He started out as a poet. One of his most striking poems so far is *The importance of Being Ernest*. He was also a spoken word writer and screenwriter before writing his debut novel, *Ready Player One*. After his first novel, Cline wrote Armada and one more book that does not have an official title yet but has been confirmed by Cline to be a sequel to *Ready Player One.*

The journey to *Ready Player One* didn't really start with writing the book, it started with Cline's dive into screenwriting. Ernest Cline is a self-taught screenwriter. He took apart John Hughe movies, reading every bit of the script and analyzing it.

Adventures of Buckaroo Banzar Against the Crime League was Cline's first attempt at a fan-fiction script, giving him prominence among die-hard fans and critics. While it did not make it to the big screen, it was the beginning of a journey that would see Cline falter then fly.

Fanboys

Unknown to many, *Ready Player One* was not Cline's first work to be made into a movie. In 2009 *Fanboys* premiered, a story of five boys traveling across the country to break into Skywalker Ranch to watch the latest Star Wars movie before its release so one of them with a terminal illness can watch it.

While it was fulfilling to see the work made into a movie after ten years of its drafting, Cline was upset about the lack of creative control. The movie was a tiring journey through production with a frustrating final result. It was thrown into a pool of over-enthusiastic financiers. There were too many hands in production and the release process dragged, causing the movie to land with a soft thud.

If anything, it inspired Ernest Cline to keep working on *Ready Player One* in hopes of getting another shot.

Writing Ready Player One

In an interview with Arab News, Cline famously describes writing the book and its initial screenplay as a long and difficult process. It became even more tasking because the film rights of the book had been auctioned off before the book was published. Cline, who had just finished writing, was caught in a web of reimagining his work in a way that it would fit in with the new authors.

In the same interview with Arab News, he was honest about the struggle, "When I started writing my drafts of the screenplay, it was before the book was even published. That was even more difficult because it was not a bestseller yet and I didn't have as much leverage to keep things the same. I could see that there would need to be major changes, because the whole time that I was writing the novel I assumed it could never be a movie, because of all the pop-culture references, and the way that I wanted to weave them into the story and mash them up and pay tribute to it in this virtual world."

Another problem that dogged Ernest Cline was how he was going to get permission from all the franchises that were featured in the movie. The intellectual property indications might have been a distant thought when Cline was poring over his notes and writing, but they were now a very present concern for him and his team.

The Spielberg Effect

While Ernest Cline and Zak Penn were trying to create a believable and achievable story to take to the big screen, someone else was dreaming much bigger. Penn, the director of other books who had made the transition from pages to the big screen, was not ready to let the magic he found in the book be diminished. Speaking about his reaction to the book he said, "They sent me the book, as well as the script, which I read first. I became completely enthralled with the idea of this juxtaposition of two worlds. Then I read the book and it really spun me out because it was so deep and so layered. It was esoteric; it was scary; it was accessible... I was hooked!"

Reimagining The Future

Cline's work didn't just have a monumental impact on science fiction but on science itself. Cline was credited for painting a world shaped by virtual reality. Steven Spielberg said during an interview in the Independent UK, "Ernest Cline is such a visionary, he has seen the future before any of us." Unsurprisingly, Cline's futuristic book published in 2011 ushered in genuine innovation in virtual reality. Cline said in the same interview, "It's the first realistic representation of virtual reality, of its potential and its potential pitfalls. It's going to change the speed with which our whole civilization adopts virtual reality. Movies are that powerful and Stevens movies are that influential. There are going to be people who try it, who never would have before. And people who will work in it who never would have done otherwise"

Like a prophecy fulfilled, shortly after the release of *Ready Player One*, Oculus, HTC, and PlayStation virtual reality headsets became commonplace, an indication that the future as imagined by Ernest Cline is very much here to stay.

Write Your Passion

Ernest Cline's story has an unconventional lesson - sometimes raw passion is enough. With no creative writing MA or features in Literary magazines, he has broken free.

A lot of writers are often swayed by what's popular. They look at the success of others and try to fit themselves into that mold. It is not surprising that usually, nothing good comes out of such moves.

Ernest Cline's success was built on a foundation of passion and knowledge. He is a self-confessed geek who poured his childhood memories and fantasies onto paper. So write what you love, write what you know and see yourself thrive.

Persistence For The Win

A constant flow of inspiration that carries you through the process of writing a book is the greatest fiction of all. Though talent and passion are not enough, you must have grit and a resolve to see things through. Cline labored for more than ten years to put his book together and added new facets every day.

You must resolve to keep honing your craft and adding to the masterpiece you are writing. Stay disciplined.

While critics may have a lot to say about *Ready Player One*, Cline has emerged as the patron saint of a new generation of writers who would not be refused.

"Concentrate all your thoughts upon the work at hand. The sun's rays do not burn until brought to a focus."

-Alexander Graham Bell

50 Shades of Success

Love rarely comes in ways we expect. Passion speaks in many languages. Incompatibles usually become complements. Sex, like all men, is a passing act of pleasure, but an act with its own history, present, and future. E.L. James understands this and portrays it in fifty shades of erotic literature.

Erotic literature has always been the ultimate reveal. It takes our deepest secrets, our most intimate desires, our darkest thoughts, and our strange fantasies into consideration. It nurses them and builds characters and intricate plots around them.

With her unique mastery, E.L. James changed the world of erotic literature and brought with her the spell of silence. Long commutes, book clubs, and libraries were quietened by a welcome elephant in the room. Anastasia Steele and Christian Grey were with them in the pages of books and smart devices.

Blessed with a story she could not hold back, E.L. James triumphed over derisory remarks of 'mommy porn' to create a new niche in writing and she's become an inspiration to writers looking to express themselves.

The Greying

Interestingly, the story of E.L. James' success does not begin with a background in creative writing or a long history as a budding writer. E.L. James began her writing journey by creating fanfiction for the Twilight series after she fell in love with the books and their characters. Writing under the moniker 'Snow queen Ice dragon', she released two kindle books and became a regular name among fanfiction communities.

Her fanfiction morphed into her own series titled *The Masters of the Universe* which was noted for its BDSM content.

It was this series that led to the first novel in the Grey series, introducing Christian Grey and Anastasia Steele to the entire world. *Fifty Shades of Grey*, *Fifty Shades Darker*, and *Fifty Shades Freed* have become major commercial successes.

The Rise Of The Grey

E.L James has become a cultural icon, not only in the genre of erotic writing but in BDSM. The Fifty Shades of Grey series was not just erotic, it brought forward a culture that was only spoken of in dark corners and hushed tones. The existence of the series opened the worlds of BDSM and created a loyal fan base that carried the books to cult classic status and film adaptations.

The character Christian Grey attained popularity ascribed to Jane Austen's Fitzwilliam Darcy and Charlotte Bronte's Mr. Rochester. The character is a quintessential romance staple - handsome and rich with an emotional vulnerability seen only by the heroine. The success formula of the Grey series is similar to many romance novels - a dashing hero, a willing heroine, and some intrigue; however, E.L. James added a secret ingredient - sex. An abundance of detailed, innovative sex that embraces a quiet culture. The books prompted love, criticism, openness, conversations, and controversy.

Even more compelling than the cultural and commercial success of E.L. James is the way she consistently defied mainstream publishing. For a long time, the opinions of publishers and agents were the only thing that mattered.

The first volume written by E.L. James was released in 2011 as an ebook and print on demand paperback from the publisher Writers' Coffee Shop, an Australian independent publishing house giving writers a head start.

The book had a relatively quiet release but readers did the rest. From mouth to mouth publicity to social media posts to blog reviews, word of the new book began to spread.

It was this growing conversation that caught the attention of Anne Messitte, publisher of the Vintage division of Random

House. Negotiations led to a deal that was closed around the million-dollar mark.

In her rise, E.L James taught writers an important lesson - the kingmakers of publishing do not hold all the power. Word of mouth amplified by the power of social media has the power to kick-start conversations that bring attention and commercial success.

A Supportive Partner

James alludes to how helpful her husband, Niall Leonard, was in the entirety of her creative process. Being a scriptwriter himself, she had the luxury of knowing someone who understood her, helped edit, and acted as a sounding board for ideas throughout the process.

She joked about how much research went into the books and their bedroom was a place for experimentation. Her story highlights just how beneficial an understanding, active partner can be to the creative process.

If you have a partner who shows interest, is willing to test out your ideas, and provide feedback, value their help.

Research

While the entire plot of the Grey series seems to flow and draw you in, it reveals nothing about the depth of research that went into it. Throughout the writing process, she devoted herself to learning about the issues at the core of the book including BDSM, luxury jets, jewelry, and psychiatry.

Talent and unique ideas are never enough. In making that bestseller come to life, you must ultimately dedicate yourself to research. Research is hard, boring, and will take hours of your time, but if your book is to stand out and command attention, research is a must.

Music Speaks

The most devastating thing that can happen to a writer is to realize their words are suddenly drying up. They start to doubt themselves and the temptation to take a break sets in.

The danger of taking a break is that they start to wait for a big moment of inspiration. They forget the power of consistency.

When it comes down to it, be prepared to write through whatever you are feeling with music helping you through.

E.L. James is able to write without taking long breaks to find her next words, but she admits there are times she needs some extra help.

For help, she turns to John Martyn's *Man at the Station* which helps her block out everything and enter into a writing cocoon.

The Grey Playbook

For one who has achieved so much success, she has remained down to earth. She shares her creative process and helps writers who are trying to come to terms with the industry.

E.L. James has made her name by saying the unsaid things. She created a loyal fan base by revealing our darkest thoughts. We look forward to her next literary exposé. But much more, we look forward to a new narrative of where closet issues are brought out in fiction. We look forward to conversations that we need to have with each other to better understand the world we live in. We look forward to more truths, more understanding, and less judgment. Most importantly, we look forward to literature remaining a driving force in modeling our society, inspiring conversations, and creating dreamers.

YouTube Freedom

Long ago, CNBC glued subscribers to their networks. With the emergence of public viewing channels like YouTube and Instagram, a revolution swept through this atmosphere. Every day, viewership turns away from private channels to focus on just about anyone who has a thing or two to broadcast about.

According to statistics, YouTube pulls in over 1.8 billion users every month. Over 300 hours of video are uploaded to YouTube every minute and there are over 30 million visitors to the site every single day. With these mind-boggling statistics, it's no question that public viewing channels have succeeded.

What does this have to do? Say you have a desirable skill that people are looking to learn, YouTube has an opportunity for you. With the traffic of over 1.8 billion users, you can reach the desired audience. Once you have a YouTube audience, your opportunities become limitless. You don't have an office, as long as you can create a video and upload it to YouTube, you're good to go. With YouTube, you're not just reaching out to people that need what you have, you are making yourself an authority in your chosen niche. Just like CNBC, you are your own broadcasting station.

YouTube vs CNBC

YouTube was launched in 2005 by Jawed Karim, Chad Hurley, and Steve Chen. In 2016, Google purchased YouTube for $1.6 billion. YouTube has users from over 90 countries with 1.8 billion users logging into the platform on a monthly basis.

As of 2019, YouTube had a database of 1,300,000,000 videos in its collection. Most of the current generation would rather visit YouTube than stick with private viewing channels like CNBC, and the reasons are not far fetched.

YouTube is designed to give viewers a wide range of choices between what they are interested in and what they want to watch. Whatever you have to showcase, there will be millions of visitors waiting to consume.

YouTube brings people audiences of like minds. You can make a whole lot of money while being passionate about what you love. The only work to be done is finding the right audience, building an account, and creating engaging content for audiences.

Earning on YouTube is easy. The question is, what are you particularly good at and how good are you?

You don't have to have a particular skill to pull in an audience. You could easily pick up an interest in a topic and explore it, giving your opinions across many related topics. It could be sports, politics, or health, among many other interesting niches.

PewDiePie

PewDiePie aka Felix Arvid Ulf Kjellberg is the brain behind the YouTube channel PewDiePie. He created his first YouTube account in 2010 and by 2012 he garnered over a million subscribers. He focuses on making video game commentary and as of January 2019, he amassed a total of 83 million subscribers. He is currently ranked 8th on the list of top viewed channels on YouTube with over 20 billion views and his network is estimated to worth $20 million.

||SuperWoman||

Lilly Singh is the owner of the YouTube channel ||SuperWoman| and she focuses on entertainment. She launched her YouTube account in October 2010 and she has over 14 million subscribers. Her videos have received over 2 billion views. She has been ranked number 10 on Forbes list of YouTube highest earners with a reported $10.5 million.

Ryan's World

Ryan's World is owned by seven-year-old Ryan and he reviews toys. One of his videos *Huge Eggs Surprise Toys Challenge* accumulated over 1.7 billion views, placing it at number 40 on the list of highest viewed YouTube videos. He is ranked as YouTube's highest earner with $22 million in revenue accumulated from his channel and product line in Walmart.

SEO Mindset

Dealing with earnings on YouTube and getting your videos out to interested audiences involves many factors and one of them is SEO. SEO stands for search engine optimization and it simply implies fine-tuning your videos and content in such a way that it can easily be discovered by users when they search Google and YouTube.

Some of the things to pay attention to in order to ensure that your videos are properly optimized for search engines include:

- Creating a unique, customized cover for your videos. Something that will attract attention while sending a direct message to users.

- Paying attention to the particular keywords that are related to your niche and the videos you upload.

- Creating content that is engaging, something that will make viewers want to click the share button when they're done.

Requirements For Getting Paid

YouTube's earning method is based on many requirements; however, once you are able to create engaging content for your viewers, something funny enough to make them never want to let go, then you are on your way to financial freedom.

Once you have monetized your YouTube channel and ads are displayed on each video you upload, you can earn as much as $5 for every 1,000 views on a particular video. To make $100 from a YouTube video, the video must have at least 20,000 views. However, to be able to monetize your channel, you must tally over 4,000 views on all your channels and have a subscriber base of at least 1,000.

All it takes to get your YouTube payday is a channel stashed with the right amount of content for the right audience. Whatever it is that your interest is, make the most out of it and put it out there for other users to watch. Whether it is a tutorial or an analysis, YouTube has just the audience to get everything going and with YouTube ads, it can only get better.

Apply the less is more approach. There are many people creating videos; however, they are not cranking down on the data, the metrics of what matters to their users.

So before you hit record, compare Youtubers that can crank out 20 highly focused videos rather than putting out 100 or more random videos. Don't forget to read the comments below the video. You can actually become part of the conversation and reply to comments on someone else's channel.

How Amancio Ortega Beat Retailers

When you have nothing, the incentive to have something can be huge. With nothing to lose but your abject poverty, nothing stands in your way to achieve greatness. Amancio Ortega is the perfect example of this. A dirt-poor foreigner upon his arrival in America, he is now recognized as the founder of Zara, a globally popular clothing and accessories line. Nothing from his background gave him advantages. All he had was the ability to fight harder and last longer than most American people.

Ortega is a Spanish billionaire with a net worth of $68.2 billion as of September 2018, making him the second-wealthiest person in Europe, and the fifth-wealthiest person in the world, according to Forbes Magazine. His wealth is largely from the fashion group he founded, known as Inditex. It may not be popular with everyone, but it's the company behind brands such as Zara, Massimo Dutti, Oysho, Zara Home, Kiddy's Class, Tempe, Stradivarius, Pull and Bear, and Bershka. His drive came from a time when he heard his mother, a housemaid, begging for credit at local stores. This was the straw that broke the camel's back. He dropped out of school and started working at the age of fourteen.

During this period, he met Mera in a clothing store where she worked as a shop assistant. She was later his wife and business partner. The two of them partnered with Amancio's brother, Antonio to create dressing gowns and lingerie designed by Mera, which they sold from their garage. It was also during this period that Ortega adopted the vertical approach that has remained at the core of his businesses to date. Whereas most retailers focused on one aspect of the business such as making clothes, distribution or selling clothes, Ortega did all three, helping him to tap into Spain's skilled workforce of female embroiderers and seamstresses. He began by organizing single women who could sew well into sewing cooperatives. The product line included lingerie, babywear, and nightgowns.

By 1963, Ortega had over ten years of experience from managing sewing cooperatives. He founded his first company, Confecciones GOA, centered around his family. He was in charge of developing new fashion trends. His brother, Antonio, managed commercial issues. Josefa, his sister, was responsible for bookkeeping. While his wife, Rosalia Mera, acted as his business partner. All of his businesses have witnessed the heavy involvement of his family members.

This business model leveraged a low-cost local workforce to deliver fast production clothing turnarounds. By 1975, Ortega opened his first storefront known as Zorba, but changed it later to Zara, which expanded rapidly in the 1980s to other Spanish cities.

By 1985, Confecciones GOA transformed into Inditex, a holding group for a number of popular brands. Ortega was not a man who allowed sentiment to get in the way of business. When he found out that the workforce in Portugal was cheaper than the Spanish, he opened stores there in 1988. He broke into the US and UK markets in 1989 and 1998 respectively.

It's no coincidence that Amancio Ortega's business empire grew rapidly. The core of his business model is the heart of a fast-fashion retailer. The key to this business model is to give customers what they want as quickly as possible. For example, Zara is known to develop and distribute 12,000 new designs annually.

Designers usually create three models a day and usually only one will survive the scrutiny of analysts and patternmakers. It's better to kill a bad design in the confines of the factory than lose revenue and brand reputation because of a bad clothing line. These analysts and patternmakers apply locally curated knowledge into their decisions. They are experts in the local or regional tastes of their respective regions, having been drawn from diverse backgrounds. They also consider reports from local store managers about changing customer habits. Every Inditex employee is trained to keep an eye on clients' styles, requests, and the latest selling trends.

It doesn't stop there, Zara also refreshes its garment stock at least twice a week; for clothes, this is on Sundays and Thursdays, while shoes come in on Tuesdays and Fridays. At Stradivarius and Massimo Dutti, new clothes arrive every Tuesday and Thursday. For Bershka and Pull & Bear, new deliveries arrive Tuesday and Friday. This is premised on the golden rule that Ortega imposed in the '70s to the effect that new orders had to be received and acted on within a 48-hour period.

This is not to say that his brutally efficient system is not without its failures. What makes it so popular is not just how positively it operates, but also, how it bounces back from its downtime. There have been failures, one such incident happened at a Manhattan store in New York when white jackets were not pleasing to the customers. As soon as the staff detected this and noted that the local clientele preferred a cream color, the white ones were withdrawn, and the clothing line was reissued in cream tones, which was a success.

The combination of these rules has put Inditex ahead of its peers in the fashion retail industry. Today, it employs over

137,000 professionals in close to 7,000 stores and facilities, across 88 countries, with annual sales revenue over $19.67 billion as of January 2015, according to Astrum People.

Another factor that has put the Zara brand at the forefront is the fact that it does not bask in the euphoria of its success for too long. It doesn't relax into the easy trap of reproducing its hits. Just because a product is doing well doesn't mean they can't do better. You can see this principle at work in most of the successful businesses. The iPhone 1 was a hit but that didn't stop Apple from releasing the iPhone 2 and going all the way to the iPhone X. You can either self-innovate into greater profitability or wait for an outsider to do it for you.

The Zara brand consistently modifies and offers varied versions of its products. Famous fashion blogger, Garance Dore, has coined the term Zaragasm, which means being seduced by the variety of choices and fashionable offers that Zara has in stock. Rather than track fashion shows, the company prefers to track bloggers and listen to its customers.

Very few companies in the world can keep up with the pace of the Inditex group. The company competes against itself, striving to beat its previous speed records. Somewhere in the world, a new Zara store opens on a daily basis, although one-third of them are in Spain, according to Astrum People.

While most people know Amancio Ortega as a fashion entrepreneur, he is also a real estate tycoon. He used profits from fashion retail to purchase prime properties. He then rents them to Zara stores and other businesses, performing the role of a fashion business' landlord. He ensures that his money keeps circulating and does not escape to third parties. His real estate empire is estimated to be worth over $10 billion.

In 2007 unemployment was at critical levels and major businesses were moving out of the country, Ortega took the opportunity to purchase their properties at great discounts.

When Harvard Business Review looked at Zara in 2004, they termed its management practices questionable and downright crazy, saying, "Zara defied most of the current conventional wisdom about how supply chains should be run... The company can design, produce, and deliver a new garment and put it on display in its stores worldwide in a mere 15 days. Such a pace is unheard of in the fashion business, where designers typically spend months planning for the next season."

This fast approach to service delivery ensures that Zara has significantly lower markdowns than its competitors. Its markdowns are usually in the range of 15%, while rival US apparel retailers and department stores are typically in the 50-70% range, according to Forbes. Even before the internet generation arrived with its focus on 'I want it now' service delivery, Zara was already providing this, becoming the natural choice for the generation. In a 2010 annual report of Inditex group, the last before Ortega resigned as Chairman of the group, he wrote, 'The customer must continue to be our main center of attention, both in the creation of our fashion collection and in the design of our shops, of our logistical system and of any other activity.'

Zara and its associated brands under the Inditex group exemplify Agile Management at work. Rather than copy them in order to beat them at their games, most established fashion brands prefer to stick with traditional management practices. They like to think the vertical management practices of Zara are beyond their capabilities, or they out rightly postpone implementing speed to market procedures. These businesses have yet to enter the Creative Economy, where the customer is at the center of the equation.

Unlike most of his competitors who have moved to China due to cheap labor costs, Inditex sources most of its products from Spain, Portugal, and Morocco, building a strong, likable brand. By controlling his supply chain, he can ensure that his company quickly reacts to new trends, giving the customers exactly what they want. It also significantly reduces the final cost of goods as he doesn't have to pay a rival to put his clothing line in their stores. He is in complete control from the design stage, right to the cashier at the storefront.

There's so much to learn from the grass to grace story of Amancio Ortega for any ambitious entrepreneur. First of all, the fiercely private life of this man disproves the theory that you have to be 'visible' to snatch opportunities. Rather than chase the limelight, Ortega focused on constantly innovating.

Another lesson we can take from him is the freedom to experiment. It's much easier to experiment when the business is still wobbly, unknown and hardly has any revenue. What is your competition either not doing at all, or not doing well? Step in and offer that service. Even if it fails, you've learned something. It's better to fail in private than when you're in charge of a Fortune 500 and the board has no other choice but to fire you as CEO.

"The man who asks a question is a fool for a minute, the man who does not ask is a fool for life."

-Confucius

Chapter 9 Productivity and Flow

"If we do not carve out moments of silence to focus our thoughts, we wind up dreaming about what is important to others."

-Andrewzee

Your Zen Spark

The Zen spark of enlightenment evades many seekers, but it can be found within one's self. Everyone needs private time - a special place, like at a park, the back of your house, or a break room, somewhere without distractions. Taking a 20-minute walk outside of the office can create the white space you need. But don't be fooled, checking your personal email, watching YouTube, and surfing Reddit doesn't count as distraction-free time. When you count this kind of personal media consumption as a 'break', you're simply replacing one form of distraction with another. Instead, disconnect yourself. Allow your thoughts to wander and your mind to rest. When you return to your work, you'll be more focused, more motivated, and more productive.

A step towards a healthier mind is avoiding environments that steal our attention. In one study, two groups of students were given the same general math questions. Before the test, one group walked through a forest for about 30 minutes. The other group of students navigated through a busy downtown for about 30 minutes. The group that walked through the forest scored 20% better than the group that walked through the city. Distractions prevent our brains from firing on all cylinders and they limit our learning abilities.

To prevent this white-space time from being sucked up by supervisors, peers, or other well-meaning people, consider scheduling a 30-minute meeting with yourself so you can realign your thoughts on a daily basis. By setting a meeting with yourself, others will see that your calendar is busy and will not call or e-mail during this time.

If you have an important deliverable due in a couple of days but you're having trouble finding the time and space to tackle the challenge, you should try scheduling yourself into a conference room for a few hours at a time for a couple of days. Working in a conference room elevates your focus because you lack comfortable surroundings, freeing you from distractions.

Being in the zone is as simple as working on one task for an hour or two without distraction. Every time we switch tasks, we lose momentum. We tend to work better if we commit our high-level lists to a notebook or a digital task list because documenting the tasks and responsibilities allows us to 'forget' the tasks, at least temporarily, so we can focus on one task at a time. The less you have on your mind, the better you can perform; furthermore, crossing out a task after you have accomplished it feels good.

Flow Achievement

With a to-do list that seems never-ending and the promise of some alone time with your favorite hobby, chances are that finding a state where your creativity is heightened is the last thing on your mind.

It is possible to not go through the same mechanical motions every day, filled with negative energy while missing out on the possibility of finding happiness in the midst of mundane work and leisure. The key to achieving this lies in understanding the concept of flow and realizing how to harness it for your success.

One man who has cracked the code is Hungarian psychologist Mihaly Csikszentmihaly. Mihaly grew up in very adverse conditions during the Second World War where he was jailed in an Italian prison. It was there that the foundations of flow achievement were formed.

Despite being in prison, he began to wonder about finding happiness and contentment with physical restrictions fading away. Using chess as a channel, Mihaly Csikszentmihaly found himself crossing into reality in spite of the physical boundaries that surrounded him. After the war, he listened to Carl Jung at a Swiss resort and he was inspired to head to America and begin a path to psychology as he sought answers to questions about the true roots of happiness.

The answer he found and one that he has dedicated his life to refining and teaching is the achievement of the flow state.

In an interview with Wired magazine, Mihaly Csikszentmihalyi described flow as "being completely involved in an activity for its own sake. The ego falls away. Time flies. Every action, movement, and thought follows inevitably from the previous one, like playing jazz. Your whole being is involved, and you're using your skills to the utmost."

Csikszentmihalyi goes on and describes the autotelic personality as a trait possessed by individuals who can learn to enjoy situations that most other people would find miserable. The autotelic personality is the height of flow achievement with the individual finding such delight in daily work and exercising it with such enthralling precision that they live a truly fulfilling life.

The key to achieving flow is focus. This means you have to eliminate things that distract, stress, and annoy you. You have to actively strip away the negative emotions of fear, self-doubt, self-consciousness, and worry. One key way to get into it is your location and atmosphere. Try playing some background music at your favorite creative spot. Let your mind do its thing. Notice the ideas that start flashing through your mind. With your body and mind in a great place, you have prepared yourself to utilize the results of your thought process. Channel these new insights into your present activity.

Achieving flow also requires intense concentration on the task at hand. It's important that all your effort is channeled to one task because it is only through this kind of focused execution that we can become valuable in one area. A clogged to do list spells failure before you begin. If a task is too complex, break it down into smaller achievable tasks. By doing this you will avoid frustration and easily move from one success to another.

Another major thing to pay attention to is the measure of your skills against the challenge in front of you. If it's too simple, you'll likely lose focus and get bored. If it is too hard, you'll grow increasingly frustrated and lose enthusiasm. The key is to find the perfect task that can keep you positively engaged while being a good match for your skills.

How do you know when you are in a good flow state? There are no flashing lights or sirens to announce it. Ultimately you feel better and begin to live in the moment enjoying every twist and turn. The fog seems to clear, you feel good about the direction you are heading in, and your mind feels relaxed as you think about the rewards ahead.

"Truly wonderful, the mind of a child is"

-Yoda

The Productive Road Warrior

When working remotely on your laptop, try to outlast the charge on your battery. The more you can operate without power or the internet, the less you'll depend on your local resources. Get in the habit of turning off the WiFi and data on your laptop and phone to save energy.

Working at a location that does not have WiFi helps to double down on focus, as you'll spend zero time wandering meaningless sites. If you have applications or web pages open in the background, beware of the rogue apps that are constantly polling servers for updates. Your phone or laptop will feel hot at times which results in battery loss. Only when you exit the rogue app or web page will you notice the temperature drop. You may also want to experiment with a black screen and white text. Black pixels in an display are essentially 'turned off' and consume far less power, try this with your laptop and phone.

Newer laptops may not be the best at saving energy. An older 2014 MacBook Air can last up to 6 hours on basic editing. With newer 2018 Macs you might not see this range of battery life. It all depends on what apps you run for your work.

Sometimes you may find yourself competing for a single electrical outlet. To help this situation, I purchased a small extension cord. Sometimes, you can even share the power cord with others. At some heavily used college locations, two-prong chargers fall out of electrical outlets. Three prong electrical cords stay in the outlet better. A trend that I had started to notice at a few different Starbucks is that they now replace the electrical outlets with a solid plate preventing you from charging your laptop limiting how much time you spend at their tables.

Prior to leaving your home make sure your devices are fully charged and synchronized. The more I wrote on the road the more important it became to synchronize DropBox and OneNote between my devices so that I would avoid version conflicts. To avoid synchronization errors, deliberately work on different pages or tabs at different locations. When arriving at your next location check that you have the latest version of your document by confirming you have the latest changes.

If you are on the road a lot, carrying a good 4X battery pack that can charge your phone at least three or four times will improve your remote experiences. If you work out of your car a lot you might want to pick up a 500-watt 12-volt power inverter to charge your laptop. Make sure that you pick a higher wattage unit as the smaller devices tend to reset easily.

Make sure you carry your headphones with you. You do not need to even listen to anything, you just need privacy amongst all of the noise that surrounds you. The last thing you need is to sit down with your coffee and then a loud conversation starts nearby.

To generate ideas, sometimes you need to place yourself in productive yet quiet areas where others are working. Here are a few locations where you can work:

- Hotel common areas. The nicer the hotel the better your experience.
- Museums with free Wifi
- Libraries
- Coffee shops

Other productive thoughts:

- Malcom Gladwell, the author of Tipping Point, Outliers, and Blink does all of his writing in coffee shops. What happens as you switch coffee shops? The scenery changes, the sounds change, the people change.
- If you work out of your car much you might want to pickup a 500 watt 12 volt to 110 volt power inverter for charging your laptop, smaller devices tend to reset easily.
- Carry a second set of earbuds in your car so that you always have a backup. Why a backup? One day I had forgotten my headphones at home and found myself at a Starbuck surrounded by 10 mothers chatting away. I felt like I was trying to work in a hen house with over two dozen chickens chirping away. The distraction level I will never forget. What I wound up doing was tearing a piece of napkin and stuffing it in both ears, this helped a little. A few months down the road I wound up buying an over ear style headphone with integrated microphone, love the unit.
- A final point I found is that listening to music in a foreign language is almost none distracting vs if you were to listen to something you would understand the words to.

A Pit Stop and Wi-Fi

Tired of asking for the restroom code everywhere you go? Document the code and location for every coffee shop you visit on your phone.

- 1130* Peet's 1 California
- 50488 Phil's Embarcadero

Steve Jobs And Jack Ma

Inspiration can come from movies, images, books, and travel. Travel has no boundaries or limitations. Sometimes, travel can change you as a person. New people, new situations, new culture, and change in mindset will trigger something new in you. Once you're triggered, all you need is a well-thought effort to work towards that trigger. The pathway is difficult but not impossible when you have the right frame of mind and inspiration to reach your goal.

When I think about successful business leaders who were inspired by world travel, two names come to my mind. These people are from different generations, different countries, and they have different personalities. They are Steve Jobs and Jack Ma. One unique and common factor in their lives is how world travel inspired them to change everything around them.

Knowledge Gained Through Travel Inspires

Steve Jobs was on a spiritual path. In 1972, Steve was working for Atari Inc. and he saved money to go to India. He traveled there with his friend, Daniel Kottke, and they stayed for almost seven months. Steve's goal was to meet Neem Karoli Baba, a spirituality guru, but he died before they could meet. His trip to India was one of the reasons why he dropped out of college. He was fascinated by Eastern spiritualism and wanted to study the culture and religion. By going to India, he changed himself completely. He shaved his head and started wearing traditional Indian attire.

After living in India for seven months, he returned to work in San Francisco. The trip changed him, clearing all his doubts. He left with the conviction that tech innovators could change the world, as opposed to political ideologues and religious leaders. He went to India allured by its spirituality and airs of holiness, but he was shocked by the extreme poverty.

Jack Ma was all about the internet and the failures behind him. After coming to America, he learned about the internet, its business, and no availability of global market. He changed his way of thinking and business style to unite small-scale industries and suppliers to create the E-commerce giant Alibaba.com, which recently went public in what has been described as the biggest IPO in history. From a one-room startup that employed just 18 people, it has grown to employ over 60,000 people and it stretches across four campuses in China. The website has over 100 million buyers daily and it's created over 40 million jobs, directly and indirectly in China.

Key Insights That Turned Into Lightbulb Moments

Steve Jobs' light bulb moment was definitely his idea to create a computer and compete with other developers. The presentation, style, and logo of the company including its name, were insightful moments. None of this would have been possible, or they might have turned out significantly different, if not for his India trip. His appreciation for spirituality was developed in India. When he came back to the United States and it was time to name the company he co-founded with Steve Wozniak, he suggested 'Apple' after a spiritual commune he discovered in Oregon that reminded him of an apple orchard. In the 1997 Apple 'Think Different' ads, Steve Jobs featured Mahatma Gandhi, a man he met during his India trip and developed a lasting admiration for. Steve Jobs was a successful business tycoon but he was also a great presenter.

The light bulb moment for Jack Ma was unique. He originally came to America in 1995 to help the local government build a highway. This was where he was introduced to the internet for the first time, at the US Bank in Seattle. His friend had an office that housed several computers. His friend told him that with the internet, he could search for anything. At the time, the Mosaic browser was still in use and it moved at snail speed. Jack was afraid of using it because computers were expensive in China and he was afraid it might break, but under his friend's encouragement, he tried it. The first thing he could think to search for was beer. He got results from Germany, the USA, and Japan, but nothing from China. He tried searching for China, and still found nothing. China didn't exist on the internet. So he and his friend created a rough webpage called China. In less than three hours of creating it, they received five emails from people so excited to see a website about China that they were proposing doing business. Jack started thinking about a global market for Chinese products. This light bulb moment helped him to reach his current heights. This proved a point that is consistent with every business idea that has eventually been scaled profitably. Businesses have to fill a need that has either never been satisfied or is inadequately satisfied. Secondly, they should be tested before a full market launch to determine the specific interests of the prospective customers so that the product/service can be developed along those lines.

Struggles In Life And Business

Steve Jobs never found life to be easy. His early life was full of confusion and turmoil, and he faced a lot of difficulties and setbacks in reaching his destination. After completing high school, he was admitted to Reed College. However, the college tuition was too expensive for his parents and he didn't like to waste their money. So, he dropped out after one semester. He continued to attend a few classes as an unofficial student, but only classes he was interested in. He couldn't afford to rent a hostel room, so he slept on his friend's floor. He returned Coke bottles for money to buy food.

Then he learned Calligraphy. This helped him transform everything. When he was in India, he used to walk seven miles every Sunday to get a free meal at the Hare Krishna temple. He slept in abandoned buildings and haggled prices until he found the cheapest one. One time, he almost got mobbed because he protested after being sold watered-down buffalo milk.

Jack Ma had no interest in studying as it was difficult for him. He failed in primary school twice and middle school three times. He failed university entrance three times. He applied for 30 jobs and they all rejected him. He applied to work for KFC along with 24 other candidates and he was the only one rejected. He applied to join the police force with four other candidates and he was the only one rejected. He applied to Harvard ten times and he was rejected every time. Rejection can be an eye-opener. Rather use it as an excuse, keep your chin up and keep putting in the work because every failure is a step closer to success.

Jack Ma spent nine years learning English. He rode his bicycle for 40 minutes every day to meet tourists at the Hangzhou Hotel. He showed them around and they taught him English because there weren't any English courses in China for him to take. He now speaks English so well, some say he has a Western accent. Western tourists opened his mind to the possibilities beyond China.

Life's Driving Factor

Steve Jobs' driving factors were Calligraphy and color gaming. His goal was to get a computer in the hands of everyone. His spiritual path and innovation motivated him to not just reach his goal, but to exceed it.

Jack Ma's driving force was his dream to become a successful businessperson in uniting small-scale businesses and spreading Chinese goods to world markets.

Poverty And Its Effect

Steve's full name was Steven Paul Jobs and he was left with his adoptive parents, Clara and Paul Jobs. The financial condition of his biological parents (Abdul Fatah Jandali and Joan Caro Sible) was very poor. They didn't want their child to live an undesirable life and they decided to give Steve to a couple who could provide him with a good education and upbringing. Paul Jobs was a mechanic and Steve spent most of his time helping in his father's electrical workshop. This environment taught him to create new things.

Jack Ma was not poor but he was poor in school. He failed the entrance exams into the Hangzhou Teachers College twice before he finally was admitted. He graduated in 1988 and stayed to teach for a few more years. His parents were traditional musicians and storytellers who barely made enough money to be considered middle class in China of the 60s' and 70s'. His father didn't believe in his ideas. When Jack wanted to launch internet-based businesses, his father denounced it as dangerous. The truth is, ideas like that could have gotten you jail time in China. In the process of learning English, he had a lot of pen pals who frequently returned his letters with corrections and suggestions. Rather than get disheartened, he took every correction to heart and made sure his next letter repeated none of the previous mistakes. On his first trip to America, he attempted to collect a debt that an American businessman owed a Chinese firm. Instead of paying, the man held him captive in a Malibu mansion for two days at gunpoint. He was only allowed to go after he promised the man that he would be his partner in a new business venture. The website that he and a friend created about China was redesigned and named China Pages, for promoting China-based businesses. It eventually failed, but Jack went on to raise seed funding for the venture that made his name, Alibaba.com.

The Effect Of A Mentor

Steve Jobs had at least five mentors and his first one was Robert Friedland. When Apple Inc. was in its early stages he met his second mentor, Robert Noyce. Then Bill Campbell helped guide him. Next came his spiritual mentor, Kobun Chino. His biggest mentor was Mike Markkula who became a father figure to Steve. He had many mentors throughout his life and following their ideas, guidelines, and suggestions changed his lifestyle and business tactics for sure.

Jack Ma had two prominent mentors. His biggest mentor was Ken Morley, an electrical engineer from Australia. Ken was one of the tourists that Jack interacted with back in China. They bonded so well that five years later Ken brought Jack to Australia for his first overseas trip where he spent more than a month in Newcastle. Ken helped Jack in many ways. His teachings helped guide Jack through his business. Ken even trained him to improve his English. Because of this, Jack flew to America for his next job. Ken tutored him through letters, then he tutored him through email. The tutoring helped Jack learn about the United States and it helped him converse with native English speakers.

Jack's second mentor was a tourist who came to the Hangzhou hotel and later became pen-pals with Jack Ma. This person gave him the name of Jack Ma. Jack's birth name was Ma Yun. But the tourist (a woman) complained that it was too hard to pronounce and decided to give him the name Jack.

The stories of these men are a testimony to what people can achieve when they allow their imagination to be fully unleashed.

"A true sign of intelligence is not knowledge but imagination"

-Albert Einstein

How A Trip On A Bus Turned Into Dropbox

When Drew Houston's father gifted him his first computer, he had no clue he was inspiring an incredible journey. Drew Houston started coding at five years old and eventually, he created a file storage solution. Dropbox started as a quick fix in a cramped office with a co-founder, and now it's a million-dollar company that went public in early 2018.

The remarkable rise of the MIT graduate can teach us profound lessons. Interestingly, the story of Dropbox is built around personal frustration. Drew was chasing his dreams and kept the bulk of his work on a thumb drive. On a bus trip from Boston to New York, he discovered that he forgot his thumb drive. He felt powerless and wanted the ability to work from anywhere so he created the first bits of code for Dropbox.

Dropbox

Described on its website as a modern workspace designed to reduce busywork, Dropbox has lived up to its promise to bring your files together in one central place, synced across all devices, and accessible from anywhere.

Early Beginnings

Born with an innovative streak, Dropbox was not Houston's first crack at creating a tech solution. His first was SAT prep, designed to help with preparations for SAT, but it was rejected by Y Combinator. Ironically, it's Y Combinator took interest in Dropbox two years later.

Finding Arash

When Y Combinator saw Drew Houston's demo video demonstrating the capabilities and functions of Dropbox, it sparked an interest but he had only one request - he wanted Drew to find a co-founder within two weeks if they were going to move forward.

This request led to a meeting between Drew Houston and Arash Ferdowsi, a man who dropped out of college with only months left until graduation to pursue Dropbox with Houston.

What looked like a shaky marriage of convenience at first has turned into a profitable partnership. In 2008, Dropbox launched publicly with initial funding from Sequoia.

Mentors And Buyers

The success of Dropbox attracted admirers and people who wanted to acquire it as an investment. Steve Jobs was one of the latter, granting the Dropbox team a meeting. He admired the product and showed interest in buying it. Houston told him that they were enjoying the building process at Dropbox and we're not looking to sell. In what was perhaps a thinly veiled threat, Jobs reminded them of Apple's domination and entry into cloud storage space.

Drew Houston considers Mark Zuckerberg a mentor after Mark sent Drew a Facebook message in 2009. Drew was concerned that it was because of the influx of Facebook alumni to Dropbox, but he was relieved to find out that it was a friendly invitation to visit which morphed into a friendship.

The Drew Houston Playbook

Drew Houston's story is not only a lesson in dedication but one in constant self-development. Thrust into the limelight early, he read constantly, taking in as much knowledge as he could find about business, leadership, and strategy.

For young innovators who find themselves in the driving seat, his advice is simple, "Whether it's just the fundamentals of business or things like public speaking or being more inspiring or being a better leader, these are all things you can get better at with practice. You should set your sights high in terms of what you aspire to do, but you also have to be patient. It's like playing an instrument. You're not going to be great as a public speaker, or you're not going to improve a lot in five days, but in five years, you might be really surprised at how much you can improve."

He continues, "No one is a born CEO, this is an acquired skill set and furthermore it's one that you learn on the job, So everyone is a first time CEO by definition at some point."

Let Your Ideas Marinate

Just how good meat involves marinating overnight, good ideas should marinate overnight too. Go to sleep thinking about how to solve a problem. When you wake up, your mind might deliver a solution through a dream. The more you think about something, whether you're awake or asleep, the more it becomes real. Your mind wants to accommodate a solution for you. Guard comes into your mind prior to sleep. If you really want to solve a problem, keep a journal by your bed and write down five ways to accomplish your idea every night. Using social media before bedtime is a recipe for disorganized thoughts that will keep you awake and unfocused.

Furthermore, wake up slowly and think about one thing before you get out of bed. It feels good to lay in bed a little longer and you are already assigning your mind to a task.

Take A Bath

Run your water, add your lavender bath salts, light your candles and breathe in the steamy air. Turn off the lights and play some subtle mood music. Playing music in the background can relax you and help you think. Whether it's pop, Jazz, or Symphony it does not matter. The point is, you want to get your mind thinking about solutions. When the mood is right, you can transport your mind to another world that's disconnected from reality.

Prior to your bath, kick start your mind by thinking about solving a challenge you are facing. When you enter your bath your mind will be primed. Close your eyes, relax, and think of a single challenge.

Phone Amnesia

People touch their phones an average of 2,000 times a day according to an article by Business Insider. Everyone around you is tethered to a digital leash. It is almost like a plague has taken over. We see people huddled around and half the group is glued to devices. They don't talk to each other, they just scroll, giggle, and say 'check this out'. While we are present among each other we are becoming more disconnected.

Ever have a slow phone moment where you clicked on an app and your phone forced you to sit there and wait? All of the sudden it feels like a hostage situation where your eyes glaze over, your mouth is stuck open and life has stopped as you know it?It's a bit strange that we have become so dependent on our phones.

The Pain of Scrolling

If you open an app on your phone you lose an average of five to ten minutes of focus time.

While writing this book I found myself reaching for my phone clicking around aimlessly, then going back to my writing. As I experienced this digital illness I noticed that working near my phone was a bad idea. To resolve this I started to leave my phone charging in other parts of the house so it couldn't distract me. As I became more focused and determined, I noticed my body started giving me warnings that I should not be scrolling. I started getting back pains after scrolling for more than four minutes. I experienced the same thing when I logged on to LinkedIn, CNN, the Huffington Post, and many other websites. What was happening to me? A case study by WebMD suggests your body's sympathetic nervous system triggers the fight-or-flight response. I know you must be thinking fight or flight right? Well the only way I was going to Live Free was by putting down my phone and applying the 4 scroll rule. These sites are designed like gambling casinos which keep you distracted with endless content that never stops appearing. I was linking app scrolling to a pain. It was kind of weird at first, but after a while, I got used to the unproductive alarms my body was sending me. I realized that I should not be wasting my time on these distractions and I had to figure out a way to kick the habit. The more particular I got with my time management, the better I felt.

Flip Phone Throwback

One time in a UC Berkeley café, an instructor with a flip phone sat next to me. The device seemed a century old. I asked the instructor about it and I thought it was a great hack to unplug from society. Our conversation about her phone was simple and she mentioned the following points:

- There is no way for the corporate giants to track you digitally
- There are no apps
- The device was simple and functional

On the flip side, your high tech smartphone is filled with sensors tracking your every move. If you have linked your phone to a Google or Facebook account beware. TechCrunch reports that some free apps can be used to gather intelligence on your offline habits which can be sold to advertisers.

Yoga for the Mind

Imagine how inefficient your day would be if you had to get in the car and drive somewhere every time you switched focus. We know better than to go randomly from place to place in our car because we have to pay for fuel, we use up our time, we have to stay awake, and we have to think about the best way to get around. Putting a cost on every activity and asking ourselves if we should be doing it can help us see our patterns. Your productivity depends on what kind of fuel you put in your engine. Fill your tank with the good stuff. Applying a consistent rhythm can get us into the groove, just as certain cars can outperform others.

Imagine setting a timer for every website, mobile app, and email inbox and all the distractions you face throughout the day. It's like you are running a faucet of time where your time is spilling everywhere causing a huge, unfocused mess.

A habit left unattended will continue to control your every move and thought, hijacking your productivity.

Processing non-important information can look like the following:

- Mobile App usage during your passenger commute - 5 days for 1 hr = 5hrs
- Mobile app usage during your work breaks - 5 days for 30min = 2.5hrs
- Reading insignificant emails and articles - 5 days for 2 hrs = 10hrs

Non-important media consumption = 17.5 hrs

Your time is like water, don't waste it.

Less Drinking More Productivity

It's time to talk about alcohol. It's very common and almost everyone on the planet has partaken at least once in their lifetime. Recent research has shown that drinking problems do not just affect chronic alcoholics as more people are underestimating its side effects. This is because we are so used to drinking liquor, we misjudge the impact of such behaviors on our health, wellbeing, relationship, and finance.

Anthony Hopkins has graced the silver screen for more than six decades and he's starred in more than 80 movies. He is known as one of the world's oldest living legends and he won a 1992 Academy award for best actor for his role in *The Silence of the Lambs*. He was nominated for and won countless awards, he also survived alcoholism and he uses his story to help others.

Anthony was a chronic alcoholic to the point where he almost lost everything. On the morning of December 29th, 1975, Anthony acknowledged his problem. Luckily for him, it was not too late. He made up his mind that he was no longer going to be drunk on set. He joined Alcoholics Anonymous and he's remained sober to this day.

Feeling terrible

After his recovery, Anthony said, "I was just tired of feeling bad all the time."

The irrational behavior and the consequences of your bad decisions will come back to haunt you once the intoxication is over. Doctors from the University of Cincinnati have shown that drinking can cause mental health problems that can last for weeks after intoxication. The famous artist Vincent Van Gogh was right when he said, "Alcohol is the greatest source of madness."

"Drunkenness is nothing but voluntary madness."

-Seneca

Better Sleep

Alcohol might help you fall asleep faster, but it alters your natural sleep pattern. Even though you are asleep, the alcohol in your system sends a different message to your brain which denies you a deep night's rest.

Staying in shape becomes much easier

Drinking sabotages our fitness in three ways:

- Alcohol is empty calories that add up to your daily limit. A margarita contains anywhere from 300 - 400 calories. It is not uncommon to hear about people who gave up drinking and lost weight.
- Research shows that alcohol in your body makes it difficult for you to build muscles.
- A study published by the American Psychology Association (APA) suggests that alcohol makes it difficult for us to control how much we eat. Thereby, people who drink before eating consume more than those who do not.

Improve Your Relationships

Drinking alcohol has become a common social activity in the modern world. Some of us started drinking in high school and have never had a social life that does not involve some shots to start the night.

Although Anthony was a lonely drinker, alcohol still affected his relationships. His second wife walked out on him and he almost lost his acting career. Drinking has a direct impact on the lives of those you love - your partner, your children, or maybe your parents. Destructive behavior, the inability to keep a job or make a good decision means that someone will suffer for your actions. This takes a toll on your loved ones' wellbeing and they may have no choice but to distance themselves from you.

One reason some people fear quitting alcohol is they fear losing their social circle. Be confident in yourself. If you lose your circle, you'll meet new people and move on from your past. If your friends only like you because you drink, then quitting will be a step in the right direction. Find people who value you as more than a drinking buddy.

You are valuable, don't hide from who you are. You can decide to move out of your comfort zone as Anthony Hopkins did.

Solitude and Working From the Woods

As I got older I surrounded myself with hundreds of books and the privacy of my 4 walls which eventually turned into taking long walks in the woods with my dogs. The more that I was alone with my thoughts the more that I could think for myself. This was one reason I started going into the woods with my dogs versus the dog parks. I had noticed that my deeper thoughts would come to me mostly when I was in the privacy of the trails with my 4 legged friends.

A walk around the block is a short time frame where your mind will be constantly tracking objects or distractions. While there is always the chance of a friendly conversation with a neighbor, this distracts you from getting into that special place for deep thought. The walks in the woods are longer and healthier for you and your dog. If you want to live a little longer studies have shown that exercising 4 times a week can help with this, as mentioned in the book *Lifespan Why we age and Why We Don't Have To* by David A. Sinclair, PhD.

As my next experiment I purchased a Norco Range e-bike with pedal assist so that I can make quick escapes to the tops of my local mountains with my laptop. With a pedal assist e-bike some of the climbs can be shortened to about 30 minutes from 1.5 hours. The views at the top of the mountains in Pacifica and in Marin California are amazing. Work from the woods when you can.

"Do more of what works for you and eliminate anything that pulls you back."

-Andrewzee

Chapter 10 Matrix Learning

"The unsuccessful person is burdened by learning, and prefers to walk down familiar paths. Their distaste for learning stunts their growth and limits their influence."

-John C Maxwell

The Future Of Learning

Maybe by the year 2036, we will be able to learn a subject by simply downloading it to our brains. Peter Diamandis predicts that by the year 2045 we will multiply our intelligence a billion-fold by linking wirelessly from our neocortex to the synthetic neocortex in the cloud. As of today, we have discovered how to send images to the mind, bypassing the eyes and ears. Time limits our learning and if we can put it aside, we will have superhuman learning power.

Peter Diamandis is a Greek-American engineer and serial entrepreneur who is best known as the founder of the X Prize Foundation. Most of his entrepreneurial endeavors have involved space travel and personal spaceflight. He founded the X Prize Foundation in 1994 with the mandate of operating a $10 million incentive competition to develop passenger-carrying spaceships. It has since expanded to create incentive challenges in other sectors such as ocean exploration, life sciences, energy, environment, education, and global development. It boasts of a star-studded board of trustees, including Larry Page, Ratan Tata, Ray Kurzweil, Arianna Huffington, and of course, the man at the center of the Neuralink challenge, Elon Musk.

The Neuralink Challenge

Neuralink Corporation is the newest start-up from Elon Musk. Elon's goal is to make the learning process similar to what we saw in *The Matrix*. At Neuralink they're developing 'ultra-high bandwidth brain-machine interfaces to connect humans with computers', according to their website. Their goal is to enable humans to compete with artificial intelligence by equipping us with improved levels of cognition. Musk has repeatedly warned us about the risks of AI and the possibility that if we continue to mindlessly develop, we might end up creating something beyond our capacity to control.

In a 2015 article published in the journal *Nature Nanotechnology,* Harvard researcher Charles Lieber who co-authored the paper said the company sought to blur the distinction between electronic and neural circuits. Antonio Regalado with the MIT Technology Review doesn't see this happening, not even within the 10-year timeline proposed by Elon Musk.

In a Neuralink presentation, Elon Musk and several engineers talked about how their solution will establish a connection with artificial intelligence with a set of wires thinner than a strand of hair. Once successfully developed, the brain implant will be introduced to humans through neurosurgery performed by a robot.

Before testing will be allowed on humans, it will start with rats and monkeys in a series of experiments which probably take years. To support his argument, Elon mentioned NeuraPace, a company founded in 1997 that sought to develop brain implants that would control epileptic seizures by sensing seizures before they start and zapping the brain to prevent them. It took sixteen years for the device to be approved.

Neuralink could start testing in 2021, a lot sooner than the original ten-year timeline, but it'll be a while before their work sees the light of day.

There's also a dark side to all of this that we should be wary about. If a private company is going to develop brain implants that give you access to a wide array of information and knowledge, shouldn't we be wary of the potential privacy violations? Isn't there a chance they might be able to read our thoughts? Isn't it possible that they will filter the information we can access, limiting the things we know? When more companies start producing brain implants, are we going to turn ourselves into products or puppets of competing brain implant producers?

Is Anyone Else Trying To Do This?

Facebook is involved in developing technology that connects the human brain to the internet. Regina Dugan, former DARPA (Defence Advanced Research Projects Agency) boss and current head of Facebook's R&D, announced in 2017 that in two years they would develop a skullcap with the ability to transmit sentences from the brain at the rate of 100 words per minute.

Unlike the Neuralink approach, Facebook won't be using invasive brain surgery. Rather, the skullcap will be designed to scan your brain, using optical imaging technology at the rate of 100 times per second. The skullcap is expected to be able to translate your thoughts to text.

A startup called Fountech.ai is also primed to develop brain implants that make it possible to learn everything without having to memorize anything. According to Nikolas Kairinos, its Founder/CEO and top AI expert, once the implant is launched, you won't need to spend time learning languages. You'll just think about what you want to say, the brain implant will supply information, and you'll be able to speak in other languages effortlessly.

Human-Computer Hybrids

Some predict that in the next twenty or thirty years, AI will supersede humans in intellectual capacity. When that happens, people like Elon Musk say we could become robot pets. Our intelligence compared to theirs would be like comparing a human to a domestic cat. If we want to remain relevant, compete, and continue running the show, we need to become like AI.

Technology similar to what Neuralink is developing will be the ace up our sleeve in the Man vs. Machine conflict. AI needs to be trained with data before it can be introduced into the market, then it continues learning with default access to the internet. Our brains are already attuned to learning. If we had access to a larger bank of knowledge that could be immediately utilized, we'd have an edge over AI. We may not be tireless robots, but human intelligence is remarkably broad.

DARPA And Neuralink

One of the biggest supporters of Neuralink is DARPA. This is not the first time they have supported similar initiatives. Since the beginning of AI, DARPA has funded and conducted research that helped develop several by-products like the internet, GPS, and self-driving cars. In September 2018, they announced a new investment round of $2 billion for new and existing projects in next-generation AI. Linking humans and computers falls right under this scope. The scientists behind Neuralink were awarded a $2.1 million grant from DARPA to test the project on rats.

How Will Neuralink Change The Face Of Learning?

The sector that will be disrupted the most when Neuralink technologies and its competitors become widely available is education. With this neurochip, the capacity of the average human memory would be amplified by 100%.

People would be able to read and comprehend more books in a shorter amount of time and they wouldn't forget anything; like a real-life Kyle from the series *Kyle XY* who had a photographic memory and could read an entire encyclopedia in seconds or the character Mike Ross from the series *Suits*. He could read large volumes of documents, and he would remember every single detail.

This technology would change the face of distribution. Whenever new books, movies, and music comes out, people would no longer have to wait to read, watch, or listen. After paying or doing whatever is required to obtain access, they would download the material to their virtual cloud storage and read or replay in their mind as much as they want.

To access the N1 (the Neuralink chip) power, users will download an app to their smartphone that connects to the chip via Bluetooth. Through the app, they will control what the chip does and its interaction with the world. In the advancement of this technology, we may see a future where users will be able to transmit knowledge straight from their smartphones to their brains.

If this technology comes to fruition, it should be able to work in a two-way fashion where information will be transmitted from the brain to the phone; however, it would probably require modifications to properly read the information passing through synapses. Imagine taking the images from your mind and putting them into a tangible form. Sharing ideas would be much easier. All you would have to do is transmit your thought to your phone and send it. The receiver would then upload your thoughts to their brains and they would literally see things the way you do.

Imagine how many years of learning could be compressed with this. Teachers across all levels of education have expressed frustration about how difficult it is to get students to understand important concepts, especially in classes composed of students at different levels with different types of cognitive intelligence.

With this technology, a teacher would only need to transmit relevant modules to a phone or a central database designed for learning environments. Students would connect to this database and 'download' the knowledge straight to their minds.

The potential of Neuralink's technology is virtually limited to what we can imagine.

The Brain And Muse

Muse is a device that helps you practice mindful meditation. Using a pair of EEG-enabled headbands, it can read your brain activity and produce corresponding sounds of weather and nature to help you stay focused and easily separate yourself from what is happening around you. Roughly speaking, when it reads a calm mind, it simulates peaceful weather. When the mind is busy, it simulates stormy weather.

It works using seven EEG sensors spread across the headband at five points - three of these points are positioned in front of the forehead and the other two go behind each ear. This device leverages EEG technology used in hospitals to detect brain disorders such as epilepsy, Alzheimer's disease, and sleep disorders.

Unlike Neuralink, Muse works with technology that is already widely available and used.

Downsides To Be Wary Of

Everything so far sounds very cool, doesn't it? That doesn't mean we should jump in heedlessly without exercising caution.

The first sector that will be challenged by this technology will be education. It will become virtually impossible for closed-book examinations to be conducted. Students will have access to the books in their memories and only have to 'open' it and mentally flip to the pages that have the answers question. Everyone would get straight A's but it would create a major crisis in teaching methods.

Another downside is it might cause the biological brain to degenerate as it is used less often. In a post-Neuralink world, people would depend on their implants and virtual memories, rather than exercising and training natural learning and memory. If this happens, our brains would gradually regress. The brain is more than just a CPU for the body. It controls other bodily functions like the nervous system, circulation, and much more. Any adverse condition in the brain would affect these functions. As such, in our bid to compete with robots, we might be sowing the seeds for our potential extinction.

As the scenes from the movies come to life, will you step to the front of the line for Neuralink and take a chance at becoming a hybrid superhuman learner? What advantage will you have that will separate you from the puppeteer's controlled by the corporations?

Until we can take a pill and learn a subject we need to be very creative with how we learn and how fast we can learn. Done right, you could theoretically obtain a four-year degree listening to audio content on your way to work. Leverage your time while performing other activities. This is where podcasts and audiobooks come into the mix. What took the author one or more years to create you can now absorb in a few sittings.

A CEO needs to read over forty books a year and implement new tactics while eliminating old ways that no longer work. If you learn just one tactic from a book you have spent some good money.

You might be thinking, "I am not a CEO", but you're wrong, you are the CEO of your life. Your past and future decisions determine your future. If you don't like where you are heading, change is the only thing that can impact you. If for every book we read we can implement a tactic to help us or our business, we will move the ball closer to the end zone. Only by hyper-focusing your mind can you start to see your potential. *Business Insider* mentioned that Warren Buffet reads five to six hours a day while Mark Cuban reads around two hours a day.

"I still believe that sitting down and reading a book is the best way to really learn something."

-Eric Schmidt, Google

Matrix Learning: How to Absorb Knowledge Like a Machine

Turn a boring task into something interesting and educational. Use that time to read or listen to an audiobook or podcast. With podcasts and audiobooks, you can learn while you cook, clean, exercise, commute, eat, or relax. Here are some auditory learning tips I've figured out along the way:

- Set your program to different speeds to better fit the task you are trying to accomplish.
- Use a waterproof case when relaxing in the bath, pool, or hot tub. Better yet, use a Bluetooth speaker or earbuds.

- Actively think about how you can use the knowledge obtained.
- Use a bookmark feature if your application allows and make a detailed, one-line description. Later on, review the sections you bookmarked. Remember, if you do not schedule this review time it will be overlooked.
- Reflect on what you learned at the end of your activity. Write down two or three steps you can take using the knowledge you've gained.
- Combine multiple ideas with what-if scenarios.

AutoPilot Jobs

Do you have a job where your work is repetitive or you have a lot of downtime? Take advantage and listen to something educational or take an online training course like LinkedIN learning at $29 all you can learn for a month.

You can also check out these sites which offer online training:

- Udemy
- Khan Academy
- Skillshare
- PluralSight

With YouTube and Ted Talks you can dial your learning into whatever niche you desire. You can absorb roughly 90% of a video's content by just listening to the audio portion. If the topic you're learning about is more visual, try viewing the presentation on a second monitor. If you are viewing content on a second monitor it helps to keep the topic aligned with what you're doing on the primary monitor. Furthermore writing down what you want to accomplish can help you remember what you were doing should your mind begin to wander. If you try to overdo it you will get frustrated. When I forget my paper notebook I write down my top two tasks in a folder in OneNote called "What am I working on".

Focus your learning on a small area vs going wide which can help you reap the benefits of freedom sooner. If you are stuck, you know your habits best on what should be cut off.

Learning On Auto-Pilot

If you have a repetitive job, try listening to an audiobook, podcast, or a video at a slower speed, but don't listen to a generic talk show for background noise. Intend to learn something new and use that knowledge for new opportunities.

If you commute to work in a carpool or you use public transportation you can work on your main project. If you have a seat, you can read, work in a notebook, or work on a laptop or iPad. If you can't find a seat, listen to something educational.

You can also listen to something educational during lunch, or you could simply think about your project and how to overcome challenges. Bedtime is another great time to think about your project and challenges.

Tips for gathering information:

- Listen to podcasts with 40 or more episodes. You want to listen to someone who is dedicated.
- Focus your listening on a single subject.

- Download episodes so you can listen offline or when you are out of service range.
- When choosing a book from Amazon, look for a minimum of 300 legitimate reviews. Also, take advantage of the free previews! Look for topics that have not been covered in your previous readings.

Avoid the following:

- Listening when you are doing work that requires your undivided attention.
- Studying multiple topics at the same time.

Target your listening to a certain topic for the week or month. When I get a new audiobook I like to take a long drive or bike ride. It's a mind cleansing opportunity that will rid you of distractions. The more you avoid distractions, the better you will retain information. Pause your listening when you have accumulated a couple of ideas. This will give your brain the chance to think about how to use the content. At the end of your journey remember to document the key lessons you learned.

As you listen to podcasts pay attention to other podcasts or books that are mentioned. These titles can pull you deeper into the rabbit hole of knowledge. Also, as you read, keep an eye out for other books and authors mentioned.

Retain What You Have Learned

One of the best ways to retain what you've learned is to review and put it to practical use. Get in the habit of taking notes for each book you read or listen to, and podcast you listen to too. Make lists of what you've read or listened to and do a quarterly review then decide what you should re-visit.

Creating a re-visit list allows you to visit the important lessons down the road. More importantly, you can use it as an opportunity to reflect on how you've been able to put the lessons to use. It's a way for you to gain new insight that you may have missed the first time around.

Be meticulous in your studies. Document page numbers and timestamps when you take notes. Remember, books and podcasts are filled with pearls of wisdom just waiting to be uncovered. Use the knowledge you gain, otherwise, those pearls will turn into nuts.

Take notes in a single location like a notebook or application like OneNote or Evernote.

. The fewer mediums you use the more focused you will be.

Here are some tactics for organizing your notes:

- Put the newest information at the top.
- Group notes by topic.
- Group notes by podcast or book.
- Identify the minute markers in your notes. For example Nurse education @ 2 minutes 30 seconds episode 24

Review your notes in reverse order. You will be surprised at what you wrote out a few months to a year ago.

To effectively retain the knowledge you must also follow through with reading, listening, and learning goals. Jumping from one thing to the next may give you a glimpse of important lessons, but you won't see the entire picture. Keep in mind that if your execution is random you won't create traction. Disciplining yourself to embrace learning and retention will enable you to make better decisions and get more out of life.

"You can't depend on your eyes when your imagination is out of focus."

-Mark Twain

Chapter 11 Don't Worry Be Happy

"Too much work and no play does not allow the mind to reset itself."

-Andrewzee

Becoming Fluffy

'Oh, I'm Not Fat, Just Fluffy'

Gabriel Jesus Iglesias, commonly known as 'Fluffy', is a stand-up comedian, actor, producer and voice actor. The obstacles he faced as a child, such as his size, trigger his sense of humor such that he always and he sought out stages to share his unique brand of comedy. His comedy is a combination of storytelling, parodies, playing multiple characters, and sound effects, resulting in a sonorous blend that makes the Fluffy we all love.

His break in comedy is an interesting story. He used to work for a cell phone company but he resigned in 1997 to go into full-time comedy. Because of this decision, he lost his home and car. In 2006 he was a contestant on the fourth season of the reality TV show *Last Comic Standing.* He made it into the top 8 and then he was kicked off the show for having a cell phone, which was against the show's rules.

Later on in his career, he was diagnosed with type 2 diabetes, weighing over 445 pounds with his blood sugar spiking above 300. Doctors gave him just two years to live. With his loved ones in mind, he reassessed his life. He started by cutting back on his comedy engagements and he adopted a healthier lifestyle that involved yoga, a high-protein low carbohydrate diet, and he took up physical exercise, especially weight-lifting. He lost over 100 pounds and outlived the predictions of medical science.

Back in his high school days, it was clear that he was headed for the stage. He frequently acted on the street in front of the school. Apart from acting and making jokes, he loved sports, especially football. In an interview with *Timeout*, he listed his favorite comedians and said how they influenced him.

- Eddie Murphy - "He has a special place in my comedy story. Seeing 'Raw' as a kid was a big inspiration for me to do stand-up comedy."
- Robin Williams - "An all-round legend and one of the funniest and kindest men in comedy. I had a chance to share a stage with him and he was always spontaneous and so animated."
- Paul Rodriguez - "A mentor who paved the way for Hispanic comedians. Even offstage this guy is silly and fun to be around."
- Billy Crystal - "Billy's produced legendary characters and he's naturally funny. He's one of my comedy heroes. I geeked out when I got to meet him…"
- Sam Kinison
- George Carlin - "Ground-breaking and boundary-pushing comedy. His HBO specials were game-changers."
- Bill Cosby - "He is very much a storyteller and I would listen to his albums when I was a kid."
- Chris Rock
- Jeff Dunham
- Russell Peters - "I thank Russell for inspiring me to perform in other countries since I never wanted to leave home."

His life story is a testimony to the power of consistency. Despite everything that life threw at him, he kept coming back like a cat keen on the mice. Eventually, his consistent investments paid off.

So, what motivates him? It's not a fancy concept or deep philosophy. He simply does it. Waiting for a good feeling will get you nowhere. In a response to a Twitter follower who asked for motivation to start working on a paper, he wrote 'GET OFF UR ASS AND WRITE THAT PAPER'.

In an interview with *Maxim*, he stated that he maximized the three days he spent with his family and didn't work at all. He said, "Everybody can relate to relationships, so I'm always talking about the situation that's at home, and then the balance of life with me trying to be an entertainer, and trying to be a dad at the same time."

Contrary to belief, his home is not full of cakes and cookies, but he has created a lot of jokes about his love for food. His series *Fluffy's Food Adventures* follows him from place to place as he savors unique.

Apart from season four of *Last Comic Standing*, he appeared on *All That* and *Comedy Central Presents*. These shows gave him a platform to hone his art but he needed content to create jokes. From his size and appearance, he coined the stage name 'The Fluffy Man'. He once said, "I'm all about showing people that I'm a little messed up, I have a lot of the same problems you have. By exposing myself and putting myself out there, people can relate to me and my act won't grow stale. I mean, nobody wants to hear a comedian say, 'Life is great'."

People like Gabriel Iglesias keep us healthy with the laughter they induce. Laughter has been shown to strengthen immune systems, improve moods, and protect against the damaging effects of stress. When we laugh endorphins are released. Endorphins promote an overall sense of well-being and can temporarily relieve pain. According to the *Red Catfish* YouTube channel, the benefits of laughing are as follows:

- It reduces stress, by increasing the production of the hormone known as cortisol, leaving you with a relaxed feeling.
- It's a form of exercise as it provides a full-scale workout of the muscles and stimulates blood circulation.
- Laughter protects the heart. In fact, those who laugh more have a lower risk of getting high blood pressure. This is because each time we laugh, it increases blood pressure temporarily, then pushes it down to levels below normal. 15 minutes of laughter every day is as good as 30 minutes of exercise 3 times a week for the heart.
- Laughter boosts the immune system by reducing stress hormones and increasing the production of anti-infection antibodies in the body.
- Laughter also relieves pain; 15 minutes of laughter can increase pain tolerance by around 10% as a result of the release of endorphins to the brain.

Gabriel's wide acceptability is a result of his ability to avoid controversy and sensitive topics. He once said, "I learned early on, stay away from politics, stay away from religion and don't talk about sports. Those three right there will get you in trouble."

His live and let live philosophy of success is one worthy of emulation. To this effect, he once said, "...you cannot be on top forever. There's always going to be the next guy, and if I'm going to go down, I'd like to know I helped the next guy take my spot. You can't prevent the inevitable, but you can join the ship."

Life will throw us many lemons, but it also equips with the supplies to turn those lemons into lemonade. If we don't carry the right attitude, we'll lose the supplies in life's challenges.

"I usually travel with a posse. I roll deep. I travel like a rapper, but without the artillery. We don't carry guns, we carry cookies."

-Gabriel Iglesias

A Pug's Life

There was a time when I worked a job that required an hour and half commute each way. Waking up every morning knowing I had to get into my car became a feeling of regret. Subsequently, I gained weight and I did not feel good about myself. I was on the road from 8:30 am to 10:00 am, then from 6:30 pm to 8:00 pm. I had no time for exercise or my family.

I found myself sitting in my car and at my desk for over 11 hours a day. If this contract lasted a year I would wind up sitting in traffic for around 700 hours or about 16% of my life for the year.

At the end of my horrendous commute home I would find my wife helping my daughter Sophia with her homework. While my life kept repeating itself for a few months it felt as if I was a character on the series *Walking Dead*. When I got home I had dinner, watched TV, and went to bed. My pattern outside of the house was:

- Wake up
- Drive to work 1 hour and 30 minutes
- Meet with team
- Write requirements
- Have Lunch
- Attend more meetings
- Drive home

- Repeat

I have to say, this is as close to a lifestyle flat line as you can get. The best part of the week was the weekend and spending time with the family. The more I thought about this the more I started asking questions of myself like:

- My family is growing without me.
- How healthy is my lifestyle?
- How much time have I really spent thinking about what I want?

While I was away at work, my wife and my daughter started to have conversations about getting a dog. My daughter wanted a small dog that could sleep in her room and she could be responsible for so we decided to get a pug.

After a few weeks I came home one evening and what greeted me at the top of the stairs was our brand new pug. He had come from a Marine that was going back into the service and wanted a better life for the pug. This little dog started barking up a storm trying to appear larger than his bark as I walked up the stairs. In a few minutes I armed myself with a treat from my Rottweiler's snack jar. Next I continued towards the pug as he barked with all his might. Without fail he could smell the treat that I had in my hand as I approached him. After feeding the pug the second treat he was much more receptive to me getting closer to him.

A Healthy Pug Equals A Healthy Owner

Our pug impacted my health. The axiom now is, "I work hard so that my pug can have a good life." The healthier my pug became, the healthier I became. I never imagined that adding a small dog to our family could have such an impact. As the dog walks increased, so did the time I spent with my daughter.

I make a big deal about my pug's active lifestyle. Pugs are normally chubby; furthermore, these dogs usually only get out of the house for 15 to 20 minutes at a time. I never take my pug to general dog walking zones with other dog walkers. I prefer to let my little beast run off-leash and it helps me avoid distracting conversations with other dog owners.

Go into the wilderness and become one with nature. It removes you from the big city attachments and it recharges your battery.

Have Your Dog Take You Out

Walking my pug changed the way I perceive anxiety, anger, and love. I became grounded. Dog walks can help people who are struggling to cope with everyday challenges. When your dog is happy and healthy, you are too. The simple act of caring for and interacting with a pet can make all the difference.

My favorite dog walks are hiking up semi-steep hills with 5 pound ankle weights that allow me to use more energy in a shorter time frame. Exercising for 20 minutes or longer facilitates information processing and memory functions. Switching from sitting in traffic to exercising generates more oxygen and helps clear your thoughts.

I try to walk my pug for 30 to 60 minutes at least every other day. Exercise has made my pug healthy and muscular. He's now closer in size to a small pit bull than other pugs. When people see him at the top of mountain peaks they're always surprised to see that a pug can make it up here. When people ask how is this possible I say people go to the gym to get bigger, what's the difference? If a pug can change so can you.

Can You Multitask?

We are not computers, we are biological beings. Somehow CEOs, managers, and executives forget this when delegating tasks to employees. In the modern workplace, heavy multitaskers are still seen as superheroes even though research has continually proven this to be wrong.

In 2009, scientists at Stanford University set out to prove that multitaskers are better than everyone else, but the experiment failed miserably. The final outcome of the study showed that the heavy multitaskers were unable to focus, were less likely to remember, and it took them more time to complete simple, everyday jobs. Not only were the multitaskers distracted, but they were not able to tell the difference between relevant and irrelevant information.

Another study showed that children who multitasked before a test had lower grades. Even worse, the kids who sat behind the multitaskers were also distracted which resulted in lower test scores for them too.

Evidence from similar studies proves that in the long run, multitasking can damage your brain. However, you don't need to wait years to see the consequences of multitasking because it is a common problem that is evident in our daily lives - it's called stress.

Americans have some of the highest stress levels in the world. Stress does not just make you feel unhappy and tired, it's far more damaging. Our stress response system has not adapted to our modern world. During the ancestral era, stress responses happened when danger was present. Today, our stress response system is activated when we try to accomplish several things at once.

Scientists proved that multitasking does not increase your productivity. It's ironic because people multitask to increase their output but the exact opposite happens. According to the *New Yorker*, only 2% of the population is known to actually be able to successfully multitask.

Other negative effects of multitasking are:

- Headaches
- Insomnia
- Road accidents
- Depression

Multitasking has serious, long-term consequences on our wellbeing.

Throughout history, people have shown and cherished the power of focus, like Lord Chesterfield who warned his son against multitasking in a famous letter. He wrote, 'There is time enough for everything in the course of the day if you do but one thing at once, but there is not time enough in the year if you will do two things at a time.'

Staying focused and working on one task at a time has amazing health benefits like:

- Healthier brain patterns
- Very clear objectives
- Better Listening patterns
- Real productivity
- Building relationships

If you want a healthier brain try going for a walk or skipping junk food and making healthier choices.

Eating the wrong types of food can drain our energy and slow us down. Eating healthier foods energizes you.

You could also listen to calming music to relax your nerves which will help you focus even more. You can manage yourself better and accomplish your goals without multitasking.

Dr. Yuval Noah Harari mentions the following in his research on human happiness: "We are far more powerful than our ancestors, but are we much happier? It doesn't seem so. Compared to what most people in history dreamt about, we may be living in paradise. But for some reason, we don't feel the part."

A Nap Does the Body Good

Treat your body like a cell phone and pay attention to your charge. Have you ever noticed how your phone charges faster in airplane mode? This happens because the power-sucking apps are turned off. If it usually takes three hours to charge, using airplane mode can cut that time down to forty minutes.

Now try putting your body in airplane mode and reap the benefits of a faster recharge. Start by taking a nap after lunch, this is a good time for a break because your mind already wants to rest as your body goes into overdrive to process food. Google and other companies understand the benefits of napping and brought in nesting pods where employees can schedule naps throughout the day.

If you recharge your mind your body will give you a few extra hours of power to get through the day. In order to fully recharge you need a clear mind. You have to shut off your thoughts or think about a blank wall.

Experiment with short naps. Twenty minutes of napping is my afternoon favorite. When you wake up your mind will feel powerful and refreshed. Listen to your body and squeeze in my naps when you can.

The Napmobile:

- Park your vehicle in a shady spot.
- Park at the back of the lot, it's quieter. Also, the farther you park the more you exercise you get.
- Keep a set of earplugs handy to help eliminate the noise around you.
- Keep a thin dark beanie handy and dark sunglasses to cover your eyes to help eliminate the light.
- Keep a sunshade in your car to keep cool.
- Keep a blanket handy in your car for chilly days or extra comfort. If your blanket is the same color as your interior you can use it to cover your valuables when you park.

If you're still wondering if napping is a worthwhile endeavor you should know that John F. Kennedy, Winston Churchill, and Thomas Edison were nappers. They each carved time to nap every day.

Night Lights

One solution to a better night's sleep is installing dimmable antique bulbs in the fixtures where you spend your evening time. These bulbs give a warm, relaxing feeling atmosphere and help eliminate the blue light that interferes with our circadian rhythm - the internal clock that tells our bodies when to sleep, when to wake up, and when to eat.

An article published by Harvard Medical School goes into detail as to why your body suppresses the production and secretion of melatonin, a sleep-hormone that induces sleep.

Here are some tips to avoiding harmful night light:

- Lower your lights so your body can start getting ready for bed.

- Enable the evening filter 'Night Light' on your Windows PCs or Android phones. This feature minimizes the blue spectrum light. For MacBooks and iPhones use 'Night Shift'.

Journaling

One of the most expensive books in the world is Leonardo da Vinci's journal, *Codex Leicester*. Bill Gates purchased the 16th-century manuscript for $30.8 million.

While you may not be da Vinci, you have many things going on in your mind. Start emptying your mind of the day's thoughts with journaling. Writing down your thoughts allows you to work on complex projects while keeping your mind balanced and running at a good pace.

I like to write down my top three tasks for the day on a small yellow notepad. Crossing out completed items helps me realize that I completed something and this becomes my win for the day. Nothing beats the speed and reliability of journaling with pen and paper.

For long-term weekly entries, I use a notebook. As I take notes I leave a two-inch margin that allows me to add more details in the future. Leaving a blank line in between your notes also helps allocate space for future thoughts.

I prefer pens to pencils because the ink doesn't fade as graphite does. Using different colored inks helps me to identify the context of my notes.

- Orange ink for project management.
- Green ink for money ideas.
- Red ink for warnings.

- Black/Blue ink for regular notes.

Two great note-taking apps are Evernote and Microsoft OneNote which synchronize across multiple devices. Beware of storing your notes, documents, or images on a platform as these services may not always be around. Get in the habit of backing up your data every couple of weeks. Beware of the symptom of endless note creation. Endless notes cause you to go wide vs going deep. Use the less is more approach.

The Sun & Earthing

Earthing

We have shut ourselves out from nature by living in skyscrapers, riding around in fuel guzzling vehicles and refusing to stray from our comfortable couches. Let us step onto the grass and enjoy a little Earthing.

Earthing is simply the process of getting in contact with the earth's energy by walking barefoot. It's as simple as kicking off your shoes and strolling through the grass or sand. For years, we have known and recognized the sun for its numerous health benefits. Unknown to us, we've been standing on a goldmine.

Earthing provides a variety of benefits that can ultimately enhance the quality of life. It's so easy and it's absolutely free. All you have to do is walk barefoot on grass, sand, or dirt.

How does earthing affect your health and well-being though?

- **More Sleep**

- Earthing helps you to achieve a deeper and more peaceful rest without stress. Consistent earthing will help you to fall asleep with ease and you'll wake up refreshed and energized for the day.
- **Recovery From Physical Activity**
  - Earthing provides a simple way for you to relax your muscles, relieve tension and get rid of nagging aches.
- **Healthy Feet**
  - Earthing gives your feet a chance to stretch with continuous sessions relieving you of any strain and preventing injury.
- **Relieves Stress**
  - Earthing calms you down by reducing your blood pressure over time and it relieves muscle tension.

Sun

While a lot of people are aware that sunlight is a source of Vitamin D, there are a lot of other untapped benefits that most are in the dark about.

- **Brightens You Up**
  - Sunlight improves your mood. The science to it lies in the release of serotonin which is known as the 'happy hormone'. When you are exposed to sunlight, you ultimately become happier and have more energy as endorphins are released.
- **Clears Up Your Skin**
  - Controlled exposure to sunlight can effectively lead to smoother skin. Sunlight can help to rid your skin of acne, eczema, and psoriasis.
- **Helps Your Immune System**

- Exposure to sunlight helps to promote the production of white blood cells which results in a stronger immune system.
- **No Aches**
  - Getting some time in the sun helps ease your muscles and relieves you of stiffness.

- **Lose Weight**
  - Serotonin released by exposure to sunlight, apart from boosting happiness levels also contributes to weight loss. It suppresses your appetite, helping you to commit to your diet.
- **Healthy Sun Exposure**
  - Use a pair of dark UV protected glasses to protect your eyes.
  - Hats are a great way to help prevent sunburn.
  - Always wear sunscreen, and reapply every hour.

Next time your batteries are running low and you feel like taking a nap. Take a walk to that park bench, take off your sox and shoes, put your glasses on and sit quietly in the sunlight for 20 minutes without any thoughts going through your mind. You will awaken feeling great.

Play Time

Legos

I remember coming home from work and being greeted by my boys Ivan and Nicky. Our rottweiler Kasha was always first to meet me then my little guys rushed out of their bedroom, and they would latch onto my legs. Then I would say, "Who's up for some demolition?"

The boys and I built Lego towers as tall as our apartment's 8-foot ceilings. At the base of the towers, I would build two-inch tall barricades to protect the tower just like government builds have. When the tower was completed I would hand my boys hard hats and the remote control for a toy Dodge Durango. Then with a few swift approaches they would bulldoze the protective barriers. With the barriers eliminated the crashes into the base of the tower would cause the tall structure to begin leaning. And then finally the tower would fall. For our tower to reach a height of 8 feet I wound up buying a few Lego Duplo kits which had the beefy 4 by 2 pieces. Each single Duplo piece was the height of 3 smaller legos. So building a tower with Duplos would take around 500 pieces vs 2500 smaller pieces.

I didn't realize it at the time, but playing demolition games with my boys was an amazing experience.

The time we spent together building the tower allowed me to forget about the realities of my day job. Seeing the smiles on their faces, listening to their words, helping their little hands build a robust structure really made our day. At times I would lift them up a few feet so that they could complete the tower by placing a few bricks at the top. I enjoyed the time with them so much that it took me into baseball.

Baseball

As my boys got older I coached them in baseball from T-ball all the way into high school. We were always the first ones on the field and usually last to leave the field. I will always remember the times we spent on the field together. It's not often you have an opportunity to positively impact a child's life. Not only were we spending quality time together, but I was getting a lot of sun and plenty of exercise. The more I played with the team, the healthier I felt. Having a little play in your life can go a long way and keep you positively motivated.

Additional Activities to Reduce Stress

- **Take the stairs** - Try taking the stairs at work which will allow you to get exercise during your work day. Use the restroom on other floors. Track how many steps you take on a daily basis. If your building does not have stairs go into another building and use their stairs or hike up any hills in your area. When in San Francisco try climbing the stairs to Coit tower from Sansome street. Taking this stair path is a hidden golden nugget in San Francisco, but make sure you are in decent shape before trying.
- **Bike / Walk to Work** - Biking / walking to work will give you the cardio your mind needs before you start your workday. Try taking a different route every couple of days. The different scenery will get you thinking about different things. Jack Dorsey of Twitter walks a few miles to work everyday and considers this an investment as mentioned on the Tim Ferriss podcast. Try to think about one problem you would like to solve during your walk. The richness of your thoughts will focus your energy.
- **Mind Map** - If you start a new project and all of a sudden have 10 responsibilities try creating a mind map. Mind maps are a great way of visually organizing topics and sharing information. Try Mindmeister or Mindjet

- **Meditate -** Focus for 15 minutes a day for the next month and focus on what 1 or 2 big things you want to accomplish
- **Adult coloring books** - As you focus on coloring your stress will melt away and your mind will unwind.
- **Read** - A good book can take you out of your head and place you in a different setting.

Other Ways To Reduce Stress

- Wake up earlier
- Smile and Laugh
- Stretching
- Volunteering
- Hobbies

"What it lies in our power to do, it lies in our power not to do."

-Aristotle

Chapter 12 Conclusion

Are You Boarding the Wrong Train?

Streatham Station (Thameslink Loop London)

In London, one could take the train from Streatham in a clockwise loop or via an anticlockwise loop; and yet find themselves at the same train station year after year. This loop is not obvious when you are on the train but when you have a look at the system map you realize this.

Let's take a final journey on the train of life. The conductor yells out, "All aboard!", before closing the doors and leaving the station. A train ride for many can be a wonderful journey where we can sit back and daydream about things we would like to do someday.

"Daydreaming", is the start of how companies are made, wars are won and bridges are erected. Many great things started out as a daydream. But the reality for most of us is we are too busy working just to survive that we are deprived of our own dreams. Each of us is given a boarding pass with a limited set of punches that are used up every few years until we die. Looking forward to the weekend is not a way to live your life constantly grinding away the remaining years. When you know that deep inside there is true potential that can be unlocked. Enough dreaming.

Next thing you know, some time has passed and the conductor is coming around again. He sees you sitting in your chair. He notices a problem, he can see in your thoughts that you are stuck. He asks, "do you need a wakeup call"? You respond, "No I'm good". The conductor then mentions "is that the same suit, the same facial expression and same thoughts you had four years ago"? You think to yourself for a moment and respond "maybe". You hand the boarding pass to the conductor and he punches your pass and continues on his way. You think a little more, "Am I stuck, am I running in place from year to year"? "Is this really my reality?"

Many of your friends and family probably told you to hurry up, get that degree and get a job. But why? So that you can buy things that you cannot afford and blend in? One might think that the more you blend in the better off you are. But the truth is the opposite, the less that one thinks allows one to be enslaved and exploited like a marionette that results in a life of struggles. Unfortunately, we are driven to work harder and switch jobs for a slight pay increase and repeat for 40 years. Regardless of the profession the more we make, the more we spend. The corporations understand that they do not need chains for you to remain in bondage since a paycheck does the job. Once conditioned, a person's beliefs are the tools of servitude. For you to go to a new station you must get on another train called ACTION. With no ACTION you will be kept in the same place. There is no need to look at what you have left behind because you will be creating the future you.

Focus Your Punches

Many of us find it safer to repeat patterns instead of trying new tactics as mentioned earlier in the OODA loop. Every leader, entrepreneur, founder, CEO, have one thing in common; they started by taking one step at a time. The results of their efforts and hard work can be found in the success of their companies. Their future didn't happen by accident, if their punches were off target they would regroup and punch in a different direction. Take the time to step back, regroup and focus your punches in what truly matters to you and your family. Punch with such determination that everything else becomes a blur.

Why not try to create assets that can make you money while you sleep? This can help buy your favorite team vs buying season tickets? The first action puts money in your pocket while the second puts money in their pocket. We must think big, to achieve big! You are rewarded for your contribution to the market. If your reality is around the latest movies or gossip, the market will reward you with minimum wage. If you can solve a huge problem for society everyone that needs your solution will line up and pay you for it. If you are not solving the world's problems during your day job, it might be time to catch a train going to a different destination. Walking away from what you don't want is a commitment to a new beginning.

Coronavirus Station Transfer Point

The coronavirus pandemic has taken the whole world by storm. How can you ensure that you continue to earn an income amidst the lockdown when you cannot go out to work? Most of us are exasperated at having to stay at home without any work. Life as we knew it seems like a distant dream now. This pandemic is a wakeup call for everyone that cannot earn an income during these times.

As your train approaches the next station you hear *transfer station Wimbledon* and see it flashing on the display inside the train. This is the big sign that you have been looking for especially since the coronavirus pandemic and the move to hire contractors is now the standard with all companies. FYI many contracting opportunities do not come with benefits. The necessity to create your own income source is more important now than ever. This book has shared the WHY we need to move and HOW to make yourself more valuable during these times.

If you happen to be 45 years old, you might have 15-years left in the workforce. How will you use these remaining years to your benefit? Will enough punches remain on your boarding pass to pursue your dream? Per a survey on Yahoo Finance, 64% of all Americans will essentially retire broke. Are you financially ready for this?

If you are just getting into college this book will help you question EVERYTHING before it is too late. This is war time and to win the game you must focus on getting the right things done.

Welcome to Freedom Fighter Station
Your Last Stop

The time is 4:30 AM when you exit the train.
You walk up the wooden stairs to the mezzanine.

The scene resembles a mix between a Japanese Dojo and a WeWork. Everyone has their own pristine spacious workspace overlooking a beautiful ocean scene. You can hear the sounds of waves hitting the shoreline in the background.

You notice people are in a good mood and smiling.

In the center of the Dojo a Zen Master explains "you will need to use the waste bins over there and then go to station two so that you can begin your reinvention."

In station one you see a few waste bins overflowing with distractions of the mind, negative thoughts, regrets and a few bins for overthinking.
The bins for overthinking are stacked as high as the eye can see with thoughts. You deposit your past thoughts and move on.

Next you see a station where you are required to drop off your cell phone before you can begin work on anything. At this station you see a Zen Master providing guidance with fellow future freedom fighters.

You sit down and the Zen Master mentions, "Welcome to Freedom Fighter Station. This place is designed to help you discover your dharma, it is a way of finding your true path, a place of fulfillment and bliss. In the end you will be able to challenge your fears and become invincible."

The Zen Master continues, "your power comes from within and for you to realize this, the path ahead has been cleared for you by stripping away the non-essential.

The riches that you seek will be returned in multiples. But you must first bring value to the masses in the form of a book, an app or a business that operates on its own or similar.
For you to keep these riches they must not be tied to an employer's paycheck or your time.
Any income that is earned from trading time for money is not scalable as your time will expire."

The Zen Master then mentions "please read the instructions on the sign behind me to begin. I wish you luck on your journey."

To help you start a life of FREEDOM the following rules have been instituted for the next 30 days so that you can begin a kick-ass life-altering experience immediately.

You must write down what important one thing you want to accomplish before going to bed.
Your alarm clock will go off at 5 am.
You must put in two hours of work on your personal project before you can read email or answer any phone calls.
Internet access to social media sites is off-limits until after 10 am.
Television signals have been blocked for 30 days on all TV's in your house.
You must now start a form of exercise for 30 minutes a day so that you can take care of your body.
Facebook now closes on Weekends.
The voice of doom and gloom or any other negative self-talk will be replaced with thoughts of "You can do it".

Now pause for a few minutes and think.

If you can think it, you can create it.

Now Go Freedom Fighter

<u>Write down that one thing.</u>

<u>Go do that one thing.</u>

Ask yourself these questions:

What is my life worth?

How much are you being paid to give up your dreams?

How do you want to be remembered?

Closing

One of the guiding principles from this book is to help you build a life that you want rather than building a resume where others are making decisions for you. The path to success is a jagged one with many ups and downs. If you had never thought of starting a business my hope is that I have provided enough reasoning on why you should at least explore the idea or become double productive in what you are already doing. Your business will grow as you start to take yourself out of the equation. The day that you hire one or more employees will be a milestone in your growth towards freedom. The best piece of advice about reaching a goal is to start with the end in mind and work backwards.

If you could send 3 pieces of advice to yourself when you were 10 to 20 years younger what would that be, use the three lines below? You can also share your thoughts at www.andrewzee.com/3things

_____

_____

_____

Reminder

Read this book again in 6 months because you will have a different perspective after you have had a chance to implement the steps covered here. Part of pushing through the resistance to creativity is repeating what works for you. The purpose of this last chapter is to reinforce what you should be thinking about on a continuous basis. If we setup a proper framework it is the equivalent of building a well-built house that keeps the rain out season after season. The rain or distractions will simply flow away from you keeping you dry, secure and focused. The stronger your mindset the better you get at avoiding distractions. Before you finish this book I want you to set up a monthly reminder of things you need to do that will keep you aligned with the future you. Then I want you to print out this sheet with these reminders and place it in a location which you will see every day. Write down 3 to 4 books that you want to re - read and by when, then repeat this process every few months.

For feedback or ideas you can write me at info@andrewzee.com

The 7 Lists

Stop Doing (Most Important)

_____

_____

_____

_____

Doing

_____

_____

_____

_____

Done

_____

_____

_____

_____

Up Next

_____

_____

_____

_____

To Learn

_____

_____

_____

_____

Books to Read

_____

_____

_____

Books to Re-Read

_____

_____

_____

_____

Recommendations

Apps:

- OneNote
- Headspace
- Trello
- Asana.com
- Google Docs

Tools:

- Timer Timer
- Notebook
- Notepad

Books:

- *The Alchemist* by Paulo Coelho
- *The Hitchhiker's Guide to the Galaxy* by Douglas Adams
- *Ready Player One* by Ernest Cline
- *Sapiens* by Yuval Noah Harari
- *Zero to One* by Peter Thiel
- *The Billionaire Next Door* by Thomas J. Stanley and William D. Danko.

Stay in Touch

I want to help you take what you're currently doing to a whole new level. To get you started go find your bonus materials at www.Andrewzee.com/bookbonus

Share this book with friends and family so they can have a different perspective on how to prepare for their future. If reading this book has made an impact on your thinking I would appreciate if you can take a few minutes and leave a positive review.

If you have thoughts or comments you'd like to share with me about the book, please email me on andrew@andrewzee.com. You can also connect with me on:

Instagram: @Andrewzee1

Feel free to tag any mentions of this book with **#livefreediehardbook**.

References

Schools Mentioned

Massachusetts Institute of Technology

https://ocw.mit.edu/index.htm

Massive Open Online Courses

MOOC.org

Notes

"Stealing Fire:" How Silicon Valley, the Navy SEALS, and Maverick Scientists by Steven Kotler, Jamie Wheal

"Elon Musk" by Ashlee Vance

"Nice Girls Don't Get the Corner office by Lois P. Frankel.

Chapter 1

https://www.technologyreview.com/s/600868/the-artificially-intelligent-doctor-will-hear-you-now/

JPMorgan unleashes artificial intelligence to automate its legal work

http://www.fanaticalfuturist.com/2017/03/jpmorgan-unleashes-artificial-intelligence-to-automate-its-legal-work/

[1] https://www.brainyquote.com/quotes/gray_scott_802410

[2] https://www.brookings.edu/research/how-artificial-intelligence-is-transforming-the-world/

[3] https://www.skynettoday.com/editorials/ai-automation-job-loss

[4] https://www.newyorker.com/magazine/2019/03/04/are-robots-competing-for-your-job

[5] https://medium.com/@gc/ubers-path-forward-b59ec9bd4ef6

[6] https://www.cnet.com/news/lyft-sees-massive-growth-brings-uber-competition/

[7] https://www.sfchronicle.com/news/article/When-are-Uber-and-Lyft-on-strike-why-san-francisco-13828909.php

[8] https://www.yang2020.com/what-is-ubi/

[9]https://basicincome.org/basic-income/history/

[10] https://www.newscientist.com/article/2193136-universal-income-study-finds-money-for-nothing-wont-make-us-work-less/

[11] https://medium.com/basic-income/what-is-there-to-learn-from-finlands-basic-income-experiment-did-it-succeed-or-fail-54b8e5051f60

[12] https://basicincome.org/news/2019/04/korea-to-launch-provincial-youth-basic-income-program/

[13] https://m.youtube.com/watch%3Fv%3D2vRe6-FzgLI&ved=2ahUKEwiwzoqt-pPiAhULShUIHfKABl8QjjgwB3oECAUQAQ&usg=AOvVaw3xfp2q62bG1po9Oo0SrXZD

[14] https://www.cnbc.com/2017/12/27/what-billionaires-say-about-universal-basic-income-in-2017.html

[15] https://www.forbes.com/sites/roberthof/2016/01/28/ai-guru-andrew-ng-government-must-play-big-role-in-rollout-of-self-driving-cars/2/#4e28a51c44ef

[16] https://www.youtube.com/watch?v=-AlVbeeLSeY

[17] https://techcrunch.com/2019/03/17/these-are-the-robots-that-help-you-get-your-amazon-packages-on-time

[18] https://www.forbes.com/sites/richblake1/2019/02/24/amazons-push-to-augment-workforce-with-automation-is-pig-in-industrial-robotics-python/#73761f3742ea

[19] https://www.oxfordmartin.ox.ac.uk/downloads/academic/The_Future_of_Employment.pdf

[20] https://www.technologyreview.com/f/609672/amazons-investment-in-robots-is-eliminating-human-jobs/

[21] https://www.nytimes.com/2017/09/10/technology/amazon-robots-workers.html

[22] https://www.theguardian.com/commentisfree/2016/dec/01/stephen-hawking-dangerous-time-planet-inequality

[23] https://qz.com/911968/bill-gates-the-robot-that-takes-your-job-should-pay-taxes/

[25] https://www.nytimes.com/2017/01/12/upshot/in-obamas-farewell-a-warning-on-automations-perils.html

[27] https://www.mckinsey.com/global-themes/future-of-organizations-and-work/what-the-future-of-work-will-mean-for-jobs-skills-and-wages

[28] https://www.pwc.co.uk/economic-services/ukeo/pwcukeo-section-4-automation-march-2017-v2.pdf

https://www.ted.com/talks/carole_cadwalladr_facebook_s_role_in_brexit_and_the_threat_to_democracy

Chapter 3

The Wright Brothers by David McCullough

Chapter 4

Barack Obama and Martin Luther King

Michiko Kakutani. Obama's Secret to Surviving the White House: Books. The New York Times: 2017.

https://www.nytimes.com/2017/01/16/books/obamas-secret-to-surviving-the-white-house-years-books.html?smprod=nytcore-ipad&smid=nytcore-ipad-share&_r=0

Andrew Buncombe. Barack Obama: The nocturnal habits of America's 'night guy' president revealed. Independent: 2016.

http://www.independent.co.uk/news/people/barack-obama-nocturnal-habits-of-americas-night-guy-president-revealed-a7115561.html

https://www.biography.com/people/martin-luther-king-jr-9365086

http://www.notablebiographies.com/news/Li-Ou/Obama-Barack.html

https://www.newsmax.com/insidecover/barry-obama-newsweek/2008/03/24/id/323286/

Golden Gate Bridge

http://www.goldengatebridge.org/

http://mentalfloss.com/article/64379/20-awesome-facts-about-golden-gate-bridge

http://www.history.com/news/6-things-you-may-not-know-about-the-golden-gate-bridge

http://theconversation.com/how-would-engineers-build-the-golden-gate-bridge-today-77846

https://www.lonelyplanet.com/usa/san-francisco/travel-tips-and-articles/14-things-you-didnt-know-about-the-golden-gate-bridge/40625c8c-8a11-5710-a052-1479d277e817

https://www.youtube.com/watch?v=-8xK3w4mvr4

Chapter 5

The Power of Broke by Daymond John

George and Steve

Reference links

https://www.theatlantic.com/magazine/archive/1979/03/the-man-who-made-star-wars/306228/

https://moviepilot.com/posts/3480594

http://www.thecrimson.com/article/2014/4/23/spielberg-discusses-sources-inspiration/

http://www.fresnobee.com/entertainment/movies-news-reviews/article85593317.html

http://www.slashfilm.com/steven-spielberg-discusses-career-inspiration-and-criticism-in-1990-video-interview/

https://movieweb.com/star-wars-last-jedi-movie-influences-challenges/

https://www.theatlantic.com/entertainment/archive/2011/07/other-unsuccessful-legal-challenges-george-lucas/353346/

http://www.mmwealth.com/overcoming-odds-george-lucas/

http://www.filmmakers.com/artists/lucas/biography/

https://en.wikipedia.org/wiki/George_Lucas_filmography

http://www.scruffles.net/spielberg/articles/article-001.html

https://www.theatlantic.com/magazine/archive/1979/03/the-man-who-made-star-wars/306228/

Ready Player One

https://www.independent.co.uk/arts-entertainment/films/features/ready-player-one-ernest-cline-intervie3w-steven-spielberg-virtual-reality-vr-a8277996.html

'Ernest Cline interview on Ready Player One, working with Steven Spielberg, and the future of virtual reality'

http://www.arabnews.com/node/1283496/art-culture

"A long and difficult process: Ready Player One author Ernest Cline on turning his sci-fi bestseller into a movie"

The Geek Genius Behind Ready Player One: An interview with Ernest Cline. Warpzoned.com, September 23, 2011. Retrieved March 17, 2017.

Schaub, Michael (August 14, 2011). Player One: A Winning, Geeked-Out Page-Turner. NPR. Retrieved July 7, 2012

Knight, Jacob (December 12, 2017. Ernie Cline Penning A Sequel Novel to Ready Player One. Birthmoviesdeath.com. Retrieved April 16, 2018)

Harry Potter

As Harry Potter Turns 20, The Franchise Still Has The Magic Touch

https://www.forbes.com/sites/leeseymour/2017/06/26/at-20-harry-potter-is-going-strong-prepping-his-broadway-debut/#29d25ec71938

https://en.m.wikipedia.org/wiki/J._K._Rowling

Entrepreneurs

J.K. Rowling reveals the routine she uses to write her best-selling novels

https://www.cnbc.com/2018/02/01/harry-potter-author-j-k-rowling-reveals-writing-routine-on-twitter.html

Mugglemarch

J. K. Rowling writes a realist novel for adults.

https://web.archive.org/web/20140730193324/http://www.newyorker.com/magazine/2012/10/01/mugglemarch

Drinking

Christiansen, P., Rose, A., Randall-Smith, L., & Hardman, C. A. (2016). Alcohol's acute effect on food intake is mediated by inhibitory control impairments. *Health Psychology, 35*(5), 518-522.

http://dx.doi.org/10.1037/hea0000320

Blais E, Bellavance F, Marcil A, Carnis L. Effects of introducing an administrative .05% blood alcohol concentration limit on law enforcement patterns and alcohol-related collisions in Canada. *Accid Anal Prev* 2015;82:101-11.

Higgins-Biddle J, Dilonardo J. Alcohol and highway safety: screening and brief intervention for alcohol problems as a community approach to improving traffic safety. Washington, DC: NHTSA; 2013 DOT HS 811 836.

http://www.imdb.com/name/nm0000164/awards

Guide to Community Preventive Services. Reducing alcohol-impaired driving: ignition interlocks. [cited 2016 Feb 5]. Available at URL: http://www.thecommunityguide.org/mvoi/AID/ignitioninterlocks.html.

https://www.treatmentsolutions.com/famous-people-recovery-anthony-hopkins/

https://www.mentalhealth.org.uk/a-to-z/a/alcohol-and-mental-health

http://www.anthonyhopkinsmovies.com/personal/how-anthony-hopkins-quit-drinking/

Ramesh Shivani, M.D., is an addiction psychiatry fellow; R. Jeffrey Goldsmith, M.D., is a clinical professor of psychiatry at and director of the Addiction Fellowships Program; and Robert M. Anthenelli, M.D., is an associate professor of psychiatry and director of the Addiction Psychiatry Division and of the Substance Dependence Program; all three at the University of Cincinnati College of Medicine, Cincinnati Veterans' Affairs Medical Center, Cincinnati, Ohio.

Chapter 6

Steve Jobs

Steve Jobs by Walter Isaacson

https://www.ted.com/talks/steve_jobs_how_to_live_before_you_die

https://www.biography.com/people/steve-jobs-9354805

https://en.wikipedia.org/wiki/Steve_Jobs

https://www.youtube.com/watch?v=4DZVRKGvWDw

https://www.investopedia.com/university/steve-jobs-biography/steve-jobs-success-story.asp

Jack Ma

https://en.wikipedia.org/wiki/Jack_Ma

https://www.investopedia.com/university/jack-ma-biography/jack-ma-success-story.asp

https://www.forbes.com/forbes/welcome/?toURL=https://www.forbes.com/profile/jack-ma/&refURL=https://www.google.co.in/&referrer=https://www.google.co.in/

https://www.youtube.com/watch?v=lYGGpc2mMno

https://www.youtube.com/watch?v=euxJhgYZXL8

Napster

https://www.lifewire.com/itunes-store-history-2438593

https://www.forbes.com/sites/hughmcintyre/2018/03/21/what-happened-to-the-piracy-sites-that-nearly-destroyed-the-music-industry-part-1-napster/#53f5cb432293

https://www.lifewire.com/history-of-napster-2438592

https://techcrunch.com/2013/02/06/charting-the-itunes-stores-path-to-25-billion-songs-sold-40-billion-apps-downloaded-and-beyond/

http://www.businessinsider.com/elon-musk-first-principles-2015-1?IR=T

https://en.wikipedia.org/wiki/Sean_Parker

https://www.forbes.com/profile/elon-musk/

http://www.businessinsider.com/the-insane-life-of-facebook-billionaire-sean-parker-2015-7?IR=T

https://www.forbes.com/profile/sean-parker/

https://www.lifewire.com/number-of-ipods-sold-all-time-1999515

https://www.forbes.com/pictures/587543a74bbe6f1f20eaa91e/sean-parker-foundation/#5ed087f87bb0

https://www.wired.com/2002/05/the-day-the-napster-died/

https://jamesclear.com/first-principles

Paul Graham

YC Winter 2018 Batch

https://blog.ycombinator.com/14-companies-from-theyc-winter-2018-batch/

10 Y Combinator questions every entrepreneur should answer

https://medium.com/vaave/10-y-combinator-questions-every-entrepreneur-should-answer-d1a9186a93a1

How to prepare for the interview

old.ycombinator.com/howtoprepare.html

The 10 most successful Y Combinator startups

https://www.businessinsider.com/10-successful-y-combinator-startups-2012-3&grqid=P

YC Alumni Go Big: The 15 Most Valuable Y Combinator –
Backed Startups

https://news.crunchbase.com/news/yc-alumni-go-big-15-valuable-y-combinator-backed-startups/&hl=en-NG

Chapter 7

Dropbox

http://uk.businessinsider.com/dropbox-founder-and-ceo-drew-houston-interview-2017-6?r=US&IR=T

Dropbox founder reveals how he built a $9 billion company in his 20s — even though Steve Jobs told him Apple would destroy it

https://medium.com/the-story-of-grip/how-two-guys-that-barely-knew-each-other-build-one-of-the-biggest-cloud-storage-companies-in-the-c41c383a952e

How Two Guys That Barely Knew Each Other Build One Of The Biggest Cloud Storage Companies In The World

Learning

https://www.usnews.com/news/education-news/articles/2017-08-31/new-study-questions-links-between-race-disability-in-students

Elon Musk

[i] SpaceX, About Us www.spacex.com/about

[ii] Bob Van Voris, Matt Robinson, Benjamin Bain, and Dana Hull, *Musk Faces US Contempt Claim for Violating Accord with SEC,* (Bloomberg Technology, February 26th, 2019) www.bloomberg.com/news/articles/2019-02-25/elon-musk-faces-u-s-contempt-claim-for-violating-sec-accord

[iii] Elizabeth Lopatto, *Why so many people think Elon Musk is a hero – or a villain,* (The Verge, November 30th, 2018) www.theverge.com/platform/amp/2018/11/30/18118414//elon-musk-hero-villain-genius-spacex-tesla-boring-company

[iv] Mayo Oshin, *Elon Musk's '3-Step' First Principles Thinking: How to Think and Solve Difficult Problems Like a Genius'* (Mission, August 30th, 2017) www.medium.com/amp/ba1e73a9f6c0

[v] Blue Origin, Blue's Mission www.blueorigin.com/our-mission

[vi] A sequential design process that involves downwards progressive steps through stages such as Conception, Initiation, Analysis, Design, Construction, Testing, Production, Implementation and Maintenance

[vii] An umbrella term for development methods that involve delivering the smallest amount of valuable work in the shortest possible time.

Chapter 8

https://www.forbes.com/sites/travisbradberry/2014/10/08/multitasking-damages-your-brain-and-career-new-studies-suggest/#7e7bbc4b56ee

https://www.npr.org/templates/story/story.php?storyId=95256794

https://www.newyorker.com/science/maria-konnikova/multitask-masters

https://www.forbes.com/sites/lisaquast/2017/02/06/want-to-be-more-productive-stop-multi-tasking/#67128d4855a6

https://www.researchgate.net/profile/Markus_Buehner2/publication/230899010_Working_Memory_Fluid_Intelligence_and_Attention_Are_Predictors_of_Multitasking_Performance_but_Polychronicity_and_Extraversion_Are_Not/links/09e4150c63b006e4ff000000.pdf

https://consumer.healthday.com/encyclopedia/emotional-health-17/emotional-disorder-news-228/multitasking-and-stress-646052.html

https://www.psychologytoday.com/blog/the-squeaky-wheel/201606/10-real-risks-multitasking-mind-and-body

Article by Martin Lindstrom on Neuroscience

https://www.neurosciencemarketing.com/blog/articles/buyology-by-martin-lindstrom.htm

Article by Arlene S. Hirsh

https://arlenehirsch.com/10000-hours-of-video-games-building-skills-or-wasting-time/